THE SINGLE WOMAN AND THE
FAIRYTALE PRINCE

THE SINGLE WOMAN AND THE FAIRYTALE PRINCE

JEAN-CLAUDE KAUFMANN

Translated by David Macey

polity

Published in French as *La femme seule et le Prince charmant* by Jean-Claude Kaufmann ©
Armand Colin, 2006 (first edition: Nathan, 1999)

This English edition © Polity Press, 2008

Polity Press
65 Bridge Street
Cambridge CB2 1UR, UK

Polity Press
350 Main Street
Malden, MA 02148, USA

ISBN-13: 978-0-7456-4049-5
ISBN-13: 978-0-7456-4050-1(pb)

A catalogue record for this book is available from the British Library.

Typeset in 10.5 on 12 pt Sabon
by Servis Filmsetting Ltd, Stockport, Cheshire
Printed and bound at Replika Press PVT Ltd, Kundli, India.

Ouvrage publié avec le concours du Ministère français chargé de la culture – Centre
National du Livre

Published with the assistance of the French Ministry of Culture – National Centre for the
Book

The publisher has used its best endeavours to ensure that the URLs for external websites
referred to in this book are correct and active at the time of going to press. However, the
publisher has no responsibility for the websites and can make no guarantee that a site will
remain live or that the content is or will remain appropriate.

Every effort has been made to trace all copyright holders, but if any have been
inadvertently overlooked the publishers will be pleased to include any necessary credits in
any subsequent reprint or edition.

For further information on Polity, visit our website: www.polity.co.uk

CONTENTS

Part III The Autonomy Trajectory

LIST OF TABLES AND FIGURES

FOREWORD TO THE NEW EDITION

It was seven years ago [1999]. The first edition of this book was about to be published and was about to leave its world of paper. It set off shock waves all around it, which was a strange experience for the author. The book was in tune with a burning question of the day: the highly charged issue of the growing number of people who live on their own. As for Prince Charming – the Fairytale Prince – I had refused to believe he existed when I began my research, but he took the opportunity to make a spectacular comeback. Although he had been reduced to nothing more than a residual archaism that only little girls would admit to, he escaped the mawkish and highly stigmatized imagery to which he had been confined and suddenly began to crop up regularly in ordinary conversations – with a hint of ironic distance, of course, but that could scarcely conceal the intensity of the women's dreams and expectations. Cinderella 69 admitted it quite openly in her blog: 'Fed up with dates that lead nowhere. Fed up with websites posting the same old profiles and promising what I imagine to be relationships that are enough to make you weep even before they've got off the ground. I'm still waiting for my prince to come, still waiting for Mr Right, the man who will understand me and carry me off, far away from this bloody drab existence, into a wonderful world, all cuddles and sweet as sugar. Has my prince gone to sleep, or what? Quick, give me a sign; I really am getting impatient.' Over the next few weeks, Cinderella 69 received 30 or so offers in response to her blog. Unfortunately, they were a bit dull and they were all the same. Not everyone can become a Prince.

I too received a lot of post when the book came out: a flood of fascinating and detailed first-hand accounts (enough for a second volume). Strangely enough, almost all of them had the same structure.

First, detailed descriptions of the personal quirks to which I had not paid enough attention in the book. Linda told me: 'Personally, and this is the big difference between me and your single women, I secretly dream about Princess Charming. Unfortunately, it goes no further than that because I don't have it in me to go through with it.' Second, a reappropriation of my analysis, followed by well-argued criticisms and proposals for variants. 'In my opinion, you underestimate the need for sex. That's another norm that's forced upon us: the obligation to perform. And as it happens, it undermines men even further. As you say, it's nice to have a shoulder to cry on, but a Prince needs to have rather more exciting attributes too! Poor things! Men feel that they have to prove themselves and they have to be good enough in that area too. Sex has become the number one topic of conversation for me and my girlfriends' (Eve). Third, expressions of thanks for the book's liberating effect. Because it stressed the power of a social trend that is making individuals embark upon autonomy trajectories despite themselves, it made it possible to remove the terrible self-doubts. 'I've finally realized that it's not my fault and that I've done nothing wrong. The worst thing of all was not knowing what I might have done wrong. Obviously, because I hadn't done anything wrong!' (Raïssa). The removal of the feeling of guilt begins with the surprising discovery that she is just like everyone else in her position and the realization that a description of certain forms of the social can provide insights into something very intimate. 'You've stripped me naked. It borders on the obscene. How did you manage to describe my life, when you don't know me? I thought I was the only one, and now I discover that I belong to a sort of secret community. It's very reassuring (I feel a bit less alone), but it's also unpleasant. Thanks and no thanks. Thanks for making the good times feel even better. And no thanks for the bad times, because you don't offer any solution and you've made them even worse. You say that the single life is a life divided, a mixture of tears and laughter. And you're quite right. But, having read your book, I feel even more torn than before' (Carline).

Although it was usually the case, reading the book did not always have a beneficial effect. The author has no control over what use is made of his book (which is, for better or worse, just as it should be). I remember, for example, one young couple who studied *La Trame conjugale* (Kaufmann 1992) too closely. Book in hand, they both watched their partner-enemy's every gesture like hawks. Their married life obviously became a living hell and I was the (unwitting) cause of the disaster. I was very touched by the story Malvina confided in me as I was writing this book; I feel somewhat guilty and I feel for her. To celebrate her 30th birthday, she treated herself to a trip to India and took *La Femme seule et le Prince charmant* with her. Reading it made the penny drop: time was passing and she needed to find a father for the children she could already imagine herself having. Our states of mind change the way we see others and it seemed to her that she had found the ideal candidate as soon as she got home, especially now that her biological clock was ticking. Being an experienced womanizer, Richard promised her the earth and lived up to all her expectations. No sooner were they married, unfortunately, than he turned into an ugly frog and went back on all his fine words. 'I liked him because he didn't run a mile when I talked about commitment – I wanted a child quickly – and what he said seemed to fit in with my principles. It was along the lines of "I don't want you to iron my shirts for me: you're not my maid." That was four and a half years ago, our daughter is three and a half and – I CAN'T STAND HIM! What annoys me most is his chauvinist attitude, things like: "What? My green shirt hasn't been ironed, and I wanted to wear it this morning" (in the meantime, the other 15 are clean and have been ironed: the green shirt is the only one in the linen basket!). Or: "What's this pigsty? You might tidy up! You've been at home all day" (I had in fact marked 35 sets of home-work, made a meal and done two lots of washing, but I had left the bin bag outside the front door). And the worst thing of all about all this is that he regularly goes out on his own with his mates while I stay at home to look after our daughter, whereas I'd like to go to see a movie or go to an evening do at school. He makes a big scene just to put me off wanting to go out.'[1] Being in a relationship is like buying a ticket for the lottery: you don't always win the big prize.

This is why the number of people living on their own has risen inex-orably over the last seven years all over the world. When the time came to prepare a new edition, I had to take stock, to see what had changed and to decide whether some passages had to be revised. I did not have to take anything out. Apart from a few minor details (the diaries have become blogs), the questions were still the same and the most detailed observations had not changed one little bit. New and very important elements have, however, obviously emerged, and they merited discus-sion. A number of chapters have therefore been added. There have been three main developments.

First, there has been a change of atmosphere. Since the first edition appeared (in 1999), we have had speed dating and *Sex and the City*.

---

[1] The story of Malvina's life with Richard will be continued in a forthcoming book on how couples fall out.

The trendy atmosphere of the big cities means that the single attitude now has a huge screen presence and seems to have become very
fashionable. All those wretched couples trapped into their narrow
domestic lives look so behind the times. Singles seem to have become
the standard-bearers of a joyous and inventive freedom.

The sad truth is that the revolution has been purely superficial. It
has certainly let some air in and has made it easier to talk about all this.
But what I am saying in this book is that society speaks with
forked tongue: 'Everyone is free to do what he or she wants, but . . .'
The more the 'free to do what he or she wants . . .' crops up in the
light banter of urban parties and TV dramas, the louder the 'but . . .'
becomes in the depths of society. The discrepancy between the two is
growing. Coupledom is not out of date. On the contrary, the settled
home life quietly asserts itself as the norm, more so than ever in a
society that makes so many psychological demands of us. It surrepti-
tiously stigmatizes the singles who thought they had freed themselves from the dead weight of its norms. Even where it should be least
oppressive: in their private domain and in the places where they meet.
As we shall see in chapter 9, a Net surfer who posts her vain quest
for love for too long is very quickly pigeonholed and begins to look
suspicious to her fellow surfers. The accusing finger can be pointed
on the Internet too (see chapter 2), and that is even more cruel
because the Net is so intimate: the traitor is inside the gates. Singles'
relationship with money is probably the best example of this. It
should allow them to indulge in all the little treats they can afford
because they are single and not accountable to anyone (and especially
not to a mean husband). But their existential fragility and their anxieties about the future put paid to that dream: two-thirds of single
women see themselves as more frugal and less extravagant than
married women.[2]

The second new element is far from being just a ripple on the
surface: the Internet really has revolutionized the ways we can meet
others. A new chapter is therefore devoted to it. Making contact has
become astonishingly easy and (apparently) risk-free. All it takes is
one click, and you can choose between an infinite number of offers,
each more attractive than the last. All it takes is one click, and a new
world opens up before the eyes of the astonished surfer, who can write
words of love, receive endless virtual kisses and even flirt at a distance.
She can break out of her loneliness whenever she likes, make friends,

---

[2] Survey (of 609 single women) carried out by IPSOS on behalf of GE Money Bank in
December 2005.

find confidantes, and become involved in passionate debates about all kinds of subjects. The Net can quickly become a drug for anyone who ventures on to it. And, as with any drug, there is a danger that she will no longer be able to do without it and that it will have painful side effects. Some of the side effects are harmless: she's had all she can take, and suddenly becomes sick of virtual reality. And some are terrible: emotional commitment becomes even more problematic. The illusion is to believe that the Internet makes everything easier. In reality, it makes it easier to make contact but makes commitment more problematic than ever precisely because making contact has become easier. Falling in love has become a problem. Christelle explains it very well: 'Falling in love is one thing. Staying together is another. Personally, I've never met a real flesh and blood man.' In the first edition of this book, commitment was already described as the real problem; the 'Internet revolution' has just made things worse.

The last element, finally, has to do with the globalization of exchanges. At first sight, it too appears in the best possible light because, having rebelled against the sinister forces of cultural isolationism, our era dreams of hybridity and has acquired a taste for the Other. The globalization of singledom also allows particular categories (such as farmers) to break out of their isolation and to find, somewhere in the world, partners who live up to expectations that their local territory can no longer satisfy. But if we look more closely, it transpires that, as in the economic domain, the globalization of the marriage market has its down side too. A profoundly unequal structure of exchange between the North and the South (to which we can add the countries of the East) is in fact being established. Men in the North are demanding (and obtaining from the South) women who are young, beautiful and submissive. Of course they are attracted to the autonomous and highly educated women of the European metropolis. But when it comes to beginning a relationship, they think of all the effort they will have to make it 'good enough' (see chapter 8). They therefore prefer old-style women and wives who can provide them with a quiet married life, who are submissive and who are good house-keepers into the bargain. What is more, they are demanding women who are young and beautiful. There is therefore a danger that men in the South, and especially poor men, will find it more difficult to find partners. At the same time, educated women in the North who have reached an age that means that there are few suitable single men available (see the Appendix: 'The Globalization of Singledom') will increasingly face new forms of competition that makes the existing age difference even greater.

As for the young women of the South, marrying a foreigner does provide them with an opportunity to escape their poverty. But that is not all it does. They often dream of romantic love too. Just as he is ubiquitous on the Net, so the eternal Prince Charming still plays the leading role in the globalization of singledom. Sadly, there have probably never been so many carriages that turn into pumpkins.

ACKNOWLEDGEMENTS

My warmest thanks are due to my colleagues on the 'Psychanalyse et pratiques sociales' team at the CNRS (UMR 6053), and especially to Markos Zafiropoulos and Denis Duclos. The studies that allowed me to write this book were carried out during the two years I spent with the team. I would also like to thank Patrick Berthier. Most of the ideas presented in this book were first expounded in the 'Philosophie de l'éducation' seminar that we run together at the Université de Paris VIII, and they owe a great deal to Patrick Berthier's patience, friendly solicitude and critical sense.

INTRODUCTION

This book tells the story of a strange couple: Prince Charming and the single woman. It is a sort of modern fairytale, but it is also a true story. Its main character is the single woman, who is present throughout. And she is very much alive: her every move is described and we can spy on her dreams and thoughts. Prince Charming is an ambiguous figure who only appears from time to time.[1] Is he an outdated cliché who is summoned up far too often in our modern era? We will have to wait for the end of the story before we can tell.

This book does not simply tell a story. I may as well admit it from the start: the story is really no more than a pretext, an Ariadne's thread that will guide us on our way as we analyse singledom. The single life is an inextricable labyrinth and there is a danger that we will get lost. The reader may, however, prefer the pretext to the analysis and, by skimming through a few chapters, can follow the adventures of Prince Charming and our modern Cinderella.

The reader is, however, advised to prefer the analysis, which is the important part of this book.

I have been working for eight years on the question of men and women who are not part of a couple, and loneliness. For a long time, all I did was to come up with new categories and more and more

---

[1] Prince Charming's constant comings and goings between the imaginary world and reality confuse our analysis: who are we talking about? Women who dream about their fairy-tale Prince are well aware that he is a fictional (but wonderful) character. But women who are quite prosaically looking for a man who suits them and call him their Prince are quite happy to sprinkle stardust on a man who would look quite ordinary in the cold light of day. They are able to believe in their Prince because he probably isn't a Prince any longer. In order to differentiate between these very different figures, the real Prince – the one in their dreams – will be given the distinction of having a capital 'P', whereas princes who turn out to be very ordinary will be denied that honour. There are Princes and princes.

specific questions: the isolation of men in the peasant world, the feeling of loneliness experienced by housewives, and so on. There came a point when accumulating more and more details without any guiding thread simply confused the issue. That is the paradox of atomized knowledge: the more we know about something, the less we know. And the less we know, the less we can say about it clearly and loudly. And that is precisely what men and women who live alone are waiting for: they want – finally – to hear a clear message that explains their strange lives and that helps them to take decisions about their future.

I have therefore decided to use Ariadne's thread to do all we can to understand the central process, even if it means ignoring marginal or particular categories. Nothing will be said here about the difficulties farmers have in forming relationships, about the loneliness of housewives, or about a thousand other problematic micro-contexts. Nor will there be anything about the isolation of old people. And very little will be said about men. Men are obviously not a marginal category, and their absence may be regrettable. But that is the price that has to be paid when we look in depth at any subject, especially when its content is complex: we have to concentrate on the central issue.

In this case, the story is undeniably centred on women, and there is nothing arbitrary about the choice of women. Nor is there anything arbitrary about the decision to concentrate on one age group: women aged between 20 and 50. It is women in that age group who are most affected by the social mechanism we will be examining in detail in the pages that follow. We will see that the single life is a combination of two contradictory component elements: the single life is a divided life. This is because the hidden model of private life assigns women of this age a different role: they should devote themselves body and soul to their families. Caught between the impulse to be autonomous and the pressures of the secret model, single women are in the eye of the cyclone. They are torn apart and constantly wonder why their lives are so divided. They also write about themselves a lot: it is thanks to an analysis of a corpus of letters that we are able to explore their innermost thoughts. My description of the most factual aspects (and especially the portrait painted in Part II) is also based upon a synthesis of quantitative surveys and studies.

In many respects, the life of single men is, however, similar to that of women. They embark on this biographical trajectory with the same carefree energy, the same desire to construct their lives as they see fit. And the time for question and doubts comes for men too. Sometimes

it is the corrosive effect of a loneliness that is just as cruel as the loneliness of single women. Sometimes it is the desire for a family, and
sometimes it is the desire to have a baby (our most vivid dreams are
about the things we do not have), the desire for intimacy, warmth and
social recognition, and for domestic peace and quiet, and normality.
Single men can therefore read this book and recognize themselves in
many passages in it: hiding away at home, the sudden decisions to go
out ('I'll meet her tonight'), and the pleasures and pains of existential
lightness. They will, however, be surprised to find a clearer and more
detailed picture of the mechanisms that structure their day-to-day
existence: looking at women allows us to look at those mechanisms
through a magnifying glass. In Part III, we will, for example, see how
the 'logic of the shell' forces single women to show themselves in their
best light and to construct their identities on the basis of how the gaze
of the Other legitimizes that half of them. Men become caught up in
this process too, but to a lesser extent, and they find it easier to admit
how it tears them apart inside. For men, the 'logic of the shell' does
not develop into the 'paradox of appearances' which eventually traps
some women who have become too intimidating and perfect to remain
approachable.

Being alone does not necessarily mean being lonely (only people
who have not come to terms with being on their own say they are
lonely), but it is true that loneliness is common. Let us be quite clear
about this: the loneliness of men is no less acute than that of women.
Although it is difficult to quantify these things, it is even likely that
slightly more men than women are lonely. This is because men are
accustomed to the reassuring presence and support of a woman (a
mother, a devoted wife), and because they are less autonomous when
it comes to organizing their domestic lives. Suddenly, an essential
support is no longer there: this is actual loneliness in a raw state.
Women too experience an emptiness when something is missing, but
they do so in slightly different forms (they tend to miss not having a
shoulder to lean on rather than not having someone who is devoted to
them), and it is sometimes experienced so intensely that it raises the
traditional expectations of marriage. It is, however, no more than one
element in their inner turmoil. The social mechanism is stronger: their
loneliness is hard to understand because it is the product of a strange
exteriority. It is obvious to the sociologist that this is where the real
questions lie.

Part I will set the scene, mainly in historical terms: why the steady
and considerable increase in the number of people who are living on
their own? Part II will go into various details of everyday life in order

to paint a picture that would not have this overall coherence if it were not the product of a social mechanism. Part III, finally, will provide the main explanatory key: the autonomy trajectory. Single women find themselves caught up in it despite themselves, and they have no option but to pursue it because it makes their lives easier. This triggers a merciless war between two radically different possible identities: devoted wife (devoted to a hypothetical family) or autonomous woman? That is the recurrent and obsessional question.

In an earlier book (Kaufmann 1997), I analysed how families are structured by becoming moored to everyday objects, and how individual identities are in their turn constructed by the weight of these objects and by family routines. Here, we see the other possible side of self-realization. Not the stability and the calm that is provided by the immobilizing mass of the concrete. On the contrary, we see the uncertainty and lightness of an identity that changes as the individual's mood changes. The fact that the revolt against domesticity is such a central issue for single women is no accident. Domestic responsibilities are of course the symbol and the mark of the alternative choice of identity (the family), which weighs heavily on women because it inserts them into a natural order that has inherited a lot from a distant past. The autonomy trajectory, in contrast, thrusts them into an unknown and open world. The greatest pleasures come from freedom in everyday life: doing only what they like, when they like, not cooking meals and living on snacks. But it is also the source of the most disturbing question of all: what is the point of a life without any structure and in which nothing relates to anything else? Women's dreams take them in opposite directions, and the Prince's face changes to fit in with their expectations of the moment. He turns into a sort of gentle husband-father when they are thinking of committing themselves to a family career at all cost; he is unrealistically perfect when a combination of autonomy and romantic ideals (which encourage them not to settle for mediocrity) remains their supreme value.

Prince Charming has no male equivalent because, no matter whether we are talking about commitment to the family or the ideal of love, men's ambitions are more limited. More and more men do dream of having a family and finding love, but much less so than women. Men can find loneliness very difficult to live with, but it is essentially a private matter. That is the big difference between men and women, for whom being single is at once a private matter and something public that concerns society as a whole. When women take the decision to embark on the autonomy trajectory, they take a decision that does not just affect them: they challenge a basic structure (the family, which is based upon the role of the devoted wife), and they pose a threat to the entire social edifice.

These are no doubt only the first questions to be raised by the irrepressible trend for women to become autonomous.

Part I

Is There a Model for Private Life?

Why are there so many people living alone? Why do their numbers continue to rise inexorably, year after year? These questions have rarely been answered, because they are difficult to understand, because they break too many taboos and because they call into question one of our society's essential foundations.

Taking all the necessary precautions, I will attempt to provide some elements of an answer. I will begin by taking a look at our past. What are the origins of the trend that now encourages millions of men and women to act in this way, often despite themselves?

— 1 —

LIVING ALONE: A LONG HISTORY

The history of those who live on their own has yet to be written (Knibiehler 1991), 'other than in terms of derision, exceptionality and even abnormality' (Farge and Klapisch-Zuber 1984: 296). Attaining the ambitious goal of writing their history in a few introductory pages is obviously out of the question, and others have already begun to write it (Bologne 2004). But an overview is necessary if we are to try to understand the origins of the long-term trend that leads people to live alone. The reader will, I hope, forgive me for my rash decision to juggle with centuries of history in just a few lines and to trace evolutionary lines that are no doubt too clear to do justice to the contradictory density of the social. It is, however, important to try to see things a little more clearly.

What Marriage Was

We now know that the earliest human societies were extraordinarily diverse. And yet they used the same instruments to establish themselves: religion, which was the primal form of the social bond, and marriage. Marriage is neither a minor issue nor a purely private question: it is one of the foundations of civilization and has existed throughout the history of humanity. Anthropologists prefer to speak of alliance. The term illustrates the original function of marriage: it allows small groups to unite, to form wider communities and therefore to avoid war (by 'exchanging women' in accordance with codified procedures).

To say that marriage was central from the outset tells us nothing about the concrete modalities of conjugal life, which were very different from those of our society and which differed greatly from one group to another. In certain societies, for example, married couples lived in separate houses. The important thing was the bond of alliance that was sealed by marriage and that united two families or two social groups. But it also brought together two specific individuals: because it was a matter of public order and collective interest, marriage necessarily involved the personal union of two individuals.

The term 'union' has to be understood in the strongest of senses. The modern couple has paved the way for an ever-more intimate intersubjective communication between partners (Luhmann 1990). At the same time, their growing individual autonomy has resulted in breakdowns in the alliance contract, and thus revealed its fragility. Our intimate exchanges were quite unknown in the earliest societies. Matrimonial unions were total. Marriage meant constructing an indestructible whole that transcended individuals.

Intolerable Celibacy

That is why the very idea of living alone was unnatural. When people did, despite everything, live on their own, their behaviour was viewed as intolerable and everyone strove to conceal this dangerous nonsense, or to do away with it by forcing the unfortunate recalcitrant to marry. A few cases of men who were afraid of having any contact with women and who refused to marry have been reported amongst the Chagga of East Africa. The problem was so serious that the chief became involved and ordered the kidnapping of a girl in whom no one had shown any interest. 'No status could be more abnormal, more disparaged or more hostile to the social body than celibacy' (Héritier 1996: 244).

Some (very rare) incorrigibles did, however, succeed in remaining single. They were suspected of casting evil spells and were described as evil spirits: the social order was restored by excluding them. The situation of a widower was slightly less problematic because he had been married. Widows, in contrast, were given scarcely any more consideration than women who had never married. Life outside marriage was even more unthinkable and insane for women than it was for men (Flahault 1996). Women who never married were, of course, even worse than widows. In Imperial China, virgins who died without ever knowing a man were 'cold demons' (Héritier 1996: 243), and were so dangerous that even other demons kept out of their way. Women who had never married were so abnormal that widows could

4

not enjoy the tolerance that was extended to widowers. Amongst the Ojibwa, widows spent a period of three to four years in mourning, living alone, their hair uncombed, dressed in rags and covered in ashes. According to Indian tradition, they no longer had the right to sleep in the marital bed and slept on the floor, eating frugally and leading solitary and unobtrusive lives. Death alone allowed them to regain their status by letting themselves be burned alive on their husband's funeral pyre.

Great Buffalo Woman

And yet a few individuals did not conform to the obligation to marry, despite themselves in many cases. Those who were ill or who had been badly treated by fate could not have access to the model's normality, and were quietly taken care of by the community. Others deliberately defied the taboos, and such deviants were quickly accused of being in league with demons. Most were men. Their single status certainly meant that they lost the trust of the community, but their attitude was more easily tolerated than female celibacy because it posed less of a threat to the social order. It was not only that a woman who never married was nothing without the community (nor was an unmarried man); she was also nothing without a man. Unmarried women were intolerable in two senses.

The few women who did dare to remain single therefore had to be cunning and display exceptional abilities, like Great Buffalo Woman, who was an Ojibwa Indian. Her story is recounted by François Héritier (1996). She had to learn to be self-sufficient and, in order to do that, she had to achieve the status of a man by respecting the rules of the hunt. Although she was still a woman, she became a real man in social terms.

Single men, in contrast, rarely developed their feminine side and tended to be looked after by the women in their families. The only culinary task to which they could devote themselves without any loss of status had to do with fire – an old masculine symbol and the antithesis of water. So they grilled the meat: some contemporary customs, such as the male speciality of taking responsibility for the Sunday barbecue, have a long memory.

Paradoxically, and in the face of adversity, the first unmarried women did therefore succeed in achieving a greater autonomy than their male counterparts. But they were the exception. The model still made all women subordinate to some man. Although there were fewer

5

of them, unmarried men were also the exception. In societies based upon the notion of equilibrium, marriage was a basic part of the social order. And yet the equilibrium was destroyed.

Celibacy Becomes Legitimate

Ideally, I would like to be able to describe in a few simple words the sequence of events that paved the way for modern singledom. It is, alas, impossible for me to do so. That is a task for a professional historian and I am no more than an amateur. It should have to have been begun by others, but it has been shelved or confined to the margins of related topics such as sexuality or marriage, which have been more widely discussed (Flandrin 1981; Duby 1983[1981]; Bologne 1998).

What is to be done? Should we begin with the nineteenth century? So many things happened before then, and I do know a little about them. I have chosen to talk about them, even though I cannot tell the story I dreamed of telling. May the historians who read these lines be generous enough to do so with indulgence.

The earliest religions were the most purely contemplative and integrative: the history of religious beliefs can be seen as the slow and gradual mobilization of the social. Marcel Gauchet notes (1997[1985]) that a first important break came with the emergence of the state in about 3000 BC, and that it is the real beginning of our 5,000 years of history growth. A new and crucial event occurred with the emergence of the idea of one God, from Persia to China and from India to Palestine. This heralded great changes to come because it established the preconditions for a personal relationship with the divine. But it was Christianity that inaugurated the decisive revolution by contrasting heaven and earth, and commanding everyone to act in such a way as to win their own personal salvation. Individual fates were no longer irremediably and collectively sealed; the individual project became part of human life, and opened up a 'crack in being' (Gauchet 1985: 47). It encouraged introspection.

The rise of individualization is not to be confused with that of celibacy. The former affects society as a whole, whereas the latter's effects are confined to one category of individuals. And yet there is no denying that celibacy, and even solitude, did play an essential role from the very beginning. Those who wished to think about the world had to be detached from it. Louis Dumont analyses (1986) how hermits were the precursors of modernity because the virtues of solitude allowed them to explore a personal relationship with God.

For our purposes, the most important thing is that, for the first time in history (and thanks to the great debates that rocked the Church), one form of celibacy became legitimate, and liberated individual creativity. The most innovative intellectuals, for example, often put on a monk's habit. It was only because he was a monk that Erasmus, who revolutionized his time, was able to do what he did. He lived alone (that is the etymological root of the word 'monk'), devoted all his time to intellectual debate, travelled all over Europe and became involved in passionate group discussions.

A Maid in Men's Clothes

The mobilization of society does not just produce heroes and geniuses in the upper reaches of society. Other forms of celibacy developed at the very bottom of the social scale, in the dark depths that were rejected by the organized world. In the world of women, the figures of the prostitute and the witch emerged. In the world of men, in the world of forests and heaths, charcoal burners and brigands also seemed to mix with evil spirits (Castel 1990). Other equivocal figures could also be glimpsed: wretched knights-errant, who were younger landless sons prepared for all kinds of adventures, students and shady monks. Were they at the top or the bottom of the social hierarchy? In many cases, it is hard to tell, as their subsequent lives could take them in either direction. They are early illustrations of a very modern component element in the single trajectory: they are deeply contradictory.

From that point of view, Joan of Arc is a veritable textbook example. She was a poor uneducated shepherdess, and her most likely destiny was to be marginalized or to be burned as a witch before she had time to leave her mark on history (and that did almost happen: on several occasions, she was described as mad or suspected of being a witch and underwent an exorcism). Instead, she embarked on one of the most astonishingly upward trajectories imaginable, moving from the status of a mere shepherdess to the highest military rank and commanding the king's armies. How did she do it? She was able to do so because her inner convictions were unshakable and because she remained resolutely celibate. Like Erasmus, Joan could not have accomplished such feats if she had been forced to play a very different domestic role and had devoted herself to looking after a family. She did quite the opposite. She lived (with great passion) only for her ideas and invested body and soul in the destiny she imagined for herself. And she fulfilled that destiny. Often quite alone, in the face of

7

the hostility of those around her, and protected only by the strength of her reflexivity and her inner voices.

Joan only hesitated once, on 24 May 1431 (though she never flinched when she was tortured). Three days later, she took a new grip on herself by remaining true to her voices. And in order to make her point even more forcefully, she once more put on a man's clothes (Le Goff 1985). It is disturbing to note that, in the olden days, the women who embarked upon the most spectacularly independent paths had to come to terms with male attributes. In a male-dominated world, Joan (like Great Buffalo Woman and, later, George Sand) had to become something of a man in order to become a woman out of the ordinary. Hence the strange figure and the totally atypical identity of a virgin wearing armour. If, however, we look at her in terms of the historical emergence of unmarried trajectories, Joan does not look so strange. She was certainly an extremist with exceptional will power and strength, but there was nothing strange about her: she was a pioneer.

These few lines may look iconoclastic or even sacrilegious to anyone who has a very different image of Joan of Arc. More so than any other woman, she has been the object of many attempts at ideological recuperation (Le Goff 1985). I think that it is mainly because we have no history of the single life that my comments sound so surprising: many biographies of Joan could be revised in completely new terms if the fact that she was single were seen as the key analytic tool. That history is, however, difficult to write (since it probably does not yet exist). This is because celibacy is intimately bound up with a much broader and much more complex process: the individualization of society.

Introspection

Throughout this book, I will be discussing two questions that are at once interrelated and distinct. I will of course be discussing celibacy, usually in the modern form of singledom. But I will also be discussing the more general trend within which it is inscribed, and of which it is no more than one manifestation: the individuation of the social. Louis Dumont has described (1986) in broad terms the primordial model from which it gradually emerged. That model is one of the holistic society in which individuals are no more than parts of a totality that encompasses them. The future is a destiny that is predetermined, truth and morality are imposed collectively, and personal identity itself is defined by the position the individual occupies within the group.

Our society opens up a new and completely different perspective. It is centred on the individual, encourages self-definition and enjoins us to choose, choose and choose again at every moment and in every domain. We choose our truth, and the number of truths on offer becomes ever-greater and ever-more contradictory as they are popularized by the media. Even the simplest actions we perform in the course of our day-to-day lives, which used to be prescribed by tradition, are now a matter of individual choice. We choose our morality from a very broad range of values that proscribes only a small number of things that are taboo. We choose our social bonds and accumulate our relational capital, and doing so involves both work and a certain competence (which is not randomly distributed across the social chessboard). We imagine our own futures, intervene on the basis of our own scenarios and projects, and thus make the idea of destiny redundant. We define and construct, finally, our own identities, and do not leave it to others – and still less to society – to tell us who we are and what we will become. This invention of the present and the future necessarily involves a subjective effort, introspection and reflexivity. This is not synonymous with isolation. Norbert Elias has demonstrated (1991) that, on the contrary, the development of greater introspection is bound up with the multiplication and diversification of ties of interdependence. Individuation is not a form of autarchic withdrawal.

There are other misunderstandings that have to be cleared up. That the groundswell of individualism is irrepressible does not mean that it is predictable or uninterrupted. On the contrary, powerful countertendencies alter one or another aspect of the landscape, sometimes for centuries at a time. For similar reasons, the fact that the individual is now, in historical terms, centre stage must not lead us to conclude that concrete individuals can be fully responsible for their acts or that their behaviours can be completely rational: reality is far removed from that model. What matters is the long-term direction of the trend: we are becoming more and more responsible for our own actions, and our desire to shape our own lives is growing stronger.

The link between the general trend towards individuation and towards celibacy is complex. The premises of individualization were originally dreamed up by celibate individuals (Dumont 1986). The link between actively taking responsibility for our lives and remaining single is now much looser. Those individuals who actively take responsibility for their own lives may well be married; individuals who are not part of a couple may well reject the idea of self-definition. It is, for example, rare for anyone to make a deliberate decision to remain on their own. And yet a growing number of those who do live alone no

9

longer wish to cease doing so (at least for a while), or are making very great demands on partners who would change their status. In some cases, singledom becomes the clearest and most radical manifestation of the diffuse and many-sided trend towards a society that is centred on the individual. It is also a reliable indicator that the trend is real.

The World Turned Upside Down

This historical trend went through a crucial stage during the so-called 'Century of Enlightenment', but that had little visible impact on celibacy. And yet this essential pivotal period in the long history that leads to modern singledom has to be mentioned. Prior to that, some individuals (Lombard bankers and navigators like Columbus) and thinkers (from Socrates to Montaigne) certainly did experiment with new forms of the 'care of the self' (Foucault 1986). But although the trend became more pronounced during the Renaissance, those pioneers were still in the minority (Laurent 1993). At some point, the balance of power between holism and individualism was inverted: minority ferments became the norm and holism began to be confined to various small private groups (and especially the family cell). Marcel Gauchet (1997[1985]) attempted to date the moment when the world was turned upside down to 'somewhere around 1700', which is when 'what is certainly the greatest break ever to have occurred in history' took place. The meaning of this break must be clearly understood. It was not sudden: almost nothing changed between 1699 and 1701, and the individualist revolution has to be reckoned in terms of hundreds or even thousands of years. But a major theoretical event did take place 'somewhere around 1700': the individual became the main principle of the social.

The result was that certain sectors of activity broke free and began to develop autonomously. As we all know, the eighteenth century was one of intellectual and political revolutions that laid the foundations for modern science and the Declaration of the Rights of Man and the Citizen. The collective effervescence surrounding the emergent individual seems, however, to have had little effect on private life. Celibacy continued to exist on the fringes of society thanks to the poverty of vagabonds, the discretion of widows and the minor escapades of erudite libertines. It was not until the next century and the Industrial Revolution that marriage once more came under attack.

The Nineteenth Century: The Main Trend Begins

The widespread view that the nineteenth century was rigid and disciplined is only partly true: contradictory forces were at work behind that façade. As we shall see, its Puritanism cast a veil of modesty over the discovery of new emotions and the rise of a new physical sensibility. Similarly, the obsessive hymns to the family and the incantatory odes to mothers and domestic virtues were primarily designed to ward off the danger that there might be another model for private life. The nineteenth century was the century of both Louis Bonald and Charles Fourier (Chaland 1998).

The contradiction between the two models (the individual or the family as the basis of society) was blatantly obvious as early as the Revolution, which, despite its attachment to family values, passed an astonishingly modern law on divorce (Bart 1990; Ronsin 1990). It was promptly repealed under the Restoration. But the supporters of a sovereign family order were powerless to resist the irrepressible trend towards individual emancipation, which found its main expression in the increase in the number of people who failed to marry.

Until then, celibacy had not been unusual but, because single people were scattered across the countryside and hidden within their families, they succeeded in disappearing into 'the grey background' (Farge and Klapisch-Zuber 1984). Younger sons who were sacrificed on the altar of primogeniture, soldiers and prisoners, vagabonds with no fixed abode, wretched day labourers huddled in garrets, maidservants tied to their masters' households, melancholy and self-effacing widows, the sick and handicapped women who were rejected as unfit for marriage, the maiden aunts who devoted themselves to their families, the nuns who lived in convents, and the women who became prostitutes after having been raped – there was a long list of specific categories of 'marginals living on the periphery of a society whose center was the family' (Perrot 1990a: 259). As a result of the Industrial Revolution and because of the bright lights of the big cities, this shadow army was still relegated to the margins, but it suddenly began to look like a more visible cohort of individuals who had chosen to live that way; by the end of the century, a new form of celibacy was beginning to emerge and was starting to take on the forms that we know today.

The first centred on residential autonomy. Being single while living in a family and living alone in one's own lodgings were two different realities. Some people did live alone before the nineteenth century, especially in the poorest milieus, where they tended to lead marginal existences rather than live in the centre of their villages (Bourdelais

11

1984). But because they were both scattered and discreet, they remained invisible and their singularity did not stand out. Their families took them in when they could afford to do so; single people who lived alone did so because they had no alternative. When people began to live on their own in the towns, they usually did so away from their families and, although their accommodation was poor, it allowed them to become independent. Their little garrets may well have been poorly furnished or even squalid, but they allowed them to dream their own dreams. Even though the future was not easy, it was becoming less hard to invent it, and individual destinies were no longer something that were sealed in advance and by others.

Despite the contextual differences, these experiments in living outside marriage were strikingly similar to the forms with which we are now familiar: it is as though we had, in the past 30 years, picked up a trend that appears to have started 100 years ago. Let us look at four examples: geographical propagation, moments in the life cycle, social polarization and women's work.

Geographical propagation. Celibacy was not a specifically urban phenomenon. Indeed, it tended to be more common in small and remote rural communities, where the demographic imbalance meant that more and more people were unable to find a suitable partner, given their age and social status. The phenomenon began to change in the nineteenth century. Whereas rural celibacy continued to exist on a recurrent basis, a new tendency for people to remain single began to spread from the big cities to the countryside, and also from the countries of Northern Europe to the South. Compared with England's spinsters, who were free and spirited and many of whom had successful careers in the retail business, the arts and the sciences, Italy's *zitelle* still found it difficult to enter the world of work in the early twentieth century. They were still marked by the atmosphere of suspicion and the need for discretion incumbent upon unmarried women, who were objects of pity and sarcasm (Di Giorgio 1992). The pattern (from the town to the countryside and from North to South) is still the same today.

Moments in the life cycle. As today, being unmarried was not a status that is evenly distributed across the age range. It was characteristic of the extremes of youth and old age. Old women have been living on their own for a long time. The number of widows living on their own did, however, rise in the nineteenth century. Working-class widows were destitute and lived in seclusion; their urban and bourgeois counterparts were active and self-confident: 'Widowhood could be a form of emancipation, a sinister way of taking revenge on the way

12

roles were distributed within couples' (Perrot 1984: 299). The phenomenon of young people living alone is much more recent, and is a product of deracination and the exodus from the countryside. Before 1850, girls living in small towns still did not dare to live independently (Dauphin 1984). When they began to work in the big towns and cities, they lived much further away from their families of origin: the growth of residential autonomy was irresistible, and it affected young people too. Living alone was an uncomfortable experience, especially for the poorest: unmarried washerwomen, seamstresses and factory workers shared cramped accommodation while they looked for husbands or, failing that, common-law husbands. But as they waited, the effects of their single status began to affect young people too. Some professions even went so far as to institutionalize celibacy for young people. Domestic servants remained single until they were 30 or even 40, and left service when they got married (Fraisse 1979). Department stores would not allow their sales assistants to marry (and sacked them when they reached 30; Parent-Lardeur 1984). The lives of many women therefore began to follow a new pattern of three successive phases: professional experience and financial autonomy when they were single, marriage and then widowhood. On the whole, they spent less time living with partners. These contrasting phases, and the tendency to spend less time with conjugal partners, are still characteristic of the biographical trajectories of women today.

Social polarization. It was more common for those living at the extremes of the social spectrum to be on their own. In the case of the poor – beggars and other vagabonds – it was a well-established phenomenon (Castel 1995). It did, however, become more common as urban poverty increased. New ways of rejecting the bourgeois model of private life began to emerge amongst the cultivated classes too: the decision to remain single was part of an assertive counter-culture. Most of those who could afford to be so daring were men – bohemian artists and individualistic dandies (Perrot 1990a: 257). For their part, women embarked upon careers *en masse*. This social polarization is still typical of today's singles, the only difference being that some women have been so successful that they have now taken the place of the old bohemians and dandies.

Working women. The number of women earning their own living rose steadily throughout the nineteenth century (Marchand and Thélot 1997). In the (non-domestic) service sector, their professionalization went hand in hand with rising levels of competence and higher qualifications. An army of women now found themselves torn between the joys of the autonomy given them by work and the pain of

13

not being married. The most committed felt that they had a sort of vocation: they were powerless to resist the trend. They were being swept along by history. They became young ladies employed in department stores (Parent-Lardeur 1984), worked for the postal service (Pezerat and Poublon 1984), became health visitors (Knibiehler 1984) and taught in primary and secondary schools (Cacouault 1984). The higher their qualifications, the more they embraced their careers, and the more difficult it became for them to find husbands. Their professions gave them self-confidence and status, and opened up new horizons. They became too self-confident, had too much status and had too many new prospects to be satisfied with those uneducated and brutal candidate-husbands who were still available, or to accept the suffocating prospect of married life under such conditions. The gap between men and women is still relevant today. And women's levels of qualification are still the main factor in their segregation (Flahault 1996).

Grisettes and Phalansteries

While the bourgeois conjugal way of life became the norm in almost all social milieus, the growing number of working women prevented it from becoming universal: these pioneers of autonomy were the unwitting harbingers of a counter-model. In many cases, they were reluctant pioneers, as this subversive ferment did not make everyday life any easier. Their peculiar status attracted attention. They did not fit in and were often suspected of being deviant: stigmatizing them was the only way that those who were comfortable with the norms of the moment could ward off their anxiety: 'Were these creatures who ventured outside the domain of their sex really women?' (Perrot 1995: 45). Their perceived failings and what was assumed to be their emotional frigidity were used as excuses to pigeonhole these unfortunate women in the ready-made category of 'old maids'. They were sometimes criticized for the opposite reason: a woman who was too free was inevitably a loose woman. The term *"femme isolée"* was in fact used to refer to both working women who lived alone and clandestine prostitutes (Scott 1990). In a period of strict morality, such suspicions were intolerable – especially as it meant having to resist temptation: a freer and more sensual life was indeed within their reach at a time when, despite superficial Puritanism, bodies were secretly discovering new desires (Corbin 1990). Unmarried women who were firmly committed to their professions, such as primary schoolteachers, therefore

14

constructed characteristic personas in self-defence: a tight bun and a high-buttoned blouse. Rejecting the opposite stereotype, they flaunted their affluence, their ability to speak their own minds and especially their elegance (fine but discreet lace, fox-fur collars). As a result they stood out from all the dried up, ill-tempered old maids who 'smelled rancid' (Perrot 1984: 300). Rejecting both the categories that were on offer, they asserted their difference: they represented a social figure that had yet to be identified or defined.

Sales assistants in department stores, who were more torn between work and marriage (unlike schoolmistresses, their single status was usually temporary), chose a rather different option. As their greatest fear was that they would be seen as old maids, their elegance was more colourful. They wore more perfume, displayed their charms and risked falling into the opposite stereotype. And yet they did often succeed in striking a balance, and succeeded in looking like autonomous individuals who were neither loose women nor old maids, and who were beginning to be part of the social landscape.

There were, of course, real 'old maids' and real courtesans, but they were relatively few in number. It was only because the imaginary categories were so vague that there seemed to be so many of them. 'Blue stockings', for example, were systematically mocked, suspected of being emotionally frigid and accused of being 'old maids'. They were in fact often pioneers in their own right, and were committed body and soul to their very individual trajectories (Flahault 1996). As for loose women, there was a vast gulf between prostitution and freedom of morals.

Take the *grisettes*. Moralists violently rejected the lifestyle of the young seamstresses of the Latin Quarter. They were carefree, and lived for flirtation, gaiety and love. They were impressed by the new moral codes they had learned from bourgeois women and were intoxicated with the way students courted them so romantically (Guillais-Maury 1984). After all that, how could they reconcile themselves to marrying men from their own milieu and to sinking into the darkness of the working-class world of the nineteenth century? They preferred sonnets, sweet nothings and caresses, even though it meant self-destruction of a different kind, a lonely old age and poverty (once they had lost their looks, their fairytale princes abandoned their pretty little sweethearts and got married). So were the *grisettes* loose women? Of course they were. But, in one sense, they were autonomous women too. They refused to reconcile themselves to a life in which there was no glamour and no excitement, lived their lives in accordance with

15

their girlish dreams and invented forms of conjugality that have now become legitimate.

The *grisettes* were looking for a new code of love. The nineteenth century was unable to live up to their revolutionary ideas. On the contrary, it was a period that wanted to reinforce matrimonial norms. Those utopias that did flourish were swimming against the current, and were doomed to remain on paper or to be restricted to a few marginal experiments. And yet the ideas behind them were very daring. The view that the married couple was the foundation of society was the prime target of most radical thinkers. In his *Le Nouveau Monde amoureux*, written in 1816 but not published until 1967, Charles Fourier sang the praises of the liberation of desire and of the untrammelled sexuality he wanted to see flourishing in his 'phalansteries'. He outlined a serial conjugality (leading to marriage only late in life) similar to what we know today. His model could not, however, become a reality in his day because he put too much mathematical rigour into designing his phalanstery, and above all because mentalities were so focused on the family (and Fourier's disciples in fact played down this aspect of his programme).

The rise of individualism within private life took other and more discreet paths, and circumvented the institution of marriage without overthrowing it. The upheaval was not the result of a radical challenge to marriage, but of slow changes in everyday life, and especially in the day-to-day lives of women. Those who became wage-earners discovered independence. And they no longer had any qualms about taking a critical view of what they might get out of marriage. Getting married was not enough: their future husbands really did have to give them a better life. Witness this reader's letter, published in *Le Petit Echo de la mode* in 1907: 'I therefore took the time to think, compare and observe; my meditations are not in favour of marriage. I am 25. I am no longer a child. Know what I want and what I am doing. I am of sound mind and I have chosen my own path. My heart knows no regrets' (cited in Raffin 1987).

The Break

In historical terms, individual autonomization is not a linear process but a series of waves that create particular generational styles (Terrail 1995). When the tide is high, men and women feel that they are being irresistibly carried away. And then the tide turns, rather as though society had to get back to dry land before embarking on a new adventure. At the beginning of the twentieth century, the wave was on the point of becoming a real groundswell (especially for women). And then one event suddenly reversed the trend: the Great War.

This analysis will surprise those readers who are convinced that, when they took the place of the men who had been mobilized at the front, women became a more significant presence in factories and offices. The reality was more complex. Women replaced men only to a limited extent, and were often restricted to subaltern jobs or jobs with female connotations, such as cleaning, quality control, keeping records, caring for the wounded and feeding the homeless. In the imaginary, however, the idea that men might lose their traditional role resulted in a collective anxiety that had already begun to make itself felt during the emancipatory upsurges of the nineteenth century. François Thébaud (1994[1992]) stresses the paradox: the progress being made by women in the world of work (and they were not making great progress) triggered a conservative closure of minds. This change of attitude probably had a lot to do with the new style women had adopted (an entrepreneurial self-confidence that marked a complete break with their earlier self-effacement, a free and strong allure that frightened men). 'What was really new was that women were living alone, going out alone, and taking full control of family responsibilities. All these things had previously seemed impossible and dangerous' (Thébaud 1992: 48). The trend for women to enjoy greater autonomy had lasted for several decades and appeared to be accelerating still further, and that was too much.

Although the women of 1914–18 seemed to have a brilliant future ahead of them, the old order was about to be restored. The restoration of the image of the dominant male took place under the sign of the brave poilu: women had to be brought back into line. First of all, they had to go back to being mothers again. How could a good mother leave home to go to work, and not devote herself completely to her children? In Germany and England, the answer was a clear 'She cannot': a woman's place was in the home. In France, women were now too integrated into production for their labour to be withdrawn on a large scale (Lagrave 1994[1992]). Criticisms of women's autonomy therefore became even more virulent, especially now that the birth rate was on everyone's mind: the real heroines were the mothers with 10 children, and from 1920 onwards they were awarded the *médaille de la famille*. In Italy, Gina Lombroso's book *L'anima della donna* (1917–18) reminded women of their procreative mission, and was a huge success (Di Giorgio 1992).

17

For men whose identity had been undermined, this return to the old models felt like revenge. For their part, many of the women who were exhausted after all their efforts wanted peace and quiet, and were happy to retreat into their families. All the preconditions were there for the great matrimonial consensus that would emerge during the inter-war period.

Dark Times

The belle époque was well and truly over. It had seemed that everything was changing and speeding up, but society was now settling back into its old ways and beginning to breathe more slowly. In the immediate post-war years, the message was not yet unanimous. The image of the 'bachelor girl', which was popularized by Victor Margueritte's 1922 novel, may have given the impression of a groundswell, but it was no more than an imaginary ripple: women quietly went back into their homes and stayed there for a long time.

The ambient discourse spread the idea of a new and modern life. Paulette Bernège and the Salon des Arts Ménagers (which opened in 1923) pointed the way to a technological revolution in everyday life. Sadly, the realities of domestic life were slow to change. For the vast majority, the revolution meant no more than a boiler for the washing, tinned food and electricity; more time was spent on housework, and conditions scarcely improved. In 1948, only 4 per cent of British households owned a washing machine, and only 2 per cent had a refrigerator. In 1954, 42 per cent of French people still did not have running water (Sohn 1994[1992]). Women had given up what they already had for an uncertain future. They had exchanged their growing autonomy for a domestic modernity that had yet to become a reality. It was a grim and narrow-minded period.

But an era's dominant voice can never drown out the descants: although they were muffled by the doleful melody of domestic reorganization, other voices were singing a different song. Women had indeed basically gone back to being mothers (Knibiehler and Fouquet 1977), the angel in the house (Perrot 1990a), and were obediently dependent on their husbands. Their bodies, however, told a different story. Their movements became freer by the year. The corsets, the starched underwear and the cumbersome hats went into the bin. Women showed their legs and took big strides. They displayed their unfettered bodies with a strength and freedom of movement that showed how much they had changed (Montreynaud 1992). Although they wanted to retreat into their families and stay there, they also stressed their individuality and were becoming aware of their own strength. The male/female balance within marriage was becoming more equal, and some women were even bold enough to ask for a divorce (Sohn 1994). In 1919, women began to take the *baccaulauréat*, which gave them access to the universities. Women like Colette, Simone Lenglen and Marie Curie were becoming important figures in various domains. It was not unusual for some women to behave more independently (given the imbalance between the sexes after the war, this was inevitable). 'But they were not part of an overall dynamic, and were smothered by the almost consensual discourse about the wife-and-mother' (Thébaud 1992 [1994: 73]).

The American Model

A comparison with the United States is not without its uses. Very active feminist movements emerged there at the end of the nineteenth century. The years between 1910 and 1920 saw more women than ever entering the liberal professions and finding 'white-collar' jobs; the idea that marriage was their only prospect was seriously called into question.

The war, which was taking place far away, did not lead to any major changes. And yet, the same withdrawal into the family could be observed from the 1920s onwards, even though its modalities were not the same as in Europe. It was not a reactionary and conservative trend provoked by a weakening of women's identity. New factors internal to the family were beginning to compete with and hold back the dynamics of autonomization.

The first was the mechanization of the home. Unlike in Europe (where it remained on the drawing board for a long time to come), it quickly became a reality and rapidly revolutionized housework. A whole nation was affected by a burst of modernization. The domestic group was transformed into an efficient unit in which activities became increasingly diversified. In 1928, one American in six owned a car and 40 per cent of households had a radio (Cott 1994[1992]).

The second factor was the revolution in married life. A new ideal couple designed by an army of experts nurtured on the human sciences soon became the norm. In contrast with the old model (which was hierarchical, rigid and rather uncommunicative), it recommended greater intimacy and relational exchanges based upon equality and mutual respect between partners, as well as an emotional and sexual liberation for both husband and wife. Modernity had arrived: it became possible to find a new personal self-fulfilment within marriage (which enjoyed unprecedented popularity in the inter-war period). What more could a woman want? As a result, women who refused to commit themselves to this absolute model were described 'as a danger to society, as irrational and unhealthy creatures, and as somewhat mannish and frigid' (Cott 1992: 80). Women who had been to university, and who tended to be unmarried, became the most ardent propagandists for this new image of marriage and abandoned the idea of autonomy. The American model of self-fulfilment within marriage was born and would (together with the mechanization of the home) spread to Europe in the 1950s. The definition of conjugal marriage had never been clearer, and marriage had never before been so stable and so widespread. It seemed that any other lifestyle could only be deviant, dysfunctional or a failure on the part of the individual concerned. Until, in the mid-1960s, a giant hurricane tore through this peaceful matrimonial sky. The parenthesis of 50 years of conjugal restoration was closed as quickly as it had opened, and the trend for autonomy took off again.

The Scandinavian Model

This time, the influence came not from the United States but from Northern Europe. A different option had been taken as early as the 1930s, especially in Sweden, where, in order to ward off the economic crisis, the welfare state had begun to intervene in family life. Relations between the individual, the family and the state formed a perfect triangle. When the state withdrew, the family strengthened its hold; when the state intervened, the individual was emancipated. The state acted as modern individualism's midwife, and guaranteed everyone the right to define their own identity (Schultheis 1991). For that to be possible, inequalities between different categories of the population had to be compensated for. Franz Schultheis emphasizes that, after an initial historical stage in which state intervention was directed at the poor, women became democracy's new beneficiaries: only the state could allow them not to be dependent on their husbands and to define their identity on their own terms.

Sweden and the other Scandinavian countries began to go down this road at the very moment when the American model seemed to be taking over the whole of the Western world. The goal of relational equality within the family was the same as in the American model, especially where children were concerned (Dencik 1995). Individual/ family priorities were, on the other hand, completely inverted. The outcome was that the usual familial schemata were turned upside down. Authentic commitment, and not stability, was now the cardinal virtue. The pivot was no longer the *pater familias* but the woman, now firmly established in the world of work and free either to remain on her own with her children or to live with a partner (Arve-Parès 1996). By 'marrying' the welfare state, women established the preconditions for their autonomy in two senses. This was especially true of women with children, who benefited greatly from the Scandinavian model. In liberal countries such as the United States or Great Britain, there was a close association between single parenthood and poverty. This was not the case in the Scandinavian countries, and especially not in Sweden (Lefaucheur 1994[1992]).

Crazy Times

The wind of autonomy blew steadily from Northern Europe, first to the central countries (Netherlands and Germany) and then the countries of the West (France and Great Britain) before encountering a certain matrimonial resistance in the Catholic countries of the South (Italy, Spain and Portugal). The change was especially rapid in those countries that had adopted social welfare policies based upon the Scandinavian model. But intervention was not restricted to those political elements. Much more progress was made in the big cities, but in the countryside the social system remained unchanged. The impetus actually came from a deep underlying historical trend: a new wave was irresistibly sweeping individuals along with it. Like that of the previous century, it would destabilize the family and in doing so provoke new theoretical ways of thinking about the family (Cicchelli-Pugeault and Cicchelli 1998).

A few indicators allow this development to be dated with relative accuracy: it occurred in the mid-1960s (Roussel 1989). Initially, few were aware that the trend had been reversed. Things became a little clearer thanks to the 'events' of 1968, even though they were dominated by a political phraseology that masked the cultural revolution that was taking place. It had an impact in the forms taken by individual emancipation (Terrail 1995). Women were, of course, in the front line and they marched under the banner of equality. The greatest novelty was, however, the sudden appearance on the scene of young people. Throughout the Western world, the ways in which they

21

established conjugal relationships and entered the adult world were revolutionized in just a few years. 'Youth' was becoming the great moment of existential creativity, and young people were free to imagine what their lives should look like: it was advisable to take one's time and not to commit oneself too soon. How to commit oneself, who to commit oneself to and for what purpose were also important issues: introspection was a way of inventing a better private world. No one should have any hesitations about breaking off a relationship if it did not live up to the dream. No one should have any hesitations about remaining on their own if the prospect of living with someone was not sufficiently attractive. This was especially true for women, because starting a family was still an obstacle to having a professional career and it therefore reduced their autonomy (Singly 1987).

The 'couple' was becoming a more flexible notion. Living with a partner was an intense experience, but it was not always one that lasted: the number of individuals who were not permanently living with partners (and who were spending more time on their own) began to rise once more, and did so rapidly and inexorably. The parenthesis of the dark times had been well and truly closed.

Uncertain Times

The tide obviously began to turn again at the beginning of the twenty-first century. So how do matters stand now? Has a new parenthesis been opened? There are no easy answers to these questions.

This is certainly not a time for individual inventiveness. We are afraid of the future, and the need for protection is reactivating traditional values. The crisis in social welfare funding is forcing the state to retreat and to re-establish the family as the pivot for socialization in every domain. Women bear most of the burden of this redeployment of the family. They appear to have accepted this and have (no doubt provisionally) abandoned the idea of entering the world of work on the same terms as men (it takes too much effort and is very destructive in terms of their identity). Faced with a future that frightens them, young people are trying to enter the adult world earlier. People who are not in relationships are no longer seen in the way they were seen in the 1970s and '80s: the 'single women' we feel so sorry for have replaced the 'superwomen', the 'new single women' (Laufer 1987) and other unmarried women.

And yet, despite the unfavourable climate, residential independence is still becoming more common, and that is the most reliable

22

indicator. In Europe, the wind of autonomy continues to blow from north to south, and it is now influencing countries that had previously been unaffected. Forms of socialization specific to young people are becoming more widespread and more pronounced: they are slow to commit themselves and are spending longer periods on their own.

It is as though independence had reached a limit that means that any backlash will be ineffective, and that it is not really possible to open a new parenthesis. Although it has obviously slowed down, the trend is quietly growing stronger.

2

A LIFE DIVIDED

Those who are now experimenting with living on their own do not really think about this long history. Society's memory is sedimented much more deeply in the depths of the implicit. Many people begin to live on their own for very pragmatic reasons, without making any real decision to do so, and without any clear awareness of the vast historical process in which it is inscribed. Which does not make it any easier to understand the specificities of this particular trajectory. Let us begin with the most important: the strange way it divides lives into two.

The 'Accusing Finger'

Living alone inevitably leads to a form of splitting: the two parts of the Self are permanently at war with one another but neither can ever win a decisive victory. 'The problem at the moment is the incoherence inside me' (Charlène). Such is the paradox of the situation: the single life is a life divided.

Uncertainty and instability are the price that has to be paid for this tearing apart of identity. Which is the real Self: the woman who laughs, or the woman who cries? Which is the real woman: the woman who feels herself to be free and strong, or the woman who feels as lost as an abandoned child? The answer to these questions shows just how complex they are: they are both the 'real woman'. The split is a structural and situational given, and it is absolutely inevitable. The extent to which it is pronounced obviously varies, but it is always there. It is most pronounced when life is perfectly divided into two equal parts. It is least pronounced when being single has a highly positive value. It is even less pronounced at the opposite extreme, or when life seems to

24

be nothing more than a bottomless black hole. Whereas the woman who cries can come close to the extreme point where she cannot see even the slightest ray of happiness (loneliness as pure unhappiness), the woman who laughs cannot succeed in being perfectly happy. There is a reason for this: society's 'accusing finger'. Lydia feels that it is pointing at her: 'I could quite easily get used to being on my own, if it weren't for the looks, the words and the situations that come together to point an accusing finger, to make me understand that I really am outside the norm, and therefore suspect.'

Outside the norm? Is there really such a thing as a norm or a model for private life? This may seem a strange thing to say at a time when the family is becoming deinstitutionalized and when a growing number of flexible forms are recognized as legitimate. Cohabitation, reconstituted families and even children born outside marriage: everyone now seems to have the right to be able to determine the structure of their private life as they see fit. It is all the stranger in that the rise in the number of people who are on their own is part of a powerful historical trend. The figures are there to prove it (see the Appendix, 'The Globalization of Singledom', at the end of this book): what was once a marginal phenomenon that concerned only widows and the excluded has become a powerful groundswell. It now affects a growing number of younger and educated women and is encouraging them to live autonomous lives. When they embark upon this new life, the most active of them often make a pleasant discovery: the lightness of being, which is the key to being in control of their own destiny, gives off an intoxicating smell of freedom. Elisa has no regrets: 'I am proud of being on my own, of being able to be self-critical so easily, of being able to have an open mind about other people. All that would hardly be possible if I had a husband and children.' And yet the pleasure is never complete: 'Why can't I take advantage of all the possibilities that being single offers? Why the depression? Why all the questions?' Sometimes it is because she would like to have someone with her. But usually, it is because the 'accusing finger' is at once everywhere and invisible.

Public pronouncements notwithstanding ('Everyone is free to do what they like'), there therefore is such a thing as a model for private life. It is hidden and kept secret, but it suddenly – and cruelly – makes its presence felt when a single woman feels that the 'accusing finger' is being pointed at her. The pleasure is ruined. Freedom begins to taste bitter, and lots of unpleasant questions come to mind.

'Weird'

It all starts with the process that pigeonholes her as 'out of the ordinary, not like the rest' (Maria). Anne-Laure feels she is 'a lonely island in the crowd, living alongside the other people that make up society'. Out of the ordinary, and outside society, like a more or less undesirable alien whose presence is merely tolerated. 'It's our invisible yellow star' (Marie-Andrée).

While public discourse officially proclaims that 'Everyone can do what they like', the 'accusing finger' pigeonholes and condemns them: 'Fails to respect the norms!' In the double-speak characteristic of democratic societies, the abnormality is no more than hinted at by silences and is never spelled out (Kaufmann 1995a). And yet this discrete message cuts single women to the quick: 'Deep down inside, you cannot avoid thinking that you might be not quite normal' (Annick). But are they abnormal? Society proclaims their right to be single and the single life does have its good side. So what is the problem? 'Weird': the word gradually imprints itself in their brains and becomes an obsession, but it does nothing to solve the mystery. It is a strange life when positives and negatives, tears and laughter are so closely entwined. And what about me? Am I a weird person, then? Isn't it precisely because I am weird that my domestic situation is seen as weird? Not realizing that all these self-doubts only arise because of the 'accusing finger', Sylvie cannot stop herself from going back to the same old question, and causing herself even more pain because she can never find an answer. 'It bothers me all the time: just what is this weird fucking life? It would be all right if I could say to myself: "Calm down, things couldn't be better. Everything's normal." But, no, I can feel them all staring at me: "Weird, weird, strange, not very kosher." But what's so weird about me? Tell me and let's have done with it! What's so weird about me as to get me into this mess?'

The 'accusing finger' has a magnifying effect. The more a woman imagines it is pointing at her, the more hurtful the message it gives out. But it also has a real magnifying effect thanks to the stigmatization process described by Goffman (1963): any imagined flaw leads to the suggestion of a whole series of associated flaws (which of course allows the individual to be pigeonholed as deviant). Then they mention veiled spiteful comments: 'They must think that it's because there's something wrong with me that I'm on my own, a good-looking girl like me' (Charlène). But the real suspicion is that a single woman must be emotionally frigid. The individualization of society secretes the need to make a show of our humanitarian virtues, rather as though

26

they were an antidote to the poison (Singly 1991). In the case of women, and much more so than for men, those virtues are centred on the ability to love and to devote themselves to their families. A single woman is rapidly suspected of being inhuman. Olivia is exasperated by the message she thinks she can hear, especially as she has completely internalized another of democratic society's injunctions (the need for authenticity when it comes to choosing a partner): 'I'm not going to fling myself at the first man who comes along just so that I can shout it from the rooftops!'

When she is walking through a crowd, Adeline 'can tell they are staring' at her and thinks she can hear them whispering: 'What is it about her that puts men off?' These are in fact the accusation's two weapons: looks and whispers. She is always being stared at, everywhere. It does not matter when things are going well, but it is hard when the loneliness becomes oppressive. Poor Juliette feels so isolated that she is ashamed of herself ('I feel that it's obvious to all that I'm on my own, and that makes people stare at me. I hate being stared at and being pitied. I'm ashamed of being on my own'). It makes Liliane feel hatred: 'I hate it when I feel that people are staring at me: poor woman on her own'). Hearing the distant whispers and the actual criticisms is like being stared at: they are everywhere but they are invisible. And yet sometimes they are suddenly spoken out loud in brief comments that contrast sharply with the soothing superficiality. 'Last week, one of my pupils asked me: "Are you a mum, miss?" "No!" "Then what are you, if you aren't a mum?" A cute 7-year-old had knocked me completely off balance. I said nothing for a few seconds. Finally, I gave him an answer: "Nothing!" And in the eyes of a lot of people, we are nothing' (Justine).

Uncomfortable Places

The 'accusing finger' points more directly in certain places and at certain times; in places and at times when, in one way or another, the secret model for private life goes on display and forces itself on everyone.

There is the terribly intimate spectacle of family gatherings (which can range from a banal Sunday lunch to intolerable christenings and weddings). The spectacle of social life in small provincial towns is on a smaller scale, but it is no less restrictive. 'Going out to a café for a drink on my own after 6 was out of the question, and so was going out for a walk at 8 on a June evening when it was too hot to stay in front of the telly. So, thank you for all those freedoms, Paris!' exclaims Géraldine, who came to live in the capital a few months ago and who immediately adds: 'But even here, not everything is possible.' The spectacle of public spaces in the big city appears to give her greater freedom, but it too has its rules, and they are sometimes just as cruel even though they are subtle and implicit. All it takes to make the intro-spection more critical is for a place to be full of individuals who sym-bolize the triumph of family values (couples who are obviously in love or the laughter of children). Even when the lovers mean her no harm and are blind to everything but their love, and even when the children are not in fact laughing at her, their very presence is an accusation. Sylvie no longer goes to the park. 'Especially not in springtime, not with all those couples smooching. I can't stand it.' The image of the lovers reactivates the model, reminds her of her abnormality and brings out the other half of her personality. 'It's like being knifed' (Nelly).

The 'accusing finger' is born of a complex interplay between the public spectacle and the woman who is on her own. The spectacle can take various different forms. There may or may not be suspicious looks and disapproving whispers; there may or may not be demon-strative displays of family values. But the way the woman who is being looked at (or thinks she is being looked at) interprets them is decisive, as the markers are too subtle and too vague to channel any real sub-jectivity. In a piece of research (Kaufmann 1995a) into the secret norms that govern how we behave on the beach, I discovered certain objective indicators: the more the women who take off their bikini tops deviate from what are seen to be normal positions with respect to a set of criteria, the more people (really) stare at them. That allows them to understand the secret rules and to adapt their behaviour to them. On the beach, in contrast, the signs are, to say the least, vague. We can rarely conclude that the behaviour we are observing is abnor-mal simply on the basis of what we see: the woman who is wandering around on her own may well be a married woman who is looking for her children, and so on. The system of gazes that indicates what is normal therefore cannot be established with the same precision. And a woman who is on her own is forced to be on the look out for the smallest clue in order to form an opinion, and there is a serious danger that she will over-react: the more she feels excluded from the model, the more she imagines that the finger is being pointed at her, and the more signs she will see around her, even when they are not obvious. We will look in more detail at an example that typifies the process: the cinema queue.

The cinema is one of the many little pleasures of the single life: single women go to the cinema three times more often than married women (Singly 1991). In the darkness, with all the lights dimmed, a woman on her own feels herself to be fully involved in a cultural communion. There are other people around her, and she is one amongst many and no different from anyone else. But in order to get into the cinema, she has to go through the ordeal of the queue. 'There are days when it is very hard to stay in the queue, with all the couples kissing and laughing, and with parents playing with their children. So I concentrate on my magazine. I can't do without it in difficult moments like that.' Géraldine imagines that a monstrous finger is pointing at her, even though she greatly enjoys her newfound Parisian freedom. What is really going on? Perhaps there was a slight look of surprise, even though it meant nothing and even though not a single word was said. The noisy, demonstrative displays of family values, on the other hand, were all too real. Too noisy and too demonstrative to be totally honest. Why does Géraldine react to them so badly? Why does she not realize that they are forced, that families sometimes have to make a considerable effort and that they have to put on a show in order to make a good impression? Because that good impression is in keeping with the ideal model that obsesses her: the model has only to show its face for her to be plunged into the dark side of her life. And then the finger becomes even more threatening.

Many other spaces are also problematic, especially those associated with evenings out and leisure (with the exception of sporting activities, which are more centred on the individual): restaurants, cafés and theatres. So are the local shops, which are traditionally places where everyone keeps an eye on everyone else, and where buying individual portions quickly attracts attention and triggers comments and jokes that are hard to take. Tired of the barbed comments, Marie-Pierre has finally stopped going to her butcher, even though he has better meat: 'At least they leave me in peace in the supermarket.' In peace, but not really alone, but, compared with the butcher, the checkout assistant is the lesser of two evils.

So there are some uncomfortable places. There are also some uncomfortable moments. Everything that happens in daylight and on working days tends to decrease the model's pressure: daylight and work give the autonomous individual greater freedom. For various reasons, other times of day encourage the 'accusing finger'. Evening does so because it is getting dark and because women who are out on their own have always attracted attention in such circumstances (Di Giorgio 1992), and still do (the same is not true of men). 'Evenings are even worse, because you cannot go out. Our solitary status goes unnoticed during the day, but at night you have the feeling that it becomes fluorescent' (Elodie). Holidays and Sundays are difficult because they are reserved for families. 'It's impossible to go out for a walk by yourself on Sundays because the streets have been invaded by couples and families' (Annick). As for Christmas and Valentine's Day, there is no need to labour the point. Edwige sums up everything that is wrong in one sentence: 'Weekends, Christmas and New Year parties, sunsets and income tax will always be enemies of women who are on their own.'

The Family: What Can Be Said and What Cannot Be Said

The secret model for private life is the result of a profuse and diversified normative production: just as there are 'uncomfortable places' (where the model is at its most influential), an infinite number of social circles also secrete specific norms. Any single woman belongs to several of these circles (family, friends, work colleagues), and each has its own points of reference (Marquet et al. 1997). Two circles within this network of contradictory influences represent its opposite extremes: the family and girlfriends.

This brings us to the world of friends and family, where the mechanism of normative production is not the same as it is in public places: the glances and whispers now give way to real conversations. The understanding and supportive conversation of girlfriends release the hold of the model. Family conversations are more problematic because, with all the good will in the world, families cannot play that role. 'My close family is hard' (Marie-Anne). 'My family are terrible; they don't understand anything' (Leila). This is because families are torn between their desire to help and a greater obligation against which they are powerless: more so than anything else, it is the family that guarantees the application of the model.

Parents hesitate between two ways of thinking and two ways of speaking. There is nothing new about this hesitation, as education is now structured around a contradiction (Singly 1996). Of all the values that families have to pass on, the most precious is the autonomy of the child, which, in theory, invalidates the very notion of 'passing on': it is impossible both to teach children how to behave and to ask them to invent their own lives. The hesitations and incoherence become even greater when children begin to be sexually active. Their parents tell them: 'You have the right (and even a duty) to listen to your heart.'

But, *sotto voce,* they are actually saying: 'There are obviously limits, and a few elementary rules do have to be respected.' For example: there is something odd about the boyfriend a daughter has brought home to meet her parents. They say: 'Of course that's your business.' But the greater the discrepancy between what he is and what the family expects (and when the relationship becomes more serious), the more their parents feel they have to intervene, and may feel that they have to take a firmer line (Cosson 1990).

They are also uncertain as to what attitude to take when their daughter does not bring a boyfriend home to meet them. At first, it does not seem to pose a problem. On the contrary, young people now take their time about settling down to adult life, and their studies have to come first, especially for girls. As time passes, doubts begin to arise: how much longer will she go on putting off getting married? What if she stays single for the rest of her life? Of course she has the right to do so; it's her life. But is it normal? That is the fatal word: 'normal'. Once it has been pronounced, things begin to accelerate. Questions about the norms of private life in fact reveal a peer-group pressure (friends, neighbours, cousins) that had not really made itself felt until now. 'Her neighbour's daughter is getting married in two months: you can just picture it.' Olivia's mother was really shocked by the news. The world suddenly becomes different and aggressive. She feels that the 'accusing finger' is pointing at her personally: you're a mother; don't you think that your daughter is weird? The first classic reflex is to try to shrug off the stigma (Goffman 1963): 'She's been hassling me ever since; she doesn't understand that I haven't found anyone yet.' Finding someone: the terminology is telling. It is too late to evaluate the criteria by which she chooses a partner or turns down suitors. The problem is both serious and urgent: she has to find 'someone' at all cost, no matter who that 'someone' might be; to make the 'accusing finger' go away. Olivia has got the message: 'It's mainly because of my parents that I have such a guilty conscience.' Flora too is annoyed and confused by the pressure that is being brought to bear by the very people who should be understanding and should be supporting her. 'It's as though my parents were getting depressed on my behalf because they don't have a "normal" daughter.'

Her parents feel that the way their daughter is behaving is making them lose face, and that encourages them to intervene. But if that were the only problem, their parental love would allow them to resist the social pressures. But there is something else, something that cannot be defined because its roots plunge deep into the secrets of the soul. Now that they are alone with their destinies, individuals are tragically

31

obsessed with the lightness of their being and the narrowness of their limits. Inscribing themselves in a lineage is one of the few ways that can ward off the obsession with death (Déchaux 1997) and 'put time into check' (Théry 1996: 22). They can turn to their ancestors by reactivating the memory of the dead as they construct a personal identity, or they can turn to their children by over-investing in their education to such an extent that they forget to take care of themselves. The bond of filiation thus becomes 'the ideal form of unconditional and indissoluble bond' (Théry 1996: 22). Individuals can become so immersed in it that they lose all sense of who they are in their own right. Hence the 'anxiety about breaking the chain' (Déchaux 1997: 297). For the parents of a girl who is still single, the anxiety centres on the fact that the chain might very well be broken, that their over-investment in their child might lead to an inexplicable existential void. That is why the social criticisms made by the 'accusing finger' have such resonance and such force: it is not only the laws of society that are being defied, but the rules of life itself. It is at this point in the debate that the arguments come closest to nature and biology: haven't women been meant to have children ever since the beginning of time? 'She never misses an opportunity, and I always get the same comments and the same questions: "When am I going to be a grandmother?". And what about me? There are times when I can't wait to have a baby!' (Bérangère).

The family pressure increases until the daughter is old enough to have a baby in the right conditions, and then it decreases. As the criticisms begin to mount, the modalities of parent/daughter communications can be divided into three typical sequences. At first, there is not the slightest reproach. Indeed, the parents enjoy teasing their daughter, and love is a recurrent theme in the jokes. When they become more serious, they advise her not to get carried away because they are vaguely aware that entering into a relationship too soon would prejudice her future. And then the tone changes imperceptibly. Her parents are worried now. 'When I was 25 or 26, they used to tease me about my love affairs. Now they say nothing and no longer dare ask me "How's your love life?"' (Justine). The oppressive silence, which is full of innuendos, makes her feel uncomfortable. The silence, which speaks through the sudden thematic gaps in the conversation, discreetly points the 'accusing finger' for the first time. 'They no longer dare to ask questions about my private life; I can feel it. All they ask me about is work' (Sabine). During the third phase, finally, comments begin to be made. To be more accurate, it is during this phase that they start to use doublespeak, or a combination of sympathetic silence and sudden barbed comments. 'That's the sentence that hurts: "A beautiful girl like you!"' (Lorraine). Parents (and especially mothers) cannot stop themselves from interfering: 'They'd really love to bring about a miracle cure; they've got whole suitcases full of patent medicines' (Loriane). With a brusqueness that surprises even them, they remind her of the demands of normality because they feel that, for loftier reasons they do not really understand, they have to criticize her. It is, in fact, society that is speaking through them. Deep down in their hearts, they are more inclined to be understanding and forgiving. Unfortunately, they cannot but have mixed feelings – in the same way that their daughter cannot but be torn in two. And, just like her, they never stop asking questions about why she is leading this weird life: why, but why? They get no answer. One final enigma torments them: 'At least she must know. You can feel them itching to ask questions: "But what's so weird about her life, what's wrong with her?"' (Loriane). They do their best not to be critical, and not to ask questions. Until the words come out unprompted. They can't help themselves.

The daughter reacts to these two aspects of her parents' language by taking an ambiguous stance. 'I know full well that, in their eyes, I'm not normal and that all this must be hiding something. I have the impression that I have to justify myself.' And sometimes, when she is forced to, Lydia (or part of Lydia: the most public part of her, the part that is most influenced by the model) has no option but to go suddenly into explanations that are too long and superficial, 'as though someone else was speaking'. The second part of her (the more intimate and autonomous part) watches herself speaking and is sickened by this flow of slightly hypocritical words that express only half of what she is thinking: she lapses back into the silence. 'The best way to get on with your life is to go your own way and ignore the comments. You have to remain impervious.' For both the daughter and her parents, silence is the lesser of two evils, even though it makes them feel uncomfortable. It allows them to preserve their mutual love and the strictly interpersonal nature of their relationship; whereas conversation inevitably reactivates the social model for private life, raises questions to which there is usually no answer and poisons the atmosphere.

Various friends – male and female – work colleagues and mates adopt positions that are midway between the extremes of her 'family' and 'girlfriends' circles. They follow the example set by the family in terms of forms of communication and go through the same three phases of jokes, silence and comments. 'Some male friends used to tease me, but they no longer dare to ask how I can stand being on my own' (Annie). There is, however, one variation on the final sequence:

the little comments are less direct and aggressive and rely more on hints and irony. On the other hand, they follow the example of her girlfriends when it comes to how they define the content of what they say: whereas the family always refers (more or less explicitly) to the central model, friends, like girlfriends, adapt to the norm specific to the group, which changes over time. During the final phase, the content of what they say certainly conforms to the central model, but they reach that phase in different ways. Whereas the family increasingly feels the pressure from outside and feels that the finger is being pointed, conversations with the group of friends evolve from within, and reflect changes in the way the group behaves. Olivia recently felt that 'the wind has changed': several of her friends are about to get married and the group's value-system changed at the same time as its topics of conversation. Suddenly at a loss as to what she should do, she felt herself forced to make up 'a trip away with a mysterious lover. In fact I was going to stay with my family, but I heard them say: "When are you going to introduce him to us?" I felt so stupid afterwards! I've spoiled everything. It's no longer the way it used to be.'

The Laughter of Girlfriends

Human beings are not, and can never be, purely solitary creatures who cobble together their identity in their own ivory towers; they are nothing without other people, and are constantly shaped by the many interactions that tell them who they are (Mead 1934; Dubar 1991). Everyone has a role in this interplay of reflected identities. The anonymous people with whom we are in fleeting contact in the course of our day-to-day lives implicitly confirm who we are, while our 'significant others' give our identities their committed and emotionally charged support (Berger and Luckmann 1967). When individuals are inscribed within a close family unit, members of their family tell them who they really are (Singly 1996). But when their family ties are looser, a peer group of the same gender usually becomes a substitute family and the 'reference group' that shapes their identity (Queiroz and Ziolkovski 1994: 51). This is what happens with a single woman and her 'girlfriends'.

In historical terms, there is nothing new about female social circles. Edward Shorter (1984: 292) has demonstrated that, on the contrary, such circles were institutionalized in 'traditional society' and were based upon a 'culture of "solace".' From the nineteenth century onwards, that culture disintegrated as women began to enter a world that had until then been a male preserve on an equal footing. Today's groups of girlfriends are in part a heritage from that period. But only to a limited extent, as they are also involved in the very modern task of confirming the individual's identity. Such groups are initially a product of circumstances, and are based on a shared lived experience at a particular stage in the life cycle (Bidart 1997). The work of friendship consists of reducing differences and of moving slightly away from one fraction of the original group. The friends then distance themselves still further, specify the difference between them and the original group and 'recognize that they have something intimate in common' (Bidart 1997: 326). 'When I'm with my girlfriends, we merge into one another. We recognize ourselves in each other' (Carmen). The group is then at the height of its socializing power, becomes the essential point of reference for her identity and relegates her parents to secondary roles, if not mere walk-on parts.

Extreme intersubjective proximity ('merging') does not have to be based on geographical proximity: unlike husbands, girlfriends do not normally live near by. If we look more closely, however, it transpires that this mode of socialization is not restricted to the moments when the group is together. Several forms of socialization overlap, with each fulfilling a specific function: support from a distance, doing things together and having a good time.

Support from a distance. Even when they are apart, girlfriends are always close to one another. There is a remedy for the slightest difficulty, an answer to the slightest need to talk. 'Fortunately, I always have my girlfriends, so there is always someone I can call' (Amélie) – thanks to the wonderful instrument known as the telephone. It often rings for long conversations (and sometimes for very long conversations late at night): secrets, kindness, being there. 'Girlfriends are a sacred bond in moments of loneliness' (Jenna).

Doing things together. The decision is often made on the phone and rarely brings the whole group together (there is often only one girlfriend involved). The goal is to go out without being alone: shopping, going to see a film, various nights out (including the ones spent looking for a soul-mate). We will see the importance of the two criteria of doing things together and getting out. These excursions are not really arranged in any hierarchy. They all have their importance, even the little trips to the shops. 'One phone call, we're off. We make plans to go window-shopping. Our trips to the shops are important. They mean a lot and at the same time they are not very important. They put us back on top of things. Besides, at moments like that, you feel normal, you're bursting with health' (Tania). Especially when shopping in the strict sense of the word is combined with more joyous moments of greater intimacy (which, while they are quiet and never get out of control, prefigure the good times to come). 'Going out with the girls, shopping, the little tea rooms where we feel so close to one another and where we can laugh at all the stupid things we've done, those are real sources of energy' (Jenna).

The real good times. The whole group, or almost the whole group, has to be together. The tenderness and the silky atmosphere give way to screams of laughter, to a vocal exuberance or even vulgarity and, curiously enough, the sharing of secrets. Everything becomes easier to say, especially if it has to do with men. The group intoxication becomes a form of liberation. It is an exorcism, a form of group therapy; the girls go wild. In this context, the 'fusion' is at its most intense, and the group becomes a central referent. And the energy it gives off does away with the questions and doubts; the 'accusing finger' is completely forgotten.

Support at a distance, doing things together and having a good time are forms of communication. Their content tends to focus on two poles (which is another manifestation of a divided life).

Relations with girlfriends do have their downside. This does not mean lamentations and tears, which are unusual (they cry in private), but a search for understanding and consolation: warmth, support, a good listener and mutual analysis. 'Fortunately, my girlfriends are there to cheer me up when I'm feeling down' (Annie); 'It does me good and reassures me' (Carmen); 'It does us good to think together, to put some order in our ideas, especially when we have our moments of doubt' (Sylvie).

They also have their bright side. There is the ever-present laughter. Laughter can take many different forms. It can be no more than an element in the intimate atmosphere ('it's light-hearted and pleasant, a mixture of tenderness and laughter' – Edwige), but it can also be the guffaws of the good times. Every kind of laughter is different and has a specific function. Just as in conversations between husband and wife (Kaufmann 1992), so ironic laughter and mocking humour allow them to overcome their embarrassment and make it possible to say things that could otherwise not be said, to think in terms of double meanings (which is perfect when they are of two minds). 'Having a laugh' cheers the girls up and gives them energy: 'I always tell my girl-friends: it doesn't matter, it will sort itself out. Have a good laugh about it and off we go again!' (Chantal). The gusts of laughter allow them to cut themselves off and to forget about the 'pointing finger' as they become completely immersed in the counter-culture of the group. 'Sometimes we laugh so much that we must look crazy, screaming with laughter to the point where we wet ourselves' (Tania). Getting the giggles has the same effect, but it is less violent and more intimate: it too is a form of communion. 'We can't stop ourselves from giggling over stupid things; we don't even know why we're laughing. It does us good. It's incredible how close we feel at times like that' (Tania). They feel close and they understand one another better than ever, even though not a word is said. That is the magic of the giggles. It is an astonishing language without any signs, and it finally banishes all the contradictory thoughts that torment them. It justifies and explains everything, and there is no need to think: the most important things are said when nothing is actually being said.

It doesn't matter whether it facilitates dialogue or does away with it, laughter is associated with the search for an inner truth, for a sort of energy that sweeps aside barriers and makes it possible to forge ahead with the help of the girls. 'Lots of laughter, truth and sincerity. Life becomes really exciting!' (Joanna).

Betrayal

Groups of girlfriends evolve in typical ways. In the initial phase, the work of friendship forges an increasingly specific and intense unity that ends in fusion. At this stage, life is carefree and almost everything is sweetness and light. And then the laughter imperceptibly dies away and the descent back into the darkness begins. The girls no longer offer each other the same support, and something is missing. At first, the signs are imperceptible. Things lose their sparkle and become less spontaneous. There is a feeling of needless repetition as they try to rediscover the excitement of old. Keeping up the ritual can scarcely conceal the fact that its content has been exhausted (Bidart 1997). They listen more critically to what is being said and disagreements emerge. The girls have changed.

For a while, it seemed as though friendship could forgive everything. The newly married girlfriend tried to stay the way she used to be in order to ensure that the group stayed the way it always was. But the apparent consensus hides a very different reality: an enemy has been introduced into the group. This is not just a matter of a few disagreements. This really is the enemy they feared most. These are the ideas they fought against, the most destabilizing ideas of all: 'Husband, baby and home' (Astrid). The finger is no longer being pointed by obscure strangers who understand nothing about their lives. It is being pointed from inside the group.

The group that seemed to be so strong and that could give off such energy suddenly reveals its fragility: it was nothing more than a provisional space for a counter-culture floating in a hostile ocean. The contamination is often very sudden, and the girls are quickly converted to new ideas. When they all do so at the same time, the group goes on as though nothing had happened. It continues to act as a reference point for the girls' identity even though its content has changed because each member inscribes her trajectory within a shared framework that is changing. It is, unfortunately, rare for all the girls to change in the same way at the same time, and the girl (or girls) who remains true to the old references is therefore marginalized. This happens all the more easily if most of the rest of the group's evolution is harmonious. Danièle found it very difficult to see that her friends had suddenly betrayed her. The words she uses are the very same words she used to express how uncomfortable she felt when she was with her family: 'They no longer ask me how my love life is.' She is now really on her own, and has to rely on herself to construct the arguments that give meaning to her life. Dorothée has just experienced what she sees as the first stage in the process. Being very lucid, she knows what will happen next: 'As they get married one after the other, I feel that I am being gradually marginalized more and more. I dread what will happen when they start having babies.' There are obviously ways to stop this happening. They can, for instance, focus the work of friendship on the things they still have in common as the group becomes smaller, even if it means parting company with the majority as they convert to the new ideas, until there is only one best friend left. But it is no longer the same, and the group's energy has gone for good. Marie-Laure and her best friend remained inseparable for several years and always went around together. Marie-Laure never went to the shops, the cinema or a restaurant without her friend. 'But now, I tend to avoid her because we were beginning to look like an old couple.'

From the married girlfriend's point of view, carrying on with the relationship begins to feel embarrassing. What is there to talk about? It is, in theory, possible to go on speaking the same language, to exaggerate the dissatisfactions and horrors of married life, and to use a single friend as an ideal confidante. Unfortunately, the tone they used to adopt was too honest and too sincere for the difference not to be obvious, and there is always something that rings false. The other bad solution is to seek comfort from the illusion that the bond of friendship exists outside the social role, that they can say anything and understand everything, and that sincerity is the only thing that counts. The outcome is even worse. 'My girlfriends were what mattered most to me. They were my life: the pictures, eating out, going to the theatre, going on holiday. The friends who used to be closest to me have different preoccupations now: husbands, babies and their home life. They ring me to say that one of the kids has just learned to walk on his own, to talk about their worries about leaving the baby at home to go back to work. And every time I hang up, I could scream!' (Astrid).

The group's content in fact begins at a very early stage in its life, long before any of the girls even begins to think of getting married: the referential norm that both bound the clan together and constructed its personal identity constantly evolves throughout the various stages of the life cycle. Paradoxically, sex is the one thing that does least to keep the group together. And yet the normative pressure is intense: young people feel that they have to conform to the group at every stage in their initiation (Le Gall 1997). Gaining sexual experience, which is a 'normative experience' within a given age-class (Lagrange 1998: 166), has less and less to do with beginning a relationship. Love is much more complicated. 'Everyone around me is talking about their love life. I never have anything to say, so I feel as though I was from a different planet' (Pierrine). The worst offenders are those who talk about their experiences and the couples who flaunt themselves. They can bring about rapid changes within the group. The epidemic suddenly spreads: all Marie's friends now have boyfriends, and they delight in showing them off as though they were trophies. 'And I'm not even seeing anyone.' She suddenly feels herself overwhelmed by despair and anxiety, and feels she has been plunged into what she calls her loneliness. She is only 23.

Girlfriends betray the group at various ages, and very different trajectories emerge. In one scenario, the group shares many passions and interests: careers, leisure activities, moments of madness and the grandiose projects young people have. Love is no more important than anything else. When this is the case, the group may enjoy a long life. The girls support each other in their attempts to invent their own lives as they see fit. They go on doing so until the group breaks up, which may not happen until they are 30 or 35. In a very different scenario, the only fixation point – and it is an obsessional one – is the couple. It is impossible for the girlfriends to form a real counter-culture. The group itself quickly reactivates the model: first it is a boyfriend, but it very quickly becomes a matter of 'husband, baby, home'. This type of brief trajectory, in which a woman very quickly settles into the traditional role of being dependent on a husband, is more common in social milieus with little cultural capital, and in which careers and leisure interests offer fewer alternatives: girls dream of love for want of any alternative. Their marginalization (differences of opinion with girlfriends, surrender to the norm, feelings of loneliness) begins when they are very young – between 20 and 25 (or even younger) – whereas it begins 10 years later in other milieus. Mathilde is 20: 'Being a single woman is difficult in the society we live in. There are days when the loneliness is really difficult to put up with.' Pierrine is 21: 'I say to myself that I am not getting any younger, and I'm frightened that I will never find a man.' Agathe is 18 (!): 'God preserve me from ending up an old maid. I feel ashamed, and I no longer know what to do with myself. I tell myself that I'll never find a man, that I'm a lost cause. I've never felt so lonely and so out of things as I have this year. I feel I look different. I am profoundly and desperately alone.'

Much of the future is determined by what seems (but only seems) to be banal chatter: girlfriends' favourite topics of conversation.

A Cycle in Three Stages

The rhythms that govern our entry into adult life are, with some social variations, dictated by peer groups. Girls from educated backgrounds embark on long journeys. Those who are in a more precarious position do not have that luxury: they have to find a job and start a family as soon as they can. At the next level, young workers in stable jobs (unlike those who are not so fortunate) are slower to start having families (Galland 1993). The higher up the social hierarchy we go (using levels of education as a distinguishing factor), the more obvious the process becomes. When individuals make a deliberate choice to remain unattached for a while (which is another way of putting off family commitments), that choice is therefore part of a winning social strategy. Especially for women.

This explains why people who have decided simply to remain unattached tend to be euphoric (the further we go up the cultural hierarchy). What happens next is less cheerful. And it is quite in keeping with a typical model of emotional development. To put it in schematic terms, there are three stages.

Go on girls! Deferring family commitments does not raise the slightest problem. With the active support of their girlfriends and the tacit approval of society, young women who are on their own create the preconditions for openness and dynamism: the future has yet to be invented, there are no limits and life is full of energy and creativity.

Storm warning. And then their expectations change. 'Until a few years ago, being single was synonymous with independence and freedom, and I liked that. Now I dream of having a man I could talk to, love and share my life with' (Maggy). After all the betrayals that have taken place in the group of girlfriends, doublespeak begins to be used. And suddenly the finger is being pointed. It is as though the sky had fallen in and values had been inverted. Being single then comes to seem weird, and something to be slightly ashamed of. At this point, they begin to torture themselves: what have I done with my life, and what decisions should I take now? Radical alternatives present themselves: go further down the road to autonomy, or 'husband, baby, home'? Inner turmoil.

Casting anchor. The torments do not last. For the opposite reason to the one that triggered them. Once women get beyond the critical age, the 'finger' tends to be less obvious. As the social pressures ease, it becomes easier to be single and to organize everything on other values, most of which centre on everyday life: the importance of little things, subtle and discreet pleasures. The price that has to be paid for at last finding some peace and quiet is that the girls have to give up the screams and laughter of the days when they were centre stage, and learn a new style based upon reserve and sobriety.

Some women find the storm terrible, and almost all of them are surprised to find themselves safe and sound in a haven of calm. 'There was a time in my life when I thought that I would die of loneliness without even needing to commit suicide. I've got beyond that stage now' (Nathalie). There is a sort of minimal pleasure to be had from simply succeeding in living, from going one's own way without being 'pointed at' and not having too many self-doubts. In the most difficult situations (and especially when the storm is violent), the only way to find some peace and calm is to lead a quieter life, to put limits on one's dreams and aspirations, and to be extremely discreet in matters of style. 'I tread softly', as Donatienne puts it so poetically. The process is the same as that described by Alexandre Vexliard in his account of the homeless: having fought society and its norms, and after feeling that their personalities were being torn apart, they find a sort of haven of peace by becoming resigned. They cut themselves off in an almost autistic manner by 'minimizing society and the "normal" world' (cited, Mucchielli 1998: 115). The difference is that the homeless are marginalized, whereas the single can succeed in creating a legitimate space for themselves (provided that they are discreet about it).

The haven can sometimes be truly pleasant, but it is always, at the very least, a moment of calm after the storm. When our moorings are elementary points of reference, we can stray away from them only if we are very careful: this is the complete opposite of the period of 'go on, girls'. Jacqueline, for example, went on waiting for what was meant to be until she was 35. She went on waiting for a dazzling prince who never came, and then sank into despair. 'All the experiments and all the affairs never brought me anything but regrets.' And then she suddenly resolved to have no expectations, and immediately felt herself to be at peace ('Even though I have to cope with it all on my own and despite the lack of tenderness'). 'I like my life: I go to the cinema, go walking, and read, and I never have time to do all the things I want to do.' Madeleine went down a similar route: 'After three years of sleeping around and bed-hopping, I decided it was time to cast anchor.' There is no going back on her decision: 'I've given up looking, given up hoping.' That allows her to feel that the finger is no longer pointing at her, and to fill her life by throwing herself into all sorts of activities: cycling, walking, travel, reading, cultural associations and even a cheerful group reunion. 'I've made my choice, and I'm sticking to it. From time to time, I do feel the anxiety swelling up inside, and that leads to tears, but I still go my own way. I wouldn't go through another love affair for anything in the world.'

— 3 —

A LIFE SHARED

Back to History

I should imagine that the reader is finding it somewhat difficult to follow the thread of my argument. That is because the subject is complex. We saw in the first chapter that the tendency for individuals to live alone is part of a major historical trend that irresistibly urges them to become more autonomous. The conjugal norm should have been weakened as a result. We saw, however, in the last chapter that this is far from being the case. On the contrary, the norm is so powerful that the slightest mention of it is enough to throw singles off balance.

So what has happened to make the couple so resilient? In order to answer that question, we have to go back to history, even though it does not give up its secrets easily. The evolutionists of the last century believed that the course of history was linear. The realization that it falters, retreats and is inconsistent in various ways then led to the belief that it was pointless to try to discover its meaning or direction. That error is regrettable as naive evolutionism.

There is no such thing as a non-contradictory phenomenon. If we attempt to reduce the antagonistic nature of phenomena, we will not understand anything: it is the discovery of the interplay of opposites that gives researchers their analytic tools. The 'couple', for example, is in reality a mishmash, with a multiple and very heterogeneous content. Its history is 'much more tumultuous than they say', and marriage has always been 'a question and a tension' (Théry 1996: 18). The same is true of its component elements. Take love. It is profoundly contradictory and fragmented: the phenomenon's unity is a (necessary) surface illusion. Niklas Luhmann (1990) emphasizes that it is a framework for the expression of emotions and that it is, in historical terms, subject to many changes. That framework has never really succeeded in becoming stable and homogeneous in any period of history. Then why do we go on talking about love (and the couple) in the singular? Because there has to be a superficial unity if the norm is to take shape. Because we need that norm. And the norm succeeds in establishing itself (despite the current diversification of practices) precisely because it is a hotchpotch of different ideas and because it cannot be defined with any certainty.

If we simply wish to go on with our lives without too many problems, it is easier to go on believing that 'love' has a single meaning. But if we wish to understand it, our only solution is to make a radical break with that idea, to abandon the idea of the singular and to look in detail at the contradictory systems that structure both couples and love.

Premonitory Experiments

The historical process is anything but linear. That is because of the contradictory nature of the phenomena involved, and because of the astonishing impetus given it by innovations. 'The new is not all that new. It has been a long time coming' (Castel 1995: 159). New ways of living and thinking do not appear suddenly or as the result of diffusion alone. When the micro-environmental climate is favourable, avant-garde ideas can in fact emerge hundreds of years before the preconditions are there for them to become generalized on a lasting basis. The process is even more remarkable when we turn to sentimental behaviours and forms: the parentheses that open up are out of step with the general context of the day, and certain aspects of them can be unusually modern. Such manifestations appear to have no future, but they leave traces of preparatory and premonitory experiments. Courtly love is a very good example.

Its origins are obscure, but may be bound up with the Catharist heresy. Its rules, which were astonishing for the time, are 'the antithesis of those of medieval marriage' (Flandrin 1981: 108). This passionate love can only be experienced outside the institution of marriage. The lover is ready to surrender body and soul to his lady. Yet this personal devotion takes the form of a constant struggle within himself in order to survive ordeals (which are dreamed up by the lady), to perform great deeds and to exalt his individuality (Markale 1987). We are already very close to the contemporary contradiction that runs through conjugal life: how can we be our authentic selves when we

44

share our lives with someone else, and when our lives are more intense when we do so? This brings us very close to the contemporary alchemy of a subtle mix of sexuality and sentimentality: love must have physical origins, and at the same time sublimate them. In certain respects, it even seems that courtly love is ahead of our times. Jean Markale explains, for example, the emergence of the state of being in love, which is a product of a patient struggle with the Self. The courtly code explains how it is possible to experience the desired emotions. This is the exact opposite of the representation of love at first sight that was to become the dominant image for hundreds of years. And we have yet to rid ourselves of that image.

Let us look at just how this idea of celestial love became established.

The courtly love parenthesis opened suddenly. The Middle Ages found it profoundly disturbing that there was no clear definition of the role of the couple. Apologias for chaste solitude had inevitably cast doubts on marriage. 'Copulation, the bodily humours, and consequently marriage – all were regarded with deeper repugnance than ever before' (Duby 1983: 27). According to St Jerome, all marriages, which did no more than make fornication legitimate, were therefore accursed. Gregory the Great divided society into two: a celibate elite who enjoyed a direct relationship with God and lesser beings who had been sullied by marriage. The more diplomatic St Augustine was reluctant to condemn a whole class of people. He defined marriage as 'a less imperfect form of copulation': better a married man than a mere fornicator (Duby 1983: 28). Yet even that form of marriage was at the bottom of the hierarchy of merits; nothing could be higher than consecrated celibacy.

Before marriage could be established as a sacrament (and therefore as the dominant norm), some complex intellectual work had to be done: a doctrine had to be defined in order to make a distinction between marriage and the sins of the flesh. Sex within marriage was therefore moralized. Although she could not achieve the purity of Mary, who was a mother despite being a virgin, a woman could, ideally, come close to that state by avoiding the throes of passion while still ensuring that biological reproduction took place. Asceticism or, at least, restraint, which were the values and signs of celibacy, were introduced into marriage. This doctrine was quickly elaborated in the twelfth century and became part of a coherent whole: marriage was in keeping with God's will and was a sacrament or a product of the love of God. Entering into marriage was a way of sharing that love. Married love was therefore closer to a spiritual and unshakeable *caritas* than to corporeal and impulsive *amor* (Duby 1993). Love brought about a miracle: love could be detached from sin despite the physical union.

Not everything was simple, of course. Rampant sexuality was not easily tamed, and there were a lot of penances. But at the end of the Middle Ages, definitions seemed to become clearer as marriage became established as the norm. In the sixteenth century, unfortunately, everything became confused. Especially on the sexual front. In the privacy of confessionals, physical love was the target of repression when it became 'exaggerated', 'too ardent' or 'unnatural'. The purpose of the act was not pleasure, but procreation alone. Sins committed between man and wife were even graver than those committed outside the bonds of marriage. There was also confusion on the feelings front. Until then, it had all looked fairly simple: on the one hand, divine love, which was unique, positive and transcendent and which bound the conjugal group together; on the other, lewd pagan pleasures which had to be curbed. An intermediate position gradually emerged: 'a sort of profane love that tried to gain acceptance as "true love" because it aspired to "honesty" and "modesty"' (Flandrin 1981: 53). Theologians rebelled against this sacrilege, which implied that a man should prefer his wife to union with God. Their protests were futile: sentimental modernity had begun its long march (Shorter 1975).

The clarification of the conjugal norm had therefore been no more than apparent and temporary. Marriage appeared to have become a solid institution, but what exactly was its content? The purely divine conception of love could not channel all sexuality, and nor could it smother the emergence of more interpersonal feelings. Marriage was also strengthened by its economic role. According to André Burgière, raising the age at which people could marry in the sixteenth century was the cornerstone of a new and austere model that allowed households to accumulate adequate amounts of capital and develop the spirit of enterprise: 'Couples were no longer simply preoccupied with producing a family, but with knowing how to manage their family and with preserving and improving its social status' (1972: 1138). How could these managerial goals be reconciled with the complex management of drives and feelings? Many points were still to be cleared up, and marriage was based on a strange blend of very different elements.

The Personalization of Feelings

Married couples, who were expected to keep their lovemaking sober, owed one another benevolence and respect. Tenderness was not included in the pact. It was the eighteenth century that saw the emergence and growing importance of tenderness. It was one manifestation of a new feeling that was midway between sex and divine love: love. Although it was ill-defined and viewed with suspicion by the moral authorities, everyone wanted to try it out by placing strict limits on their impulses. It therefore emerged in the restricted form of a 'domesticated passion' or a 'tender and reasonable feeling' that was close to virtue and even duty (Flandrin 1981: 88). Initially, this revolution in the depths created only a few ripples on the surface: marriage seemed to go on as before. It was as though it were being filled from within by a new element that could easily be assimilated. The personalization of feelings was, however, the harbinger of an earthquake, and we have felt only its first shocks. For we are far from having made a break with the heavenly conception of conjugal love. Many women are still waiting for love to designate the chosen one: 'Mr Right', 'the only man for me' or 'Prince Charming'. 'I am convinced that there is a man for every woman: her Mr Right, the one who was made for her, her better half' (Elisa). She will immediately know when she has met him. Ideally, it will be love at first sight, the love that 'turns a life into something magical' (Schurmans and Dominicié 1997: 148). What we now experience as the feeling of love is the product of a strange mixture of disparate notions. It is an unstable equilibrium structured around an antagonistic pair of opposites: the growing personalization of the feeling, and its transcendental nature, which has been inherited from history. We are being swept away by an irresistible revolution, but in subjective terms we still feel the influence of a distant past.

The rise of sentimentality did, however, change the conjugal landscape. Its first manifestations were erratic and were not centred on the couple: the eighteenth century channelled it by domesticating it in the form of a tranquil passion that could be quietly cultivated within an established marriage (Flandrin 1981). But what had to happen did happen: the initial choice of partner, on which the institution was based, was affected in its turn. This led to the emergence of what was then called marriage by inclination (as opposed to marriage by arrangement) which, as we know, became a popular theme for novels and plays. This did not happen overnight, and it took almost 200 years for the idea of marriage by inclination to become part of official morality (during the Third Republic, roughly speaking), and still longer for it to become a reality.

Once more, it produces the same illusion of continuity. Once more, there was, however, a profound change. There was another dissonant element in the combination of conjugality and love. When passion became part of marriage by inclination, the outcome was anything but peace. Passion itself proved to be burning and all-devouring. Inspired by romanticism, it ventured into 'the mystery of dream-filled nights and the fluidity of intimate communication' and experimented with 'the extraordinary discovery of the Self and the way in which it changed the relation between Self and others' (Perrot 1990b: 455). The outcome was a strange combination of *jouissance* at a distance and immediate emotional commitment (Luhmann 1990). The revolution in private life seemed to be entering a decisive phase because this new sentiment was uncontrollable, destabilizing and hostile to the institution of marriage. And also, or mainly, because it masked a form of self-assertion. Unlike tenderness, an outburst of passion makes no secret of the fact that it is primarily a personal impulse, a throw of the dice that can change destinies. The emotion masks the fact that the Self is being reshaped and that the individual is in control of its reshaping. 'We say that we love something that we are in the process of creating and that is in the process of recreating us' (Alberoni 1995: 18). The emotional halo is sometimes so bright that we scarcely notice our choice of partner; in other cases, it is so dim that the decision seems to be a matter of crude conjugal consumerism. The sentiment is, however, always associated with reflexivity and with the inexorable rise of individualism, with our growing control over our own lives. In theory, this appears to be incompatible with a long-term commitment to a shared life. It is no coincidence that the nineteenth century also saw the rise of a new type of mass celibacy (see chapter 1). It was also the century of utopias offering alternatives to the married couple as a norm for private life (Schérer 1996). Saint-Just had already concluded that love, like the individual, could be regarded as an enemy of the institution of marriage. Claire Démar (2001) was denouncing marriage and demanding the right to be unfaithful. Charles Fourier (1967) was dreaming of a city of love in which everyone could change in accordance with their feelings of the moment.

The political and moral authorities understood the extent of the threat, and society was inundated with edifying discourses which took the family as their main theme. Various sensibilities and ideologies produced variations on the family theme, but the goal was always the same: only the family could calm the passions and confine the individual to a basic cell that could restrict their destabilizing excesses (Cicchelli-Pugeault and Cicchelli 1998). After the First World War, the long break in the trend towards individualism (see chapter 1) gave this conceptual framework the opportunity to ground itself firmly in reality; as it stabilized inside its bourgeois comfort, the conjugal family became a hegemonic and unquestioned norm that endured until the early 1960s. It appeared to have been established as a 'canonical form' (Segalen 1993: 282) and looked triumphant. Nothing seemed to be able to threaten it. Once again, the family had outwitted the false prophets who were proclaiming that its death was nigh.

The surprise was all the greater in that every demographic indicator was changing in the mid-1960s: the family had suddenly entered a new revolutionary phase. We had reached the end of 'a cycle of almost one thousand years in which the institution of marriage that had been at the heart and foundations of bio-social reproduction was falling apart before our very eyes' (Lefaucheur 1995: 9). The 'canonical form', which once seemed so solid, was being smashed to pieces. This was not so much because new utopias had come into being (those of the post-'68 period had already fizzled out; Mauger and Fossé 1977) as because a sudden explosion of individualization had destroyed the established conjugal structure. People were marrying later, the divorce rate was rising, and there were more one-parent families and more people living alone. All these signs were convergent. Even couples who did stay together were challenging the need for exclusive relationships, and partnerships were becoming 'sectorial, temporary and unstable': the 'I' was reclaiming its rights (Kellerhals et al. 1982: 226). Was this the final onslaught and the end of the conjugal norm?

It was not. This hotchpotch of an institution proved once more how supple it could be by integrating elements taken from the cutting edge of modernity. Although it was in crisis and had been destabilized, it succeeded in reinventing itself by absorbing ingredients which did not seem predestined to become part of it. Especially the rise of all kinds of emotionalism and sentimentality. The process began with: sexuality.

Let us go back to the nineteenth century. While the moralizers were busy moralizing, new emotions were being experienced in the privacy of the alcoves: the body was experiencing an intimate revolution (Corbin 1990[1987]). An inversion was taking place. Until then, it had seemed that sentimentality took the form of an external virtue that was in conflict with the animal drives and of 'rational control over the passions' (Luhmann 1990: 148), but the second half of the century discovered, not without a certain frisson, that it was possible to listen to the depths of the Self, and to both release and control the energy that flowed from it. It used a subtle mechanism which, in another study that draws on the work of Norbert Elias (1991[1982]), I describe as the second phase in the process of the civilizing of manners (Kaufmann 1995a). 'The contemporary history of sexuality began around 1860'

(Corbin 1990: 594), and it had the potential to destabilize the marital order. According to Michel Foucault, a *dispositif* of doctors, pedagogues, psychiatrists, priests and all sorts of other experts was immediately deployed. It was designed to control deviancy. Although it focused initially on extreme cases, it became recentred on 'the legitimate and procreative couple' (Foucault 1979[1976: 3]), which 'took custody' of sexuality by subjecting it to norms. Once its base had been consolidated, it was possible to experiment with new advances, and to set free conjugal sexuality prudently and in a controlled manner. This has continued through to nowadays, when it seems that the wild beast has been tamed. So much so that studying positions and orgasmic techniques has become a sort of compulsory homework for all couples who are both honest and serious.

Sexuality in the strict sense was not, however, the most important thing. The use of the body as an emotional tool had much broader and far-reaching implications (Kaufmann 1997). Individuals were now in charge of their own destinies, and were constantly expanding the unstable and unsettling world in which they lived: there were more and more problems to resolve, and the answers and points of reference were less and less clear. Sensory intuition, which was the quickest way to reach a decision (Damasio 1995), seemed to be the only way out. This is why the modern world makes such an extravagant cult of the emotions and sensibility, and works on bodies to make them even more receptive and even more expressive. Passionate love is an extreme example. It becomes even more passionate by feeding on the eroticized body. It does so in order to go beyond and mask (at least partly) a choice which, if it were described coldly and in its entirety, would undermine the couple's foundations. Tender gestures are a more moderate example. The history of kisses and cuddles is not a long one. Until 1900, most women made love for the first time without ever having kissed their partners first (Lagrange 1998). And traditionally, slaps, pinching and beatings were more common than caresses (Flandrin 1981). It was only in the second half of the twentieth century – very recently indeed – that young people began to kiss and cuddle without having sexual relations (Lagrange 1998). Ordinary tender gestures such as a peck on the cheek and even gentle caresses within established relationships (and towards children) are an even more recent development, and are, as it happens, now becoming more common. When seen against a background of familiar points of reference and a musical and visual setting (the consumption of music is on the increase, and DIY is the family activity with the fastest growth rate), they become the warmest element in the sensual envelope in which every member of the family curls up: it calms them down, shuts them in and rocks them to sleep.

The modern individual, who can be seen as an open and complex system (and one that is becoming more and more open and complex), is attempting to stabilize and fence in his or her identity; individuals need an anchoring point and boundaries, or fads that make them settle down or make them change (Kaufmann 2004). Identities that have been weakened are using all kinds of tools in a desperate attempt to create focal points for their grievances. One study of mental health (deliberately) lists some in no particular order: medication, alcohol, subservience to the family, cults, drugs, television – they provide a 'feeling of coherence' (Joubert et al. 1997: 362) and ward off uncertainties about responsibilities (Ehrenberg 1995: 301). In less extreme situations, similar results can be achieved by gentler means. Emotionalism and intimacy help individuals to become attached to people and things. We are moving closer and closer to 'more intense personal relationships' (Luhmann 1990: 24), to mutual support for one another's identity (Singly 1996) and concrete sensoriality. Outside the family, but also inside it. The hotchpotch known as the institution of marriage once more succeeds in absorbing everything: all-devouring and foundational passion, calm tenderness (in which the conflicts are rarely serious), domesticated sexuality and the economic interests of the household business (personal and collective), the need to fence identity in within the family home, and the culture of sensibility within the world of intimacy. The family is an anomalous and unstable gathering, but it also brings these things together in the name of something that has not changed for 100 years: the loving couple.

A Model for Private Life

To sum up: the repeated blows struck by individualization have thrown the component elements of love and the family into confusion. The latter institution has, however, displayed an astonishing suppleness that has enabled it to integrate and amalgamate new elements, and it has therefore succeeded in remaining the referential norm. Although it has changed greatly, the couple is still the model for private life.

But which couple? Can we describe its present form with any accuracy? We can, provided that we limit the exercise to the model's kernel. We have to understand that it is both one (at the centre) and multiple (on the periphery), and that the centre/periphery division is, in historical terms, becoming more and more pronounced. This has deceived the many observers who believe that it is no longer possible to speak of the family in the singular: 'The family was becoming families': families now take many different forms: one-parent families, reconstituted families, non-cohabiting couples, and so on, and they all tend to look like 'legitimate options' (Chaland 1994: 130). Jacques Commaille has demonstrated (1996: 55) that we are witnessing an upheaval in the 'normative economy'. The norm is no longer dictated from on high, no longer has a universalist goal, and is established 'from below' (p. 208) on the basis of increasingly diverse innovatory practices. Hence its new form: it is pluralistic and relative, and that makes it difficult to control, especially for the juridical apparatus. But let me make it quite clear that I am speaking here of the model's most visible and explicit aspects (which lie on the periphery), especially when the courts have to make a decision. In the centre, by contrast, the family (in the singular) is still the gold standard, especially in the depths of the implicit. And it is from here that 'the finger' is suddenly pointed.

The kernel of the model is changing, but it is doing so slowly, very slowly. Under the influence of the periphery, it integrates new notions (in homeopathic doses), and they imperceptibly change the whole model. It is, however, always out of step. It is always behind the times and uses its deep historical roots to establish itself. Most of the changes have to do with the articulation between love and marriage: we have gradually moved (in the space of a few hundred years) from taking the loving marriage and then the loving couple as our central point of reference, rather than marriage itself. The couple, then, exists in the singular. The simplicity of the definition is disarming. People who live alone and single-parent families enjoy only a superficial legitimacy, and it is called into question on numerous occasions.

Everything centres on a single idea, and it is extraordinarily simple (which is why it has such force): the idea of the couple. It is not that it is impossible not to be part of a couple. Ideally, we must, on the other hand, be able to justify that situation on the grounds that we are young, that our marriage has broken down for legitimate reasons, or that we have been widowed. So we live together as couples. But living together as a couple is not enough either: the couple must display certain characteristics, and is required to be authentic, so much so that it is better (from the point of view of deviations from the norm) to break off the relationship when it becomes too stormy. Living on one's own is better than being in a bad relationship. But we cannot break up in just any old fashion. This is a new development: there is now an authoritative model for the good divorce (Théry 1993). This brings us back to the couple, which must be resuscitated (in a different form) despite the crisis: the parental couple must survive the death of the conjugal couple.

A couple has to be a real couple based upon mutual choice, within reasonable limits. It has to be acknowledged that it is the basis on which we can construct a united team, an efficient organization, intimate relational exchanges, a pleasant atmosphere and respect for one another's autonomy. And the couple must also know how to construct a persona and how to promote an image that will sell. An insidious hierarchy tends to become established: some couples are better than others because they come closer to the idea of the true couple and because they are more representative of the kernel's purity. In such couples, the wife succeeds in adopting the perfect position (which involves a difficult balancing act) of being neither a 'careerist single woman' nor a 'housewife' (Singly 1996: 29). The husband (in his role as father) succeeds in developing an emotional style that is subtly different from that of his wife, and a delicate 'non-authoritarian authority' (p. 193). Despite the diversity of seemingly legitimate forms on the periphery, the centre in fact conforms to a very specific image. It is of course the product of definitional struggles but, when it stabilizes, it develops a constrictive power that is at odds with its clandestine nature. Take the example of family pets. First, having pets becomes a common practice. It then becomes a lifestyle that attracts media coverage (adverts for houses show a lawn, happy children and a puppy) but which is, as yet, only one lifestyle amongst others. Finally, it begins to influence the kernel, as there appears to be a growing trend to stigmatize families that have no pets, and which prove (paradoxically) to be less 'human'.

The clarity of the secret schema that structures the kernel is at odds with, on the one hand, the various peripheral options that are officially legitimate (single-parent families, people living alone) and, on the other, the anomalous nature of the multiple aspects that are amalgamated into the couple and love (the household-firm, support for individual identities, etc.). The very principle behind the model is now based on that contradiction. The interplay between the opposites is, however, coming dangerously close to the limit beyond which its suppleness loses its virtues and threatens to destroy the model. The same is true of the growing respect for the autonomy of the partners: how long can they go on being themselves and cultivating their own tastes and personal dreams without destroying the family? The same applies to the related issue of the personalization of feelings. Roch Hurtubise's analysis (1991) of more than 100 years of love letters demonstrates that the central tendency to seek personal happiness releases us from the obligation to establish a family group. Feelings become more and more personalized and begin to lose their sacred aura. Given the ideal of authenticity, which implies evaluating one's partner, 'the lexicon of romantic love can no longer be used to describe him or her' if it is to remain credible (Chalvon-Demersay 1996: 86). The ideal therefore has to negotiate a new and difficult path between the need for enchantment and the need to take real situations into account. And if it is to do that, it can no longer wait for Cupid's arrow to strike: the individual must (also!) learn to construct his or her own emotional world.

Is this another minor shift, or does this multiform individualization really herald a weakening of the model? Anthony Giddens (1992) comes close to taking that view: the revolutionary process of the democratization of private life and of the 'pure relationship' between partners really does appear to have begun.

One element does, however, appear to be slowing down the predicted revolution, which would no doubt be more advanced if the conjugal game were still a game for two players: children.

The Mother/Children Group

The criticisms that have been made of Philippe Ariès (1962) do not invalidate his basic thesis: the family has gradually become centred on the child. The child now crystallizes the future of the family. Children show couples the way forward, allow partners to avoid difficult face-to-face encounters, and ensure that relations continue to exist in a parental form once the marriage has broken down. Children are an incarnation of the ideal of indissoluble love, whereas actual couples are increasingly thrown into chaos by their elective loves. Children mean that individuals who are tormented by their mortality live on after their deaths (Théry 1996). In short, children sum up all the good things about the emotional and sensory stability of the intimate world. For all these reasons, and many others, children have undeniably become the central pivot. The child has become the household deity who, as soon as he or she comes along, allows the family bond to be knit.

The family stands at the unstable point where the very different expectations of the couple and the child intersect, and the child is the more structuring element. Especially for women, who become so intensely involved in their careers as mothers that their conjugal partners are often relegated to the background. The mother/children group is the key component in the model, and conjugal love does not remain centre stage for long. This becomes particularly obvious when the two elements are amalgamated. It is no coincidence that the 'accusing finger' is pointed at single women who have reached a certain age. Nor is the fact that not being part of a couple and not having children are factors that increase the suspicion that they are abnormal. In post-divorce family constellations, the circulation of children is usually organized by the women. And the vast majority of single-parent families consist of women and their children. To sum up: once the couple is undermined, the mother/children group takes over. This process can be analysed in two ways. The mother/children group can be seen as the most stable and long-lasting element, but one that must not be divorced from the couple, which is the model's other strong point. It can also be argued that we are dealing with opposites and not complementaries, and that the mother/children group is the embryonic model for an alternative to the couple-based model. In historical terms, there would in fact be nothing new about that: mother/children group is the most common component in the many different forms of family that existed in the past, and especially in matrilineal kinship systems (Fox 1967). It might be objected that democratic society, and the principle that men and women are equal that comes with it, opens up completely new horizons, that children who are fixated on only one of their parents are an archaism, that fathers protest when they are not granted custody of their children after a divorce, and so on. Personally, I am tempted to invert the argument. Yes, women do object to being confined to a traditional role (EPHESIA 1995). Yes, men are changing and are developing new emotional bonds with their children (Singly 1996). Yes, the withdrawal of welfare states is reactivating woman-centred familial solidarities and does work to the disadvantage of women who want to get by on their own, and especially single mothers (Lefaucheur and Martin 1995). My point is that none of these contradictory developments prevents the mother/children group from becoming steadily and inexorably more important. 'It seems that the mother–child relationship will increasingly become the axis around which family life revolves' (Schultheis 1991: 36). The hypothesis is daring, but it is worth positing it. It is possible that, despite the simplistic way we usually think about these things, we are seeing something new, that practical developments are beginning to overthrow the model and that we are moving towards a family that is primarily based upon the mother/children group rather than the couple.

The Model Undermined

Whatever the answer may be, a diversified periphery is gnawing away at the centre and displacing its centre of gravity (from the couple to the mother/children group). The fact that violence can impose norms does not invalidate this finding. Tyrannical regimes are at their bloodiest when they begin to lose their grip on power, and the model is in crisis precisely because its foundations are being shaken. It is slowly retreating into the depths of the implicit (from whence the 'accusing finger' suddenly begins to be pointed). In the explicit world of codification, and especially that of legal codification, by contrast, 'normative plurality' (Commaille 1996: 214) is gaining ground: the family as such is becoming less relevant as a category. In countries where, as in The Netherlands, the emphasis is on the rights of the individual, we are seeing 'a relative erosion of the notion of the family and a growing desire for neutrality with respect to all the different ways private life can be organized' (p. 223). As it becomes more and more fragmented and more and more difficult to find on the surface, the model is plunging into the social depths, but suddenly re-emerges in times of uncertainty or crisis.

We saw in the previous chapter how certain situations (family meals, cinema queues, etc.) make single women feel uncomfortable. Such situations are characterized by a strong family presence, and therefore brutally reveal the abnormality of individuals who are not part of a couple. Marie-Laure feels 'ill at ease' when she goes to 'a party on [her] own'. Listen to her as she goes on with her analysis. She feels ill at ease (more so at parties than in a cinema queue) mainly because her presence makes other people ('normal people') feel ill at ease ('I'm the odd one out'). 'They can't help it. They're embarrassed, uncomfortable and stop acting naturally.' Because the simplistic self-evident truths on which their lives are based are being undermined, and because the comforting model for private life proves to be unstable and weak. Couples feel ill at ease in the presence of a woman who is on her own because there is no clear system of classification. And especially because they feel that something is looking at them with a critical eye. They are being seen through the eyes of Marie-Laure, for example: 'When I look around me, I don't have any image of what a successful couple should look like. I don't know a single man between the ages of 25 and 35 who is faithful to his wife. I tend to see couples who are sharing the same house but leading parallel lives.'

— 4 —

PRINCE OR HUSBAND?

Building relationships has become difficult, but we can always hope (and it is precisely because our hopes are so insane that building relationships has become so hard). A woman has to hope and dream in order to give a human face to the man she expects to meet. Just who is this man she would like to meet? This is where the imaginary figure of Prince Charming comes in; he is the filter she uses to elaborate scenarios for the future.

Facts and Fairies

'Every morning, I get up and say to myself: "Good morning, life. Today's the day I'm going to meet him" ' (Nelly). Prince Charming is everywhere in the innermost thoughts of these women; the letters in which he does not put in an appearance are in the minority. He is obviously not centre stage from the first line to the last; he makes fleeting and unexpected appearances, like an enchanting vision that suddenly appears in moments of doubt. 'A handsome Prince', 'A Prince of my own'.

And yet there are Princes and there are princes. Sometimes there is no doubt: it really is Him. He is dressed in shining armour and riding a white horse (the white horse is often mentioned). In this wonderful compensatory imaginary, dreams are meant to remain dreams. Sometimes it is very different, and he is a cut-price prince, or a prince in name only. It is not that princes are mediocre in this imaginary other country. The problem is that the dreams that are dreamed there are not meant to remain dreams, and are scenarios for wishes that might come true. There is a simple reason why such princes are less dazzling:

this performance is a rehearsal for an encounter with the real world, and it articulates magnificent ideals with strategies for coming to terms with the facts. A wave of the wand adds sparkle and a few opportunistic alterations will produce a good result.

The various figures of Prince Charming are not randomly distributed. The real Prince will be met in two typical situations and they are, paradoxically, very different. A woman may firmly believe that Love is something that is made in heaven. The purity of that conception means that she is waiting for her Prince to arrive. When she does meet him, it has to be an absolute and immediate revelation. This is because she is destined to meet him, and a cut-price prince is therefore not acceptable. 'My life is empty. Nothing ever happens to me. But I have faith, and I know that he will come one day. I will be able to tell immediately, and I will know that it is Him' (Marie-Laure). In such cases, the Prince is confined to the realm of the compensatory imaginary. When he does appear in the other kind of dream, or one that represents a more realistic scenario for the future, he is still a real Prince. He is spectacularly, luminously handsome. As for the cut-price princes, they appear in the dreams of women who desperately want to escape the 'single' category as a result of their own efforts. The most ordinary of men can (more or less) be transformed by a wave of the wand. Countless pumpkins are transformed into carriages (at least for a while).

Not everything is always so clear-cut. The single life is a life divided. The doubts are structural and permanent. There is a constant movement to and fro between the real Prince and cut-price princes, between a refusal to compromise and the compromises that are needed to find a soul-mate, between assertions of autonomy and surrender to the 'accusing finger'. Justine is always seeing potential Princes everywhere, but the spell never lasts: 'There have been a lot of men in my life. They were all going to be Him.' Angéla cries for the moon, and denies that that is what she is doing: 'I'm not asking for the moon, just for a man who suits me and to experience something magical.' Adeline, in contrast, did ask for the moon and thought: 'I was destined to find my one true love on the boundaries of the impossible.' She no longer believes that: the men she has met are far removed from the boundaries of the impossible. 'Quite frankly, not many of them were worth crossing the street for.' She cannot stop herself from pronouncing that this implacable verdict upsets her: if she goes on being so demanding, there is a danger that she will end up on her own. That is why a new dream has invaded her nights and days. She is kidnapped by a very banal sort of prince. She cannot really see his face, but he forces her to surrender and marry him. Whilst not everything about this story is rosy, she finds it irresistibly attractive: it puts an end to the mental strain of living a divided life. She is free at last. Because she is deliberately suppressing her own freedom.

The Prince with a Thousand Faces

There are also wonderful dreams about real Princes who have stepped straight out of fairy tales. 'Cinderella' is one of the most significant of all fairy tales. Cinderella is the loneliest of the lonely (the child of a first marriage who is despised by the new wife). She has to sleep on a wretched bed of straw in a garret, and is so poorly dressed that no one ever notices her. Until the day when, thanks to a fairy's magic, the Prince sets eyes on her and reveals the truth about her to the world: she has a heart of gold and a luminous beauty. The tale was first published at the end of the seventeenth century. The Prince is mentioned only briefly, and in order to show Cinderella in a flattering light. The princely title is rarely mentioned: the Prince is described as 'the king's son'. Because that is what he really is: a good catch. There is no physical description of the Prince (we do not know if he is handsome) or of his feelings (he admires Cinderella's beauty, but does he love her? We do not know). There is no love scene, no sweet nothings and no caresses, just an ordinary marriage: 'He found her more beautiful than ever, and married her only a few days later.' Which is not surprising: the story is consistent with the way a couple was defined at the time.

What does Prince Charming really look like? It seems that, in the original version of the story, he did not look like anyone in particular. All that mattered was his status as the king's son – in other words, he was both a good match and a potential husband. In later versions, right down to Disney's film adaptation (in which Cinderella falls in love without realizing that he is the king's son), there is a gradual change of emphasis. The Prince takes on a bigger role, and becomes more and more charming: he is handsome, radiantly handsome (his beauty even rivals that of Cinderella) and the personification of Love. Despite the medieval etiquette and the white horse, the stereotypical image of Prince Charming is therefore much more recent than one might think. It was slowly developed and became more elaborate over a long period of time and it draws on an old stock of images, but the Prince took on his contemporary face thanks to the diffusion of modern feelings. What does he look like in contemporary versions?

At risk of disappointing the reader, it has to be said that it is difficult to say.

Of course, the Prince is handsome, indeed very handsome. That much is obvious and universally recognized. His good looks are, however, defined in many different ways and in accordance with the taste of the woman who is dreaming about him. There is something magical about his beauty, and that is of course the difference between him and a cut-price prince. Why is it so magical? Because it shines, is luminous and is so obvious. And because it strikes a chord within her. And there we have it: the Prince is a Prince not just because he is handsome but because of the vibrations he gives off. He takes poor lonely Cinderella away from the grey, everyday reality of her garret and carries her off to somewhere that is unknown and wonderful. There is a name for this rapture: passionate love. Robert Castel (1990) analyses one of the purest forms of love ever to have existed: the myth of Tristan and Isolde. The strength of their passion is inversely proportional to its inscription in the real world. It is because they completely abandon their previous loyalties that the two lovers experience an absolute love, 'a completely self-contained experience' (Castel 1990: 159). Quite apart from his beauty, this is where the Prince's magic lies (his good looks are its support): he is the one who sweeps her off her feet and allows her to leave her old Self behind. The stronger the passion (and it can take the form of madness), the more likely it is that the prince will become a real Prince. 'I want a great Love, I want to be thrilled, to share strong emotions with a man who drives me crazy' (Charlène). And her mind is made up: an understudy will not make up for the absence of the Prince. 'I'd rather be on my own than trap myself into a perfectly ordinary affair with a perfectly ordinary man.' For the moment, her mind is made up: Charlène is only 23. Life often teaches us to control our passions. Because absolute love is synonymous with social death (Castel 1990). The madness has to remain sober, and the Prince has to be taken in moderation.

This does not make it any easier to try to describe what he looks like; his appearance changes a lot. For the same woman, and in the course of the same day, he can go from being the real inaccessible Prince to being one of the ordinary princes of everyday life. He also varies, depending on whether she wants to be swept off her feet and carried away or needs immediate comfort in the here and now. The man who takes her in his arms and comforts her may not be a real Prince, but she acts as though he were because it is in her interest to confuse the issue. As it happens, the issue has already been confused, and the anomalous couple/love combination has done a lot to confuse it (the various faces of the Prince correspond to the very different expectations women have of marriage). Take the question of sex. Is he opposed to marriage, or is he a partner who will revolutionize it from within? How is sex articulated with feelings? We do not really know. The same uncertainty surrounds the Prince: is he a sex machine or a creature of diaphanous virtue? Different women dream of very different versions of the Prince. And the same woman can dream of different versions. At times, the escape from everyday life demands thrills and passion, and the Prince is therefore very physical. At other times, a woman's expectations have more to do with a meeting of hearts and minds, and the Prince is therefore an understanding man. This can also relate to the need to be comforted: he then becomes just a prince who can gently mend her broken heart. Without any sense of contradiction, Julia describes two contrasting expectations in two sentences: 'I am looking for a great love that is absolute and shared, and I have resolved not to have any minor scenes that lead nowhere. In the meantime, I miss not having a man's arms around me.'

We can, however, note certain constants. Thus, the figure of the Prince undergoes changes characteristic of the life cycle. For girls, he is often someone who has stepped out of a fairy tale. In many cases, that does not prevent them from seeing and describing him in terms of the latest canons of beauty. A few letters describe how the writer met several Princes in the course of a single summer (my first Prince Charming, my second Prince Charming, and so on – and some of them have something in common with well-known actors or singers). For mature women (who are more dazzled by his ability to understand, and slightly less fascinated by his looks), he takes on a more human aspect, but real Princes are in short supply. For divorced women, finally, he often – and prosaically – becomes 'my ideal man' or the 'love of my life', and is described in terms of a list of fairly strict criteria. Second loves are indeed more 'sensible' (Le Gall 1992). This is because divorced women have learned that the spell will not last. And because past experience teaches them that managing day-to-day life is more complex: embarking on a new relationship is neither easy nor something to be undertaken lightly. The day-to-day problems of running a household come first, and the Prince comes second.

'Like a Love Story'

Love is a 'symbolic code' which 'encourages us to develop feelings appropriate to it' (Luhmann 1990: 18), a 'myth made real' (Raffin

1987: 67) and a trajectory that is inscribed within a 'canonical form' (Péquignot 1991: 42). It is to a large extent a product of the poetry of the troubadours, of plays and novels and, more recently, of the films and television programmes that have told us – and never stop telling us – thousands and thousands of love stories. This does not mean that love is an illusion, by any means. The feelings and emotions involved are very real, can be measured by the chemistry of hormones, and can take the extreme form of being shot by Cupid's arrow or of love at first sight (Schurmans and Dominicé 1997). The stories define the context that provokes the inner turmoil.

The narrative framework is not always the same. Just as what makes up the couple is so diverse, and just as the Prince has many different faces, so love stories can follow different types of scenario. Photo novels preserve an imaginary similar to that of fairy tales: heavenly Love, a real Prince and predestination; the encounter is fusional and transcendental (Henry 1993). Films and a certain category of soap operas explore reality in more or less realistic and concrete ways (Chalvon-Demersay 1996). Hence the bitter-sweet tone and the subtle alchemy of a disenchanted enchantment that combines 'a certain distrust of sentimental love and the impossibility of escaping its laws' (Chalvon-Demersay 1996: 87). Between these two extremes, more classical television series and Mills and Boon novels attempt to introduce a perception of daily life that is just critical enough to lead to the essential happy ending (Péquignot 1991; Houel 1997).

'Between the ages of 35 and 40, my life was like a beautiful love story, the most beautiful I've ever known' (Madeleine). Films and novels do not just establish a framework for the expression of feelings; they teach us to inscribe those feelings within a real story. The word is not to be taken lightly. For someone who wants to be in a love story, the story is just as important as the love. There must be a setting, characters and, above all, a plot. Someone like Karen has to be carried away as the plot unfolds, and has to be able to tell her diary or girlfriends what has happened to her. Her memories have to take the form of a story. 'Four years ago, I left a man I had a wonderful scene with' (Karen). The dream is always constructed like a story, like a very beautiful story. It is the face-to-face encounter that spoils things. 'I've never had a love story, or a boyfriend of my own to introduce me as his girlfriend. They just slept with me, and that was all there was to it.' Juliette is as devastated by the lack of emotion as by the fact that there was no story. In her case, it is obvious: she was never even introduced as a character, and nothing happened apart from the sex. There is, however, often a little more to it than that: the secret is to construct and pad out the story so as to turn everyday life into the real story she goes on telling herself. 'It was a story you could never imagine happening to you, a story out of a novel that happened to me as though I was someone else. Besides, I wrote down the details about every time we met, and even thought of turning it into a book. I was carried away, as though I was in a living soap opera. I kept asking myself: "What's going to happen in the next episode?" I'm still all of a quiver' (Véronique).

It seems that love is increasingly destined to become part of the stories these women tell themselves. Justine, for example, insists on describing her life as a novel even though she admits that there is not much to her story. 'What's my life like? Like a novel, but not a schmaltzy one. It's more like a story that is devoid of interest.' This narrative form appears in letters written towards the end of the nineteenth century. Although it was originally institutional, it then became much more personalized and centred on a subject who was both actor and narrator (Hurtubise 1991). The protagonists try to see themselves in action-packed stories with elaborate settings and Princes who look like fashionable stars. This is because we are now inundated with stories and images. But it is also because these stories represent an ideal form precisely because they are so ambiguous: they are both a destiny and a strategy. Pure destiny, or a Love that is made in heaven, is difficult to imagine in a world where everyone is supposedly responsible for his or her own actions. For its part, pure strategy means the death of love. We therefore have to invent an intermediate modality that combines enchantment and a critical vision, the surprise of the emotion that carries us away but leaves us in control of the situation. A love story is all those things at once: we do not know whether the woman who is acting it out has carefully staged it, or whether she has been thrown into it against her will. That is the magic of a story: it can include everything. Such as love and its multiple contents. And such as a Prince with a thousand faces.

The Prince Settles Down

Before any encounter with the real person, the Prince is a dream and someone she is waiting to meet. Which explains why he has a thousand faces: she may have to wait indefinitely, and her expectations are often contradictory. Sometimes they are essentially negative: putting an end to the mental pressure, escaping the divided life by becoming one half of a couple. In such cases, the dream espouses the form of the norm and the Prince plays the part of the husband. 'Marriage, children and a house mean social success: a relationship that is above all suspicion' (Roseline). When she is very tired, the dream can cling to the pettiest details. Forget about the carefree life, and forget about the real Prince: the only thing that seems to matter at such times is settling into a day-to-day life that is problem-free: 'If they only knew! I very often envy them their lives, even though they seem so narrow to me!!' (Marie-Christine). As individuals are forced to take on more and more responsibilities, the more they aspire to peace and quiet (Gullestad 1992). But the modalities vary in accordance with the position of the individual concerned. Married women who are well protected by the norm often dream, in contrast, of an element of surprise (there are real Princes in her compensatory imaginary), whereas single women dream mainly of serenity and rest. Women who do experience something resembling a real love story that might turn their lives upside down, and who do meet men who might turn out to be Princes, are more likely than others to dream of an uneventful peaceful life. 'I'm waiting. Waiting for what? To be happy. For inner peace' (Gaétane). This brings us back to the life divided. Single women are torn between the attractions of passion and a search for limits, which are very different ways of defining an identity that has become spread too thinly. Passion means the real Prince and a dynamic life of perpetual self-renewal. Limits mean a husband, a settled life in a protected world at last.

For young women (who still have their future ahead of them), the real Prince obviously plays the star role. And then, what was initially no more than the secondary role of the colourless husband gradually becomes more important: 'love-as-friendship', 'nice and uneventful' (Caradec 1997: 92), replaces burning passion and a modest prince who has settled down takes centre stage. It has to be said that he gets a lot of help from another character.

'Husband, baby, house', Astrid told us. The husband is there because, while he is not indispensable, he is very useful when it comes to having a baby, and the house is there because it provides a home for the happy family. But doesn't everything still centre on the baby? 'That is the beginning and the end of the story: women are meant to have babies and to be loved by men.' One Prince can conceal another. The so-called 'real Prince' she first meets is quite quickly transformed into a husband, and then makes way for a new character who is wreathed in smiles: the little Prince. With a gentle, devoted chamberlain at his service: the husband-turned-dad. Small as he may be, there is no mistaking it: he is now the real Prince. Once a single woman who has never had a child is no longer young, the issue of babies gradually becomes an obsession. Deep inside, she expects that she will have a baby, but the baby is also the focus of an anxiety that comes from elsewhere. Claire, who is 30, is already fixated: 'I'm counting the years that come between me and my hypothetical first baby.' And Claudia, who is 38, is plunged into despair: 'It's terrifying to say to yourself that you might never have the babies you dream of having.' Like many others, Claire and Claudia now need not so much a real Prince who will carry them off on some wild adventure as a calm husband-dad for their little Princes.

It is, however, unusual for them to admit openly that this hierarchy exists. The very approximate combination of contradictory contents once more allows them to cherish the illusion that Love still rules the world, just as it has always done. Listen to Elodie: 'A life without love, without children and without someone to share it is not a happy life. I'm still waiting for my Prince to come. And it seems to me that he's taking his time about getting here.' What does her Prince look like? He certainly has many different faces and is hard to describe. It would, however, seem that the princely terminology scarcely conceals the fact that she is really waiting for a husband-dad.

The amalgam is an illusion. But it is an illusion that can delude a woman for a long time: it is unusual for the contradictions to be clearly thought through and spelled out. The comments from Martine and Michèle (who are both married and have children) are therefore all the more valuable. To begin with Martine. In Act I, she was single: 'My life was fabulous, and I had loads of friends, both men and women.' In Act II, the idea of having a baby dawns, and that implies finding a husband. 'And then, all at once, I began to feel that I wanted to have a baby. So I said yes.' And then what happened? 'I no longer existed in my own right.' Having written that, she then feels that she has to give her story a different, and less tragic, ending. She escapes her dilemma thanks to a very diplomatic combination of two very different sentences. The first is designed to give her a clear conscience and to avoid making a fuss, but the second allows her to express a truth that is at once harsher and more profound. 'Conclusion: ten years later, I have no regrets because I adore my husband and daughter. But I am sure of one thing: if by some misfortune I find myself on my own, I will never again live with a man.' Michèle has no time for such caution. Her letter is incredibly violent; she is livid with anger, and wants to denounce the trap she has fallen into. She used to look after her body, but now that she has family responsibilities, she realizes that she is letting herself go; she used to enjoy her intellectual freedom, but now she sees herself dying of boredom because her routine never varies. She dreams nostalgically of the life she has lost: singing, writing, the theatre, friends and political activity. 'Now that I'm married and have children, I'm living on a planet where, unfortunately, I no longer exist. Old maids are not what we think they are: they are the women who, because they have a bloke or a kid, become completely depersonalized and give up the right to be themselves.'

When the Carriage Turns Back into a Pumpkin

'I recently fell head over heels in love with a drop-dead gorgeous guy. We spent a few nights together. Love, madness, a dream and all the rest of it. And then nothing. He moved on' (Charlène). The letters are full of stories of Princes who all at once disappear in a puff of smoke, and of carriages that suddenly turn back into pumpkins. The speed with which the Prince vanishes is typical: it is as though he had to disappear as quickly as he appeared, as though that were the only way for him to go on being a real Prince.

There are reasons for this. Sometimes the man the woman has met lays it on thick in order to look like a Prince, but he eventually proves to be very different. In the cold light of morning, he is mediocre and unpleasant. When that happens, the metamorphosis is his doing and the disillusionment is bitter. But the deceit is usually on a smaller scale and means nothing more than the excitement of a few crude attempts at seduction. In that case, the metamorphosis is her doing because she insists at all cost on seeing a Prince when there isn't one: the carriage very quickly becomes once more the pumpkin it always was. 'Sometimes a man comes into my life. I always imagine that he is the love of my life. Then he moves on, or he is not free' (Emma). The Prince was no more than an imaginary excrescence of a fragment of the real world that was ill-suited to her purposes. He may well be imaginary, but he can also prove capable of being very resilient, and the same carriage can go on being turned into a pumpkin for years. Brigitte, who is 39 and divorced, describes her behaviour as 'that of a girl of 18: I am always emotional when I go out on a date, and it's magic.' Even so, she admits that she also needs to know how to control herself: 'Women give in too easily.' But she obviously cannot stop herself. Her prince was obviously a false Prince who was selfish and manipulative. She wanted so much to believe in him that she fell for him at every opportunity. 'The trouble was that he wanted to retain his freedom, and wanted me to be available whenever he wanted. I spent six years waiting for the phone to ring. Six hellish years. But whenever he did ring, I dropped everything.'

There is, finally, one other kind of metamorphosis: the Prince turns into a husband, and that central process allows the single woman to make the transition to being a married woman. When this happens, the Prince is nothing more than a means to an end. A few memories are all that remain. And a few regrets if the couple forgets the initial passion of the early days too quickly. 'For me, the first moments were the best, before we decided to start living together. Then the routine set in. What I'd really like is to be single again for a few moments' (Malorie).

The Prince Plays Musical Chairs

Joëlle believed in Prince Charming for a long time, and often imagined that she would see him before he vanished. Now, she does not believe in him at all, and has no wish to do so either. Disillusioned and worn down by life, she is looking for a hole to hide in: 'I couldn't stand being on my own any more. So I went back to live with my husband. I don't love him any more. It's hard sometimes. I've often told my diary that I want to die, just to die.' Could there be anything worse than no longer believing in anything? Even though he may lead women down blind alleys and disillusion them, Prince Charming is not all bad when taken in reasonable doses.

The contrast with Laura is striking. The comparison should obviously not be taken too far, as the two women's biographies are very different. It is, on the other hand, worth pointing out that, because Laura believes in Prince Charming 'without believing in him', her day-to-day life is positive and has a certain dynamism. She starts with a fairly radical statement of principle: 'A little fling, a one-night stand? No thanks, I've already done that. A real love story is what I want.' But she immediately adds that she does not expect that to happen and that she is perfectly happy on her own. The real love story is something she dips into from time to time in order to flesh out her dreams as she quietly alternates between believing 'without believing in him' and dreaming of events that will sweep her off her feet even though she no longer expects that to happen. 'Even though I do still have my dreams and reflexes (whenever I go to a dance, I look around me to see if Mr Right is there), it's little more than a habit. It does me good, but I don't actually wake up every morning expecting a miracle to happen.'

The swings are often much more violent because her Prince's many faces can take her in many different directions. At such times, her life progresses by fits and starts, with bursts of passion followed by disappointments, conflicts between real Princes and husband-dads, and clashes between an imaginary fairyland and a problematic reality. Take Julia's story. In the space of a single letter consisting of a few sheets of paper, she comes out with all sorts of contradictory things. As we have seen, she was looking for true love, for a love that was absolute and shared, and would therefore not 'make do with little flings that lead nowhere'. She makes it clear that: 'I dream of meeting a man who looks as much like Prince Charming as possible.' So far, all is clear and she has high ambitions, but the picture suddenly becomes darker when she begins to describe her Prince: 'Perhaps Julia's girlish dream of having a nice little husband and having children with the man she loves is not destined to come true.' So, Prince or husband? We will never know, because Julia suddenly decides that there is no difference between them and rejects both of them in the name of her autonomy as a woman. A woman should learn to come to terms with being on her own and reject the model for private life that society is trying to force on to her. 'Women are supposed to get married and have children, but is that the key to being happy? I'm not convinced that just one lifestyle can make you happy.'

Part II

Portrait of a Single Woman

No two lives are the same. This is especially true of the lives of single women. The way their lives are divided in two makes their trajectories bumpy, and means that they are constantly zigzagging between opposite extremes. Their lives sometimes seem to be perfect, but at other times they are in a state of utter dejection. At times, they laugh until they cry, and other times they fall prey to a doleful melancholy. At times they are active and outgoing, and at other times they curl up in a foetal position and hide away at home. And yet despite all the differences, the specific categories and the constant changes, and regardless of the psychological characteristics of individual women, an overall portrait does emerge, and it is surprisingly clear and coherent.

— 5 —

INTROSPECTION

'The Disease of the Infinite'

According to Emile Durkheim (2006: 299), marriage brings a married man calm and moral tranquillity because it consolidates his 'mental bedrock', limits his horizons and curbs his desires: 'The salutary discipline to which he is subjected makes it a duty for him to find his happiness in his situation.' The bachelor, in contrast, 'can legitimately attach himself to whatever he wants . . . aspires to everything and nothing satisfies him. . . . One dreams of the impossible – one thirsts for what is not.' Hence the 'disease of the infinite' or the series of disappointments that leads to a 'feeling of weariness and disenchantment'. The disease is a product of what Durkheim calls 'anomie': the absence of norms that can support and structure the individual. It would be a mistake to dwell on the author's moralism, as it is a feature of the time when these lines were written (at the end of the nineteenth century). The important point is the thesis he is defending: deviations from the norm (the conjugal norm in this case) produce specific types of lives and individual lives are characterized by a distinctive mode of being.

The most characteristic element is the permanent reflexivity, the way people who are on their own constantly watch themselves: isn't there something 'weird' about my life? Where is it getting me? What choices should I be making? This is the price we pay when the normative framework is weak; when we do conform to the norm, it provides the comfort of an identity that has some support. But we pay a high price when we are abandoned to our own existential creativity. The protective framework tells the subject-position what it is and what it will be: 'husband, baby, home'. Reforms – and they are minor – are restricted to subjective adjustments. The indecisive restlessness and mental discomfort experienced by the single man or woman are, in direct contrast, effects of their freedom to invent themselves. That freedom is very intoxicating – perhaps too intoxicating. We suffer from the 'disease of the infinite' because life is full of possibilities and because the future is not predetermined, because we always have to choose between very different paths. The 'disease of the infinite' should therefore not be analysed as though it were just a curse: it is the dark side of the coin, but the other side is bright and shiny. For the same reason, it would be a mistake to overlook what can often be deep suffering. We have to take into consideration both the bright side and the dark side, because they are closely connected. The single life (which deviates from the conjugal norm) is, in structural terms, a life divided, a never-ending struggle between thousands of pairs of opposites within us.

From Laughter to Tears

Take emotional life. Emotions are never gratuitous: they play an important role in the regulation of our actions. When a situation is open and weakly structured by a norm, the emotions take over in order both to guide us on our way and to attempt to force a normative framework on us. The most obvious example is what happens when we meet the man or woman we love. This is the apotheosis of a cycle of emotion that ends when we settle down into coupledom. The single, in contrast, are in the paradoxical situation of being caught up in an emotional cycle that never closes and never comes to an end. 'Being single makes you receptive, intense and profound. Being single catches at the emotions, which take on the most astonishing dimensions' (Adeline).

Although they are more intense, the emotions are also more unstable. They appear suddenly and take the form of sadness or cheerfulness for no obvious reason. They are the outcome of an indecisive struggle between the opposites that are, deep within us, trying to lay down the law. 'I often go from laughter to tears' (Hélène). Albertine regularly experiences a swing between moments of euphoria and 'Kleenex parties after I've over-dosed on myself.' She calls this her 'double life'.

The tears and the laughter are not symmetrical. Although there is usually a mixture of the two, the proportions can vary greatly, depending on the history of the individual concerned. Some laugh a lot and others cry a lot. What is more important is that these two emotional poles are not expressed in the same way. A woman can scream with laughter with her girlfriends, but when she is alone at home, laughter is a very private and vaguely guilty pleasure. Tears are expressed more strongly. This is because they have more to do with ordinary depression than with crises. Crises are far from being a universal experience (some women often experience crises, while others never do so). Everyday life is full of questions, self-doubts and constant questions to which there are no answers. And it is difficult to be reflexive and bright and breezy: reflexivity is a serious business. Hence the common tendency to 'start brooding' (Hélène). Brooding really is the only way we can take a critical look at ourselves, and it inevitably prevents us from thinking about anything else. Pleasure, by contrast, is more diffuse or irregular: it can be either a deep, latent feeling or something that suddenly comes to the surface. And sometimes it never comes to the surface at all because we ask ourselves too many questions. 'I tell myself that I have everything I need to make me happy, and that women who ask themselves fewer questions are less tormented' (Hélène).

Double Reflexivity

The mind is tormented by questions. They seem always to be the same and there never seem to be any answers. They come up again and again, night after night and day after day. The questions do not, however, all have the same importance and it is possible to put them into two main categories.

'The unavoidable "why" often crops up again and again' (Marie-Christine). Why this weird life? Why me? 'Why am I alone in my little flat at the age of 37?' (Evelyne). These questions arise, and constantly nag at her, because her real life is out of step with the model for private life, and because the gap between the two cannot be bridged. When a single woman really does come to terms with her autonomy and laughs more often than she cries, the questions she asks herself tend to be about the weird spitefulness of the 'accusing finger'. When the accusing finger makes single women feel ill at ease, they tend to wonder about their weirdly tormented lives. When single women cry a lot – and they usually cry because they accept the model – they are asking themselves: 'So why am I being excluded? Why me?'

This first group of questions, which arises because the women in question do not conform to the norm, has to do with the norm itself. The mechanism behind these questions is simple. When a single woman fully conforms to the norm, she is socialized by that norm and her critical perception of it is blunted: there is no point in asking questions because everything is 'normal'. The more she deviates from that norm, the greater her need to question its meaning in order to become more socialized. The extent to which she questions it is inversely proportional to the norm's socializing power (Kaufmann 1995a).

The second sphere of questions is very different. The first set of questions is the focus of obsessional fixations and the questions are always the same. There is no answer to them. The second set of questions is both diversified and creative. Appearances are deceptive and they are not always the same: the painful 'why' may well be in the forefront of her mind, but it conceals some very different questions.

These new questions are not being asked in order to get an answer (which never comes) but in order to make choices, and those choices are both everyday and concrete. They have to do with the openness of life and with the inner conflicts of a divided life which constantly forces single women to take options and to choose between what are often very different alternatives. 'For someone in my position, every day is a mystery' (Judith). Even when nothing is happening, she has to be ready for all sorts of eventualities because the future is still open. 'I would define this weird state by saying that part of me is lying fallow and waiting for something to happen' (Dorothée). It is a good definition: her identity is still a work in progress, something that has yet to be invented. Dorothée quite rightly says that part of her is 'lying fallow'. It in fact seems she is never fully involved in her own life. Only part of her is involved at any given moment: 'the rest of me limps along as best it can to keep up appearances' (Dorothée). It is a difficult task, as revolutionizing one's identity on a permanent basis is no small undertaking, and it is not unusual for it to be experienced as a painful obligation. 'That's the difficult thing about being on your own: you have to constantly make up your own life as you go' (Joanna). Especially as the mental effort that goes into reshaping the Self is not her only problem: she has to manage everything, including her day-to-day life, while remaining totally autonomous. 'The hardest thing of all is having to bear the whole burden on my own' (Gabrielle). 'You have to admit that organizing your own life is hard; putting up with it all on your own is killing' (Marjorie).

From Diaries to Blogs

Alone. Alone with herself. For anyone who is alone with the divided Self of a divided life, introspection is a permanent dialogue. In this imaginary little cinema, two different characters often begin a conversation: the Self talks to the Self. Sometimes the director-actor dares to speak out loud. 'Sometimes I suddenly shout at myself: "Get a move on, girl! We've got a bright future ahead of us!" And the girl does get a move on. But you never can tell, and there are times when I collapse into my chair and another voice speaks from inside me: "Bright future, bright future" (I'm doing my Arletty impression). "You're a pain in the neck, you and your bright future, I'm quite happy just lazing about!" Sometimes, the voices answer each other. It's like a little play' (Viviane).

The tool of choice for this inner colloquium is, however, the written word. First, a word about books, which play a key role in the lives of single women. Reading is the most individualistic of cultural practices and books therefore play a central role: lots of bedside books to be read late at night, snuggled up in bed. So much for leisure. The books they read in connection with their studies – and education is a historical factor in the emancipation of the individual – are closely associated with the autonomy trajectory. Some women owe their academic success to books, and that encourages them to pursue their careers without looking for husbands. Books are all these things at the same time: tools for academic success and reflexivity, for self-assertion and for the deconstruction of the Self. They also stimulate dreams of love, especially for women; girls still lose themselves in the delights of love stories (Singly 1989) simply because they enjoy them. And because they can identify with the characters in them as they try to fathom the secrets of their future lives.

But, when it comes to introspection, nothing can rival the personal practice of writing. 'Writing is the one luxury in my life' (Marie-Andrée). Some women tell themselves the story of their lives as though it was a novel. A diary is a never-ending story that has to be made up, written and read all at the same time. 'The female temptation to use writing as both an intimate support and a solitary confession is one of the typical effects of romantic culture' (Di Giorgio 1992: 378). Feelings become heightened, their lives become stories and they become introspective. The last point is decisive, and the function of the other two (important as they may be) is to provide window dressing. Turning a life into a story is a mechanism that constructs an identity (Demazière and Dubar 1997: 304). Telling stories is a form of written introspection.

'My diary is my only ally. It allows me to express myself without having to be judged' (Liliane). She can tell her diary everything: the guilty secrets she can never admit to having, questions of life and death. A diary never judges. It listens in silence as the woman holding the pen talks to herself and changes her mind as her divided life unfolds, and as something resembling a story emerges from its meanderings. A diary has a beginning and an end (a sudden end). The story often begins in adolescence. 'I've been keeping a diary for 15 years. When I was 13, I began to write about how I was feeling, my emotions, my secrets. As the years went by, the secrets of my life were revealed' (Justine). This is no coincidence: adolescence is an important moment in the reformulation of our identity, and diaries always reflect our identity crises. A diary is an instrument for a dialogue with the Self, and the dialogue is at its most lively in times of crisis. The deeper introspection characteristic of the single life often comes later (the crisis comes all the later if the woman in question has come to terms with her independence). Lise's life was so busy and everything was moving so fast that she did not ask herself any questions for 15 years. 'I've spent the last 15 years studying, travelling and meeting people because I was curious, and had an appetite for life and an irrepressible, vital need to be free. The time passed quickly. And now I am paying the price for that freedom.' At the age of 37, she began to have her first doubts. She mercilessly dissected her life, putting her comments down on paper in an attempt to find out who she was. It is unusual for someone to begin to use the written word as a form of self-exploration at such a late stage in the life cycle. As I have already said, the process normally begins in adolescence, often in the form of the sentimental diaries girls fill with their dreams and love stories. And it goes on, with all the ups and downs that reflect life's difficulties, until the crisis in their divided lives becomes acute. The diary then becomes an essential tool and takes the bleaker form of the diary of a woman who is worried because she has come to the parting of the ways.

The crisis is at its height for only a short time; after the storm, life finds an anchorage in calmer waters. The diary then breaks off, sometimes right in the middle of a story that will never have an ending. And the diary that was so precious, that seemed to be an intrinsic part of her, suddenly looks like something that is alien and useless. Or even, in retrospect, like a symbol of the time she wasted on telling herself stories rather than doing something. Agnès went on keeping a diary until she was 45. And then she suddenly 'threw it away, just like that. One day, I said to myself that I'd done with all that nonsense.'

A lot of emotion goes into keeping a diary. This is because of the subject-matter: there is a lot of talk of emotions. But it is also because the writer is emotionally attached to her diary: the bitterness of the final rejection is proportional to the love that came before it. The diary

used to be her closest friend, and was privy to countless secret pleasures: the caress of a tender word, the pleasure of coming up with just
the right idea, the sonorous aesthetics of writing on one's own. 'When
there were long silences in my life, I always had the sound of my pen
scratching on the paper' (Léa). Her diary used to be a reliable partner
who could make her feel strong and self-confident. 'Just having a pen
meant goodbye to anxieties and goodbye to loneliness: I was stronger
and more powerful than ever' (Gaétane). But a diary can also become
a false friend, an enemy within who forces her to go on and on doubt-
ing herself to an unreasonable extent or until her Self shatters into
pieces. 'Take this pen away from me! It's destroying me more and more
with every word' (Gaétane).

There is both a bright side and a dark side to Gaétane's life. She
therefore loves and hates her diary with equal intensity. She puts her
whole self into it, both because of the pleasure it affords her and
because of the depths of the introspection in which she is drowning. A
diary is often a quiet companion to whom the writer tells her story
because she is waiting to hear what will happen next and not because
she wants to indulge in painful self-doubts. The focus of the introspection shifts from one episode to the next. Léa was very surprised
(and disappointed) when she recently reread her diary (which was
something she had not done for a long time). She thought that she had
been undertaking serious self-analysis, but found herself plunged into
a rather aseptic fairytale world (especially in the early years of her
diary). 'I hung on to these pages in the belief that I had found a fantastic ally: my diary. Fifteen years of writing with only one goal in
mind: meeting Prince Charming.'

Is it a case of farewell, dear diary? It took only a few years for the
landscape of writing as self-analysis to undergo a radical change. It has
suddenly become unusual to hear the sound of a pen scratching on
paper. It has given way to a keyboard and a screen, and diaries have
moved en masse on to the net. Diaries are no longer hidden away in
secret drawers; on the contrary, the intimate Self is now on display in
the full light of day. The strangest thing about this revolution is that
those who brought it about scarcely notice that it has happened.
Women write the same things they once wrote in their diaries in their
blogs, as though nothing or almost nothing had changed (apart from
their writing instruments). They open up in the same way, note the
important events of the day and their thoughts of the moment with the
same sincerity and with the same goal in mind: they are trying to arrive
at a better understanding of themselves and to guess what tomorrow
will bring. In fact, there has always been another motive ever since

diaries were first kept: writing for the sake of it, leaving some trace of oneself, proving how rich one's inner life is, and creating a work of literature, albeit on a modest scale. Transposing this dream to the Web immediately brings the dream to life. It is not just that the work takes shape; it is also recognized (to a greater or lesser extent) and finds its audience in the form of a crowd that is at once anonymous and intimately close, understanding and warm. 'Thank you for all your messages,' writes 'Juliet-with-no-Romeo'. 'You are so kind, and your messages are heart-warming. I reread them during my moments of depression. Even when my bad thoughts spew out their filth, you still love me. Wait until I take you deeper into the darkness of my trashiest dirty talk.' When it is converted into a blog, the diary loses its pastel shades! That is the new law that governs the genre: those who do not boldly plunge into the darkest labyrinths of their secrets are in danger of being rejected because they are being trite. They will fail to find an audience. Mawkishness is out of fashion. Filth pays.

An audience that is at once close at hand and far away can, however, easily become a drug it is impossible to do without. It breaks the loneliness and expands life's surface. How could anyone allow it to shrink again? The writers of blogs do, however, sometimes break off their confidences. They have been glued to the screen for too long and feel that they are living in a virtual world. They suddenly need a more substantial diet. The dialogue does not break off for long. They have the suffocating feeling that something inside them has died. The irrepressible need to get back to their audience is too strong, and they want to go on and on talking to everyone. Especially as a blog can be more than a way of finding virtual friends. It can also be a way of establishing a loving complicity, precisely because it is so intimate. Increasingly, the quest for a 'soul-mate' is something that goes on in blogs.

The Mirror and the Clairvoyant

Then there is the mirror that reflects the passage of time. 'Mirror, mirror on the wall, tell me I'm the fairest of them all. You show me an image I did not expect to see, and you throw my hatred back in my face! Putting on a mask or lots of make-up doesn't make a difference. I can't fool you. You are everywhere, laughing at me and you always win!' (Gaétane). The mirror is a central object. As for all women, it is a support for an introspection (in both the literal and the figurative sense) that revolves around the twin questions of beauty and the

78

passage of time. A woman who is on her own takes a much closer look at herself. In her case, the dialogue between the Self and the Self becomes more lively (and takes the place of a conversation with a husband); the mirror plays the role of the man who is not there (it is as though she was seeing herself through a husband's eyes). There is no avoiding the face-to-face encounter with this symbolic object.

Questions about beauty and the passage of time are more important for single women than they are for other women; these are decisive issues when it comes to inventing the future, which has yet to be defined. When a single woman peers at her own face in the mirror of beauty, she is examining all of herself. She is examining the depths of her being and her possible identities. The face-to-face encounter with her reflection is an important moment in this inner dialogue. That is why she lingers so long in the bathroom. She is looking far beyond the image in the mirror.

She goes through the same process when she sees a fortune-teller. There is no need to dwell on the occult epiphenomena: the important point is that consulting a fortune-teller is, like looking in the mirror, a way of looking at herself. 'I consult a fortune-teller about once a year, when I really don't know where my head is at' (Justine). The need is at its greatest when the inner confusion is at its worst. Single women do not consult clairvoyants often, but they do so on a regular basis (once a year, or every two to three years). The practice is widespread (almost as widespread as that of keeping a diary); it is mentioned in a lot of the letters. Isabelle is unemployed and has no money, but she skimps on food to pay her fortune-teller. Knowing the secret of this weird life – at last! – is more important than eating.

A clairvoyant's main skill is that she is a good commercial psychologist: she must be able to guess what her customers want. Her job is then to read the message they expect to see in the cards or the tea-leaves. And that message is far from being individualized. It is a social code. All the letters say that the answer is always the same, and it is articulated around three themes: love, marriage and children. And that is what encourages Isabelle to make so many sacrifices. 'My fortune-teller has been predicting that I will get married and have three children for two years now.' Marie-Laure sees a fortune-teller every two years. Every time, she is told that she will meet Mr Right, get married and have the first of three children within the year.

The clairvoyants have not got together to perfect their only answer. The answer is always the same because of its social nature: it is simply the model for private life. Or, to be more accurate, what the clairvoyants imagine that model to be, which is why they happily stress its most archaic aspects: love is, naturally enough, something that is made in heaven, and the man is a real Prince. Given the complexity of the model, clairvoyants have to be selective: the emphasis falls on marriage and children, and love tends to be a necessary preliminary. Nor is there anything random about the number of children: there are usually two, but there is now a tendency for the figure to rise to three because changes in the tax system promote that new model.

The stereotypical nature of the answer sometimes misfires in business terms. Marie-Laure is very disappointed. Although she does not really believe in fortune-tellers, she feels a need to consult one on a regular basis. But this time, she has had enough: married within the year, and then two children, even though she told her fortune-teller that she is violently opposed to marriage and has not the slightest desire to have a baby. Usually, however, there are no disagreements, and the fortune-teller senses that her message is acceptable: she does not have to guess what particular women want and gives them all the answers they wish to hear. 'I've often consulted fortune-tellers, and the message of hope they give me does me good: he is waiting for me somewhere out there' (Fabienne). The fortune-teller is also confirmed in her belief that her message is the right one, and that it is not worth making the effort to change it so long as it is worth its weight in gold.

And yet the fortune-tellers are wrong: what the women expect to hear is not quite what they imagine it to be. The message is ambiguous and confused. Only half the Self is satisfied and relieved by what it hears. But it is precisely the half that is looking for consolation: the haven of peace and a mental pressure-drop. As Fabienne says: 'It does me good.' Faced with a fortune-teller, the other half of the Self remains silent. Especially as occult messages do seem to have their advantages. If Love really is heaven-sent, there is no point in torturing ourselves. All one can do is wait. And while a woman waits, she has to get on with her life as best she can. This works to the advantage of the other half of the Self.

Waiting in this way quickly becomes a problem: we cannot put our minds on hold indefinitely. On the contrary, an offensive on the part of one half of the Self (Prince-husband-baby) often leads to a new outbreak of internecine warfare. And if we look more closely, the war never actually ended. Few women really believe in fortune-tellers; they consult them out of curiosity and partly because they want to be told something nice. But there is often a certain distance, a hint of scepticism and an internal splitting. Only one half of the Self goes to the fortune-teller. In the case of Danielle, part of her lapses into radical scepticism after having been given the same message over and over again, even though it flies in the face of the facts. But when the other part of her is in a bad state, she still feels that she has to go to a fortune-teller. 'She always tells me the same thing: love, marriage, two children. And yet I still go back whenever I'm down in the dumps.' Justine is in a similar position: 'OK, it doesn't get me anywhere. She contrives to see Love, marriage, children – but where are they?' That only one of an infinite number of possibilities is realized finally confuses the issue and frustrates her patient attempts at self-definition. It has precisely the opposite effect, does nothing to help her to repair her shattered identity, and does not relieve the mental pressure.

This is one of the characteristic features of the divided life: even those elements that are not especially conducive to reflexivity actually encourage it. Everything becomes a pretext for introspection.

— 6 —

AT HOME

Fixtures and Fittings

We all have our own lifestyles and personal tastes, but the average single woman's home and the way it is furnished differ from those of other households in several respects. This is in part for obvious organizational and financial reasons. Single people are, for instance, more likely to rent than to own their homes and to live in the city centres (it is not unusual for them to have no car). This is, however, also one of the effects of their particular position and of the way their lives are split into two.

Let us take a look around this average home. The first surprise is to find that it is so big. It is spacious and light, as though to ward off the idea of being shut in; in some cases, the shutters are not closed at night (Lavigne and Arbet 1992). Although it is cluttered up with various knick-knacks, it is still quite bare. This is especially true of men's homes, which have little furniture and few domestic appliances (apart from microwaves). Single women have more furniture and domestic appliances than men, but fewer than the average household. It is not that they (unlike men) do not invest in their homes, but that they are more concerned with decor than with domesticity. There are often a lot of fabrics, and they create an atmosphere that is warm and soft to the touch. 'Everything is pink, with subdued lighting, soft music and incense' (Léa).

It is also surprising to find that they have fewer pets than families. This is simply because single women go out a lot, travel and spend a lot of their time at work. When they do have a pet, it is more likely to be a cat than a dog. And they watch less television. When the television is on, it is used mainly as a distant presence and as background noise (Lavigne and Arbet 1992). Music, on the other hand, provides a reassuring blanket of sound: there is a top-of-the-range stereo and a lot of CDs. The fact that the spaces tend to be bright and open should not, however, disguise the fact that the very different envelopes we find inside them mark out special moments of intimacy and protection: the musical ambiance, the bed they snuggle up in, the door that remains closed while they are using the bathroom, and so on.

This constant interplay between open spaces and niches is typical of the way their lives are split into two: the secret niches are next to appliances that provide a link with the outside world, and especially the telephone (which usually has an answering machine). Single women use the telephone much more than families: it is the privileged vector for their social bonds, the wire that keeps them in touch. They talk to their families, and especially their girlfriends. And they talk at great length: 'I daren't think about my phone bills. They can be up to 500 euros' (Gabrielle).

Bed

We are often wrong about objects. Our relationship with them is intimate and complex (Kaufmann 1997; Desjeux et al. 1998). Objects fool over-hasty analyses and observers who are in too great a hurry. Take the example of the bed. Given that it is a symbol of coupledom, one might think that it is something especially problematic for a single woman. And to some extent it is (especially in the evenings). But a bed can also be a special ally that provides warm, cosy mornings and freedom and that encourages foetal regression. 'Sleeping all day or at least staying in bed all day are two of my guilty pleasures' (Frédérique). 'When I snuggle up in bed, it is as though it was holding me in its arms. It calms me down and I let myself drift off' (Aurore). It is a den inside the den, the reference point that determines where everything else is. In a return to certain forgotten traditions (Dibie 1987), it is therefore often used in many different ways: sleeping, dreaming and reading, but also for making phone calls, working and eating.

It is true that, as night falls, the ally can turn traitor. It is not obvious at first: the first contact with the bed is always warm and soft and brings relief and comfort. Single women snuggle up luxuriously for their evening activities: eating a TV-dinner, reading a book, writing in their diaries, writing letters or dreaming. The reflexive process spirals out of control as the evening goes by: they can't switch off and have difficulty in getting to sleep. 'So I get caught up in a book or, worse still, start talking to myself! Oh dear, oh dear' (Françoise). As a result, single women go to sleep much later than married women (Grimler 1992). Even though she gets up early, Marie-Pierre reads until midnight, and Marie-Line until one in the morning. Christelle stays glued to her computer screen until even later.

As the evening goes by, the bed loses its warmth. The cold feeling is of course psychological: there is no one to share the bed with, and the cold spots tear apart the protective envelope. It is often the feet that feel it first. Adeline's feet are freezing. She cannot do anything about it: it seems to her that a man is the only thing that could warm them up. Feeling cold shows that something is missing, and the fact that something is missing makes the bed feel cold. Géraldine's bed feels like ice: 'I go to pieces when I'm alone between the sheets at night. Alone without a man.' She is not asking for a lot. Perhaps a few cuddles. But above all, to have someone there, just to have someone there. Albertine is even more specific about what she misses: not being able to say 'See you in the morning' before she goes to sleep at night.

Meals

Meals are more problematic than bed. Family meals are rituals that play an essential role in the formation of the domestic group. Even when the family members do not have all their meals together, the well-known call that rings through the house ('Food's ready!') tells everyone that an important event in their collective life is about to take place, and that it will bring them to sit down face to face to exchange sensations, words, tears or laughter. Sharing meals brings the family together in an emotional sense, and the table symbolizes the family (Kaufmann 2005). For anyone who does not live as part of a family, the table becomes, on the contrary, an enemy that represents all the values that are not there. 'What could be more frustrating than setting the table for one and sitting down for a meal by yourself' (Frédérique). This is especially true when the family dining table is empty, so the best solution is not to have one. A kitchen table lends itself more easily to small meals that are eaten quickly and on one's own.

The most common practice, however, consists in deconstructing the ritual by taking radically different options, so as to demonstrate even more clearly that having a meal has nothing to do with family symbolism. Not a lot of time is spent on preparing the meal, which consists of individual items of food, and the order of things inverts the usual codes. Meals consist of 'quick snacks' (Annabelle), of 'dolls' tea

84

parties' (Georgina) that remind her of when she was a little girl. Without the complicated ingredients: 'Tomorrow will be the same as today: Sweet corn, a tin of tuna and half a baguette' (Sabine). The food is often simple, with two dominant themes: natural and organic food. There is a lot of fruit and yoghurt. Mixed salads are best eaten in restaurants; it takes too long to prepare them at home, even though they are healthy. The shopping is quickly done. 'A quick trip to the shops to buy food for a dolls' tea party: fruit, yoghurt, ham, cheese and tea. And ten packs of Kleenex' (Joanna).

High tables and the conventional seated posture are avoided. It is as though some force drew singles towards the floor and softness. It is the TV dinner that allows this displacement. Placing it on a low table or the bed, the woman sprawls on a couch or cushions (and reinvents, so to speak, the Roman custom). Sometimes, even the tray, which is the last structural element bearing a distant resemblance to a real meal, goes. She survives on snacks, preferably eaten at odd times and as the fancy takes her, or precisely the things that children are not allowed to do. And she has a very marked preference for chocolate, which is often mentioned as being one of a single woman's special indulgences.

Breakfast in bed is another pleasure that is often mentioned. Especially on Sundays, when it is possible to have a long lie-in. The statistical mean (Grimler 1992) shows, however, that single women do not get up later than married women. Could the letters be lying? I do not think so. Primarily, because the important thing is not getting up late every Sunday, but being able to do so: it is a sign of freedom. And especially because 'getting up' (or talk of getting up) often means getting up and then going back to bed. It might, for example, mean getting up to make breakfast and then going back to a comfortable bed.

Wrapping Up and Regressing

Single women are drawn to furniture that is low and soft, but they are also drawn towards hollows in which they can curl up. The image is that of a 'full roundness' that 'helps us to collect ourselves . . . and to confirm our being intimately . . . from the inside' (Bachelard 1969: 234). In our society, which is characterized by the shattering of identity, we feel a growing need to wrap ourselves up in something warm. Dense socialization with a family can play that role. But single women (who are not immersed in that relational intensity) must invent other refuges, particularly as their reflexivity leads to even greater fragmentation. 'When I get home, the flat is too cold, too empty, and smells of death. I just need a noise, a smell, a human presence.' Elisa is especially struck by the cold, the emptiness and the gaps in her being. Odile, on the other hand, has learned to turn wrapping herself up into a real art form. Her favourite technique is to spin a cocoon of pleasures for herself. And, naturally enough, she weaves them around that primal hollow: her bed. 'On Sundays, I wake up at noon and have breakfast by way of a meal, then laze about in bed, making phone calls, reading and writing. I take a real pleasure in wrapping myself up in a cocoon made of all those nice things.'

Wrapping can cure the 'disease of the infinite' and contain the self. Some do this by getting caught up in the imaginary world of a novel, a film or a beautiful dream. Others do it by swaddling themselves in something warm and round, such as a bath or a bed. The latter are 'isomorphic . . . with the mother's breast' (Durand 1969: 278) and plunge the self into a primal calm, a foetal life that drowns out questions about identity; we can at last let go, do nothing and, above all, stop thinking. Letting oneself go is another great source of pleasure. It is a way of resisting the obligation to take care of everything ourselves, and the mental pressures that result from it. We can live as we wish and act on the spur of the moment, without having to respect good manners and ordinary conventions. 'There are such things as simple but intense pleasures: staying in a warm bed as long as you like, and not answering the phone or the doorbell if you don't feel like it' (Ernestine). Hiding away from the laws that govern the world and out of everyone's sight. At least for a while, just to recuperate. When she is all curled up in a ball where no one can see her, her thoughts calm down and peace and quiet is restored. Or should be restored: the inner divisions and the introspection and the reflexivity that is associated with it can pierce the warmest of refuges, and burst in unannounced; it is impossible to escape the introspection of the divided life. Wrapping oneself up is a quest rather than a reality. It is no more than the start of a process that is constantly subverted from within. Parodoxically, remaining motionless (nice and warm in bed or in the bath) can also encourage introspection. This is especially true at night, when the bed she thought was an ally betrays her.

Freedom from Domesticity

It is therefore not unusual for these regressive attempts to wrap up to end in failure. But the regression also has another object, and this time it does achieve its goal: the revolt against domesticity.

This is primarily a revolt against the social role that history has bequeathed to women by assigning them heavy domestic and family responsibilities, and thus frustrating their attempts to spread their wings as autonomous individuals. Unmarried women, in contrast, can spread their wings. 'Not much housework, not much shopping – just for the things I like – and being able to stay out without having to let someone at home know where I am' (Frédérique). This is a radical historical innovation: women, who have traditionally devoted themselves to others, can now think of no one but themselves. 'Breakfast in bed, and an hour to myself every morning' (Joanna). Then there is a rebellion against all the norms and conventions, and the pleasure of not having to submit to any collective constraints, not even the codes of family life and the gaze of others. 'But there's always the freedom to lounge about if I want to, to spend all Saturday or Sunday reading, in a Mickey Mouse tee shirt and slouch socks, eating nothing but cakes if that's what I feel like eating, and spending two hours on the phone to my best friend. It would be hard to do without those little pleasures' (Claudia). Martine is now married, and a lot of the nostalgia she feels for her lost happiness has to do with moments like that: 'I used to savour the bliss of my Sundays in bed with my books, my crosswords, my music and my dog. Pure bliss!'

This immediate pleasure is replicated on a different level: the enjoyment of enjoying herself, of admitting to herself that being single does have its advantages. Hence the tendency to lay it on thick and to become less and less organized quite deliberately: 'Not getting out of bed, eating snacks and not cooking' (Frédérique). Hence the tendency to let things go, to enjoy both the joys of regression and the pleasures of the liberated Self: 'Self-indulgence: leggings and a sloppy jumper, hair in a mess, no smiling because I have to, and a good book' (Joanna). Having no qualms about being more and more provocative or playing a game in which the world is turned upside down, as it is at carnival time. Danièle takes what she calls her 'domestic strike' to extremes by making sure, for example, that there is nothing in the fridge for her evening meal, and enjoys having to 'make do with whatever comes to hand'. Or pulling 'clown faces' in front of the mirror and laughing out loud. She can do whatever she likes: there is no one there to see what she is doing.

The letters never stop going on about this regressive, liberating insubordination. There is a lot of talk about enjoying a long lie-in, wearing big socks and nibbling chocolate. 'I'm so lucky to be able to lounge around in bed with my nose in a book and eating my bar of chocolate' (Katia). 'I tell myself that I'm lucky to be able to spend my

Sundays lounging about in a shapeless tee shirt, with my socks around my ankles, and stuffing myself with chocolate' (Marie-Christine). It is almost too much: is this what the private lives of single women look like? Is it possible to imagine that sloppy dressing and chocolate are enough to fill their days? Obviously not. The reason why these acts of domestic rebellion are mentioned and emphasized so often is that they play an essential symbolic role. The fact that they exist is more important than the frequency of their occurrence. Listen carefully to Marjorie: the real pleasure lies in the freedom to be able to do as she likes rather than in what she actually does. 'I'm too fond of my lazy mornings in bed, of being able to lounge between the sheets, of being able to decide whether or not I eat, of being dependent on no one but myself, and of knowing that I can go away tomorrow without having to tell anyone.' The reason why she emphasizes these things is that they are tangible signs of a greater and more profound freedom that is difficult to explain. 'I discovered that I was free, that my life belonged to me. If I feel like doing something, I do it. Being free is wonderful' (Charlène). Boundless freedom is frightening when it roams unchecked in her thoughts. It encourages her to cast anchor and to seek protection but when, in contrast, it takes the form of concrete, everyday activities, it becomes a simple and obvious pleasure. It is an implicit revenge for the hundreds and hundreds of years of sacrifices on the part of women, and this boundless individual freedom crystallizes around a few supports. Lazy mornings in bed and chocolate express a great deal if we read between the lines.

The Lightness of Being

The pleasures of the revolt against domesticity can also be experienced thanks to the fluidity with which a single woman can make decisions. She is not shut in and has no obligations to anyone; everything is possible at any moment. Her life is governed by disconcertingly easy changes of direction. She can do what she likes. There is something intoxicating about freedom at its purest. Sabine cultivates her freedom by suddenly 'running away'. She does this on Sundays. She does not plan ahead, and allows herself to indulge in the classic delights of flexible time and her desires of the moment. 'It is true that I relish the hours I spend reading, on the phone or in the bath, and indulging in those pleasures for as long as I like.' Having established this comfortable basis for her life, she has got into the habit of improvising sudden escapes. On the spur of the moment, she relinquishes the languid pleasures of being in a steamy bathroom, carefully puts on some make-up and gets ready to go out. 'My weekends consist of walks, lounging around in my bathrobe or going to the cinema. And of sudden escapes.' Inside-outside, laziness-activity; the sequences can alternate spasmodically, and their logic is unpredictable. For that is where the real pleasure lies. Just as wearing big socks and eating chocolate can be outrageously regressive, so her periodic escapades have to be sudden and unexpected, because that way they demonstrate the reality of her free will.

The single life is fluid and unpredictable, but it is also typified by the feeling of lightness it gives. In an earlier study (Kaufmann 1997), I demonstrated how families construct themselves by becoming firmly rooted in a day-to-day domestic routine. The identity of each of its members is gradually defined by that routine. Here, we are dealing with precisely the opposite situation. Life seems light because a single woman's identity is defined less by fixed points of reference than by what she imagines herself to be. The wonderful thing about dreams is that they can move mountains.

This pleasure comes close to the intoxicating feeling of being completely free to invent oneself as one sees fit, of enjoying an existential fluidity; the discomfort comes from the unbearable lightness of being. Once more, a single phenomenon gives rise to two contradictory sensations: lightness is at once exhilarating and difficult to live with. The basic characteristic of being able to manage one's identity (life seems light because it is easy to change direction) impinges upon the more concrete perception of the Self as substance: life seems empty. 'A cocoon of flat, pyjamas and a TV dinner, a lover for a couple of hours every three months. That doesn't add up to a full life' (Flora). The sudden feeling of living in a void spoils the pleasure, especially during 'the lightness of the hours when I've nothing to do' (Sabine). 'I stayed in bed until 11 today; no tears, just the heaviness of the silence' (Joanna). 'Good God the evenings are long! To say nothing of Sundays!' (Manon).

She is not adequately wrapped up. Her attempts at containing her Self are too mechanical not to look like ways of filling her empty days. It becomes obvious that something is missing, especially when she contrasts her life with her dreams of being wrapped up in other ways too. 'No cuddles, the weekends spent in front of the telly, always having to force yourself to do anything, no encouragement, no compliments, and all those tears . . .' (Dorothée). Living in an atmosphere in which there is so little to support her identity, Dorothée, who is currently unemployed, is, like many others in her position, doomed to 'force herself' in order to construct a positive self-image. Maggy manages this quite well. Except when she finds herself in what she calls a 'hole'; she suddenly collapses and there is no one to hold her back from slipping into a state in which she cannot move, or even dream, and in which she has 'no interest in anything.' Her sudden collapses have something to do with the fact that she is not fully enveloped. Dorothée's moments of crisis, for example, are no more than an exaggerated form of a daily life that is already problematic. But, as with Maggy, the divided life does sometimes create sudden 'gaps' in a day-to-day existence that is dynamic and optimistic. Take Violaine's life, and the never-ending battle between light and darkness: 'There are days when I plan everything: work, leisure, activities, an evening meal with friends. And then there are the days when I feel really down, when I feel that I'm ugly and useless. Sometimes I see no one for days on end, and eventually I can't even eat anything. Life becomes gloomy, lifeless.'

At such times, even the telephone – the friend on whom she can always rely – can let her down and remind her that something is missing. Rather than forgetting about it because it has not rung for so long, Frédérique finds it painful to listen to the silence. 'Sometimes, I find myself staring at the phone, and waiting and waiting – I'm sure it's going to ring, I know it is. And it doesn't.' Justine cannot stop herself from running to pick up the phone as soon as it rings, 'like some mad woman'. Until the day that a caller noticed how quickly she picked up. Since then, she has forced herself to let it ring twice before picking up, even though she is desperate to do so sooner. Waiting of any kind (waiting for the phone to ring, waiting for the sudden, miraculous arrival of Prince Charming) is in fact a poor technique, as it makes the absence it is supposed to ward off even worse. It is better to use various substitutes to fill the void. Olivia finds her weekends too long, but organizes them in such a way as to ensure that 'I don't even have time to think about it.' Justine uses the same method, and plans her activities meticulously. 'I try to plan ahead, so as not to feel lonely, so as to keep myself busy.' The apparently rigid programme does, however, have its good side, as it gives her the illusion that she has a disciplined control over her life. Her detailed programme in fact allows for long periods of aimlessness: 'The nicest thing about it is the way that I can lazily go from one little treat to the next; watch telly, nibble something, read endlessly and spend ages on the phone.' She has succeeded in reconciling the opposite poles of her life: her structured activities have gradually become part of her regressive wrapper.

Keeping busy and wrapping up are usually defensive mechanisms (blindly forging ahead or retreating into a protective environment) that are used to ward off a fear of the void or a deadly insight into the lightness of being. Now there is no such thing as a void, just the feeling of emptiness. The only difference between the two is at the level of their content. The context in which identity is defined has been turned upside down, and some elements have been replaced by others: the stable weight of an everyday, relational domesticity has been replaced by introspection. The former element is of course heavy and stable, but the latter is volatile and elusive. And that suggests that lightness has replaced gravity, and that that lightness is nothing, compared with gravity. But the lightness is not nothing. It is another way of constructing the Self, but most of the Self has yet to be invented. The feeling of emptiness arises because the most normal constituent elements that define our identity are missing: a stable relational and domestic framework that is at once narrow and dense. An introspective face-to-face encounter with the Self, in contrast, gives the impression of a lack of substance. Life seems to hang by a thread and the thinking Self has constantly to reinvent itself and find new reasons to go on. 'On top of the loneliness, which is difficult enough to live with, it is so hard to motivate yourself to do anything at all, especially on mornings when you have the day off. It feels like a constant battle against a lack of motivation. At times, there seems to be no reason to do anything, because you're doing it just for yourself' (Nathalie).

— 7 —

THE OUTSIDE WORLD

Going Out

The soothing effect of snuggling up in bed and day-dreaming does not last, and the feeling of emptiness is an irresistible incitement to do something. And then there is the equally irresistible idea that doing something is unimaginable without going out: we have to get out in order to feel alive. Some love staying at home, and some love going out; it is a matter of individual taste. Those who like going out are, however, usually better at coping with their situation. Going out should therefore not be analysed only as though it were a form of escape, even if it is often experienced as such. It also represents another way of constructing a relationship with others, albeit somewhat reluctantly.

Some people (and most of them are men) take going out to such extremes that they can be regarded as non-permanent residents who are often away from home and spend a great number of weekends and nights elsewhere (Lavigne and Arbet 1992). Single women, by contrast, usually spend their nights at home but go out a lot during the day. We have already seen how they go for little trips to the shops, for walks, to see their girlfriends and to go to the cinema. It should be added that they often go out to take part in cultural activities (single women go to exhibitions and museums more often than married women) and in order to relax. Received opinion notwithstanding, going to the beach alone, for example, is a common practice. People who live alone spend much more than other households on going to the cinema, the theatre and concerts, as well as on going to restaurants and cafés.

They go out to meet people: nameless strangers, girlfriends and the hypothetical Prince Charming. They go out to see interesting things and to discover other cultures. They also go out just for the sake of it, or in order to feel that they are truly alive, or to give their lives some ballast by keeping on the move. Géraldine reacts to the slightest feeling of emptiness: 'It comes over me unexpectedly: Oh, there's nothing to do. So I got out jogging, for a walk, or to have fun on my bike.' Sport plays a special role. It is the ideal way of compensating for the lightness of being and proves that one's identity can, on the contrary, be packed into a palpable body that is in good shape. The whole Self is devoted to the task. Hence the tendency to make more and more effort in a frantic quest for a more concrete Self, and hence the tendency to take things to extremes (Le Breton 1991). Nelly spends hours in the weights room at the gym in an attempt to develop 'abdominals worthy of Rocky, with the idea of meeting Him.' Looking after one's body has one further advantage that is subtly bound up with the creation of a more solid identity: it gives substance to the imaginary encounter, and constantly renews the premises of a strategy that is already well developed. It does not matter if the outcome is disappointing: the pleasure of having a good body is still there, as is the mirror-effect of the compliments and the lingering looks that confirm that the time we spend on looking after ourselves has not been wasted. Sport aside, it is therefore quite logical for single women to spend more time than married women at the hairdresser's or the beauty salon.

They take active holidays for the same reasons. 'Long weekends walking in the mountains with a rucksack on my back and spending the night in refuges. It clears my head' (Marlène). Or, which is another variation on the same theme, well-structured holidays, cultural activities and especially travel (singles travel much more than families). Holidays have to be carefully planned, as they can represent both what is best and what is worst about being single. In theory, they are the perfect antidote to the poisonous effects of a life that has become too weightless, and mark a radical break with a problematic day-to-day existence. 'They allow me to forget my day-to-day existence and represent a break in my life' (Laura). Unfortunately, the slightest organizational mistake can transform heaven into hell. This is because holidays are also a crystallization of the joys of family life: the world is full of families who are proud of their radiant happiness, and it echoes with their noisy laughter. The accusing finger becomes even more intolerant in the sunshine. And if nothing is planned in advance (holidays spent at home or with the family), another disaster can be guaranteed to happen: the lightness becomes lighter than ever, the emptiness is emptier than usual, and time seems to drag on endlessly.

It is in a sense forbidden not to be active and well organized during holiday periods.

They go out to flee the fragility of their existence when they are at home. But being hyperactive away from home eventually produces the same feeling of killing time, of the volatility of one's identity and of tiredness. 'You feel energetic and you have complete freedom to go where you please when you please. But you mustn't spread yourself too thin. There are times when I get fed up with always being on the move, and I suddenly really want to be having a quiet time at home' (Viviane). Bold sorties into the outside world alternate with regressive withdrawals into her private life. They alternate in fits and starts. This can sometimes be a violent process, and it dictates the rhythm of her divided life. If she goes too far in one direction, she immediately has to make up for it by going in the opposite direction.

Other Ties

Single people go out for the sake of it and in order to do something, but they also go out to see other people; people who are on their own develop different forms of relational inscription. 'When you don't turn towards the Other, the more you turn to others and to yourself' (Julia). Curiosity, a liking for human contact and the intensity of fleeting encounters mean that single women see lots of new faces. The number and variety of these episodic contacts compensates for the lack of intimate and lasting contacts.

This shifting network is, however, centred on one or two more structured groups of more stable and closer ties: the family, sometimes a lover and especially girlfriends. 'I could no more do without my girlfriends than I could do without my writing. Without them and without that, I am nothing.' Both her girlfriends and her diary are central to Joanna's life. She flits from one to the other because she is equally fond of both poles, but they are very different. 'I drink cups of tea in front of my electric typewriter and when I've had enough of living my life by proxy, I run straight to my girlfriends, who tell me "You're brilliant".' Whereas keeping a diary is a way of working on herself, her girlfriends provide her with immediate and unconditional support. In that sense, they play the role of a husband, and they play it to perfection. Her best friends are in fact better than a husband because she can confide in them. Women who live alone have more friends they can confide in about their emotional and sexual problems than women who are in relationships (and those friends almost always have

94

someone they can confide in too). Eight out of ten single women have confidantes, as opposed to two or three married women out of ten (Ferrand and Mounier 1993). Relatively few women have male confidants: they tell them less and are less sincere about what they do tell them, but they enjoy the charms of a gentle ambiguity. 'I have a good friend and I can confide in him. Like me, he's had a number of flings and has lived through a number of disasters. We can talk to each other and we understand each other. It's a special pleasure' (Marcelline). There is also a special pleasure when a single woman remains on friendly terms with an 'ex'. 'I smile at him and listen to him. There's no nostalgia, just tender affection: the past is the past' (Joanna). 'With some "exes", it's like being with my girlfriends; you become their special confidante. Well, it might end with a furtive kiss, with a burst of romance that takes us back to the time when we had not a care in the world. But we quickly resign ourselves to the fact that it wouldn't work because it didn't work the first time around' (Jenna).

There is obviously a pleasure to be had from episodic contacts, with no strings attached and no overall commitment. What Mark Granovetter, in what has become a classic article (1973), calls 'weak ties' can, paradoxically, be stronger than closer and more lasting ties, and can be more helpful when it comes to solving certain problems. This is another reason why single women who have come to terms with their independence and who are very involved in their work have such good social lives. Their network of contacts is in keeping with the most efficient model; it is supple, open, diversified and wide. It is, on the other hand, less useful when it comes to providing close support for their identities, and has no dense or stable centre. Girlfriends often play that role to begin with, but the group then tends to break up or to undergo a change of content (see chapter 2). When that happens, there is a great temptation to fall back on the family.

The Family

It is fairly difficult to say how things stand with family ties and, in more general terms, with contacts with relatives. Do they still matter (or even matter more than ever) in contemporary society? In quantitative terms, there is nothing to indicate that they have become much less important; kinship still plays a very important role, and the desire to stay in touch remains strong (Donati 1998). Such ties do, however, now take an elective and occasional form, as each unit in the family network clings to its autonomy at all cost, and 'goes its own way' (Coenen-Huther et al.

1994: 328). The principle of 'intimacy at a distance' formulated by Leopold Rosenmayr and Eva Kockeis (1965) still applies.

The ambivalence of relations with the family is even more pronounced in the case of single women. In theory, their need for 'close protection' (Martin 1997: 287) is more pressing, and should encourage them to develop stronger family ties. This is indeed the case in specific circumstance (moving away from home, periods of crisis, material difficulties, and help with childcare when a single woman is living with her parents). But outside these particular contexts, single women have no more contact with their families than do married women. This is especially true of single women who live near their parents; they have less contact with them than married women (Bonvalet et al. 1997). And when, despite everything, the contacts and the help become too important, they become a source of dissatisfaction: the more important they are, the more they are seen as a necessary evil (Coletta 1979).

Why are close family ties so problematic? We have only to compare single women with their girlfriends to find the answer. Because, with all the good will in the world (and no matter how much a single woman wants to see them), a single woman's parents are the embodiment of the familiar model of private life and are a permanent source of unease. Unlike her girlfriends, they live on a different planet: the planet of the normal, the planet that points the 'accusing finger'. And certain little comments that are meant to be kind are some of the cruellest that anyone could hear. Anonymous criticisms do not hurt so much.

Another danger lies in wait when a single woman's ties with her family are close-knit: there is a danger that her parents will become a real substitute for a relationship, and will irremediably involve her in that very particular type of socialization. That is what is so frightening about Sundays with the family and family holidays: it gives a single woman a whiff of the very different life that could so easily be hers. 'If I go on holiday with my mother, I really do feel like an old maid going out with her old mother. Oh my God!' (Flora). As their parents grow older, the danger becomes even greater; when there are brothers and sisters, it is usually the single woman (who is seen as having more time on her hands) who is tacitly given the task of looking after them. That she is available is a sort of self-evident truth, and it has the great virtue of at last putting her on the side of 'normality' (she can feel the approving glances). The disadvantage is that it forces her to go down a path from which there is no way back: her life will always be like that. She will lose what independence she has, and it becomes much less likely that she will one day find herself in a relationship.

That is why, despite their emotional impulses, single women (more so than married women) have no option but to keep a safe distance between themselves and their families.

Work

Work, like girlfriends, does not create these difficulties, and is less problematic than the family. This disturbing and inadmissible hierarchy offends the order of contemporary values, in which families come at the top and work at the bottom. Opinion polls show that we all feel obliged (by an invisible moral framework) to state that, even if we do not object to work itself, we do object to the fact that we have to take too great and too exclusive an interest in it.

Women who enjoy their jobs find themselves being torn apart. They are torn between their desire to throw themselves into their work, and the fear that they will once more be criticized, be told that they should not go too far down that road, and that another accusing finger will be pointed at them. Involvement in work often begins with a headlong flight that compensates for the emptiness at home. The emptier it feels, the more work is likely to offer compensation. 'I've been on my own for a year now, with no male or female friends, not even a one-night stand. In short, my job takes my mind off things because it takes up most of my time.' Chloé can take her mind off things even though her job on the check-out is not particularly fascinating. She does, on the other hand, get a lot out of it: a disciplined lifestyle, a framework that allows her to socialize and a close, living world that surrounds and supports her. And, above all, a few friendly contacts with some of her colleagues. Edwige cannot take her mind off things completely, and spends too much time dreaming about her Prince Charming. 'My only remaining option is to fling myself into my work, whereas what I really want is to be in the arms of the Man of my Dreams.' But the outcome is the same; as she waits for the hypothetical change in her life to occur, the energy she expends on work (and sport) provides her with the outlet she needs. Bérangère also dreams of her Prince and, as she waits for him to come, she contains her impatience by immersing herself in her job. In her case, however, the compensatory effect does not take the form of a split between two different worlds. She can see his face if she tries hard enough: 'I devote myself to my job for his sake.' And when it is at its most intense, the extreme exhaustion becomes a secret pleasure. 'When my head's spinning because I've overdone it, the exhaustion becomes a sensual pleasure. And then I see him in my dreams, and he admires and supports me. He thinks I'm dazzling, and he's with me.'

The desire to escape can sometimes be so strong that any job will do, provided that it takes her mind off things, as Chloé puts it. Marie-Pierre, who is a lowly toilet-attendant, puts in so much overtime that she never takes a day off: no holidays and no Sundays off. 'At least I see people when I'm at work, and I can knit and read.' But most of the time the appeal of work is the decisive criterion. This is because, in the absence of any other poles of identification, everything becomes focused on work. 'It's just as well I like this job!' exclaims Géraldine, who is terrified by the idea of losing it. This can lead to a situation of dependency in which her moods can be influenced by even minor events, and nothing that happens in her private life can change them. 'At work, everything's fine, I promise you. But when things are not going so well, or when I come across someone nasty, then I do feel very lonely'.

The central role played by work in the worlds that socialize single women encourages them to create a favourable working environment (whereas married women are more tempted to retreat into their families when the slightest problem arises). Doing so costs them almost nothing, as being energetic and active is in itself a form of compensation, a way of warding off the emptiness and sublimating the self-doubts. Provided that the job is sufficiently attractive, everything combines to give them even more impetus and to motivate them even further: they put a lot of effort into their jobs because they are good at them, and a spiral gets under way. 'I have to make up for what I don't have, so I work very hard' (Claire). This is all the more likely to happen because single women are in a position that makes them ideally available. They have time, a lot of time, and often too much time on their hands, and they are happy to work all hours. They are not weighed down or restricted by the heavy burden of family responsibilities, and they are therefore flexible and adaptable. They are available for work in both mental and material terms; their minds are not on something else and they therefore have time to think and to be creative.

When a woman commits herself to family life, she reduces her chances of being successful at work (because the sexual division of labour still exists): 'Marriage has an adverse effect on the professional lives of women' (Singly 1987: 76). Conversely, everything works in favour of single women. In recent years, a remarkable number of women have made the breakthrough into the most highly qualified jobs (Terrail 1997). This is directly related to the fact that women, and especially women aged between 25 and 35, have begun to spend periods of their lives on their own. The process begins when they are at school or university: academic success encourages them to embark upon autonomous trajectories. They enjoy their studies and are good students; trying to establish a relationship is of secondary importance. That is something that can be put off until later; for the moment, they have more important things to do. Those 'more important things' appear to be academic success and then success at work; at a deeper level, they are the discovery of autonomy, the ability to define oneself and personal competence when it comes to the task of constructing a Self. Married women are doomed to having to strike a balance between their family life and their work on a permanent basis and to develop some delicate strategies (Commaille 1992). They often have to do both at once by first ensuring that they have a secure position at work and by not embarking on relationships too early, and then by committing themselves to family life before it is too late to find the right partner. This is a dangerous and complex change of direction. It sometimes ends in failure: it is either too early or too late, or the conditions are wrong even though the time is right. The autonomy trajectory sometimes propels women so far that they cannot resolve to change their lives, and relations with men are restricted to brief experiments.

Being Oneself in the Outside World?

Some women are so torn between their private lives and work that it can sometimes become difficult to say just where 'home' is. The usual hierarchy of values can even be completely inverted: Emilienne feels more at home in the office than in her empty flat, and going home is as much an effort for her as going to work is for others. 'Everything is fine at work: the job itself, my boss and the atmosphere are all pleasant. I put off going home in the evening more and more. Today, I got home at 8.30.' Marlène used to be in the same position. 'Work dominates my life. It's true: when I'm at work, I forget everything and have a really good time.' Unfortunately, she has been looking for a new job for a month now, and it is as though her world has collapsed around her. Her two children make no difference, and her private world is not enough to compensate for the unbearable emptiness of not having a professional life. 'So, at the moment, it's dreadful: no more seminars, no more meetings and no more drinks parties. I feel a bit out of touch, you know. I can't wait to get back to work!'

Having a family is not everything, and it is possible to construct an identity by using work as a central point of reference. It is even possible to construct a very positive identity by using work as one's sole point of reference. That is how Adeline organizes her life. The whirlwind of her working life was originally a form of escape that allowed her to break the stranglehold of reflexivity. Being caught up in the whirlwind then became a pleasure in its own right. She dances to a frantic beat, is always between planes at some European airport, and is surrounded by men who are in as big a hurry as she is. 'I enjoy life in a way that not many people have the opportunity to.' And that is why she does not feel ready to 'drop everything'. Am I really going to find a reason to stop running in this crowd of smooth talkers? I'm weak enough to believe I'm worth more than that.' Joanna's story is even more disturbing because of the way it inverts conventional values. She used to live with a partner who was 'kind and considerate.' It was a peaceful relationship and there were no major crises. It was just that Joanna felt that there was 'something missing, a sort of inner inertia', that she was not really able to assert herself. Finding a new job had a decisive effect. She felt liberated and found out who she really was. She speaks of her job in the same way that she might speak of a lover: 'It's taught me to be attractive again and given me a new self-confidence. It's given me new wings and allowed me to escape what had become a suffocating, restrictive cocoon.'

But is it really natural to prefer having a job to having a partner who is kind and considerate? It takes unusual strength of character not to give in to the social pressure to re-establish what is defined as the legitimate hierarchy of values. When the construction of one's identity is too exclusively focused on work, whatever the outcome, it is unusual for the question of normality not to arise. 'Almost every day' Annabelle asks herself the nagging question: 'Is a life without love a real life?' And that question cannot but spoil her pleasure: 'While I admit that I enjoy studying and working, I find it hard to accept the idea that the energy I put into it is a screen that helps me mask something unsayable and shameful: in emotional terms, I am lonely.' Even though she is only 25, Bérangère already knows the answer to this question. She wanted to be a 'free woman' and not to be 'dependent upon a man', so she sacrificed everything for the sake of her studies and made a very successful debut in the world of work. 'But now I wonder if I haven't left it too late. I have a job that I love, but it's no longer enough. There's more to life than work.'

— 8 —

MEN

Arms

A life divided is a life that is full of contrasts between tears and laughter, inside and outside, and between withdrawal to the foetal position and bursts of activity. The sequences follow one another and their content veers suddenly from one extreme to the other. It is unusual for the lack of an intimate presence to be experienced as a permanent source of resentment, and it is usually counteracted by the pleasure of being in control of one's day-to-day life. 'I've been on my own for 10 years now, and I think I'd find it difficult to put up with the presence of someone else' (Ida). The perception of how empty life is, and the pain that is associated with its emptiness, is sudden and intermittent. The dream then takes the form of the very concrete image of arms. What is missing is a comforting arm or strong arms that can enfold her. 'As for the evenings, it depends. Sometimes I'm happy being on my own, and glad there is no one to get on my nerves and prevent me from doing what I like. But there are other evenings when I need someone to take me in his strong arms' (Ida).

Although the image is specific, it in fact relates to many different expectations: 'arms' do not always mean the same thing.

'Arms' can, first of all, actually mean a shoulder. 'Sometimes, I really miss not having a man's shoulder to cry on in the evening' (Georgina). She dreams of having a shoulder she can rest her head on. She can't switch off, and she is worn out by all the self-doubts that come from leading a divided life. When things are really difficult, Anne-Laure would like to have a man beside her, just to be able to lean on his shoulder and pour out her feelings. In more general terms, a shoulder is a symbol of support; it calms her down, reassures her and 'makes everything feel better' (Marjorie). It means that she does not let things get out of proportion. It also means just that there is someone there, and having someone there is what gives being part of a couple its spice. It makes the trivia of everyday life easier to bear. 'Having someone to share a meal and my worries with, to mend the lock or change the oil in the car, someone to look at me, the short phone calls, the small talk: "A small coffee?" "Let's go and see a good film this week".'

The second and more active arm is one that can enfold her whole body. Being held is like snuggling up in bed, but it is better than that. It is at once stifling and protective. Being held means that she is enclosed for a brief but very important moment. From that point of view, two arms are even better than one, as she can be completely enfolded in them. The letters therefore start to begin speaking in the plural, and speak of 'arms' rather than 'an arm'. But the use of the plural inevitably leads to a third expectation: being taken in his loving arms. 'I dream of cuddles and tender arms' (Manon).

Caresses and tender arms go far beyond the reassuring presence of a shoulder. The shading is gradual and subtle, and women's expectations are often complex and ambiguous. When Joanna states that 'The only way I want to be slowed down is by being hugged to death', she is not talking about wild love-making. She is talking about being enveloped. This is a tender, loving version of the arms that enfold. These arms are more active than the passive shoulder she can lean on, and they gently trace the whole outline of her body. In many cases, the longing to be loved seems less important than the simple need to have someone there. But the ubiquity of the model for private life means that her expectations quickly become conjugal. Marie-Christine suddenly feels how empty her life is after listening to nice music or getting up on the first fine day of spring: 'It brings tears to my eyes, and I would like to be able to share it with my man.' And that inevitably conjures up the image of 'being taken in his arms'. That image encapsulates both the fact that there is no one to hold her and the fact that she wants her life to be like a love story. It is a perfect summary of all her expectations. There is only one problem: this image focuses all her expectations on coupledom (because the model is so powerful), and the mere sight of a love scene is therefore enough to remind her of all the other things she does not have. 'So far as men are concerned, I suddenly burst into tears whenever I see a banal love scene on television. It's been years since anyone took me tenderly in his arms' (Gabrielle).

The image eventually shades into something else; the arms she dreams of become very powerful and the movement becomes very physical. 'What I really want is a man with strong arms, and a hairy

102

chest', admits Ida, who immediately adds: 'And lots of little hugs.' It is unusual for the need for tenderness not to be all-embracing.

Sex

What sort of sex life do single women have? Like so many things about their lives, it can vary a lot and is affected by the way their lives are divided in two. The most constant, and the most nagging, problem is the lack of an arm or arms, of presence/support/tenderness and of someone to pay them attention. The feeling of sexual need is much less constant. It is sometimes grafted onto the need for a presence and some tenderness, which makes it more urgent. Sometimes, it becomes suddenly apparent. At certain points in their biographical trajectories, they go through some liberating experiences. From that point of view, Adrienne's story is exemplary. She had a very strict upbringing which was strongly influenced by religion (she was allowed to go out with her fiancé only when a chaperone was present) and her divorce allowed her to make the intoxicating discovery of her physical freedom. She had lots of lovers. 'Nights of passion! It drove me crazy. We made love every night, in the afternoon, everywhere.' Then the disillusionment set in. The affairs ended badly, and sex lost its liberating attractions. And now, 'I really don't want all that.' 'I've tried going out with men two or three times. Men are awful. What am I doing here dancing?' She now goes to bed at 8.30 every night, alone and resigned to her fate.

For women, sexual freedom is one of the most concrete images of autonomy, and it represents a complete break from the hundreds of years when sexual freedom was a male preserve. They therefore have to experience it in one way or another in order to enjoy their freedom and to assert themselves as truly autonomous beings. It is all the more easy to do so in that it is in line with the expectations of the many men who still tend to divorce sexual relations from emotional commitment (Bozon and Léridon 1993). The experiments do not, however, last for long because, unlike their partners, women 'find it more difficult than men to imagine having sexual relations without being in love' (Bozon and Léridon 1993: 1183). The intoxication of freedom gives way to weariness, disappointment, the feeling that they can't take any more, and sometimes even nausea. 'I got fed up with being seen as the attractive young woman who is available and easily seduced. Since then, my sex life has become almost non-existent' (Anne-Laure). As the stories of Adrienne and Anne-Laure show, it is not unusual for these torrid episodes to be followed by an almost monastic retreat, and a radical rejection: they will agree to have sex only if it is part of a real love story. As a general rule, however, they behave rather differently and do not reject sex completely: the act is engaged in regularly, but not very often. Once in a while. 'I like my life, provided that I can have a fling or two every year' (Olivia). Angela has affairs on a similar basis, but is more specific about their timing: 'When I really do not feel like living the life of a nun, which happens every six months or so, I treat myself to a fling that lasts for three weeks, just to prove to myself that I'm better off on my own.' Nathalie also treads a delicate path between desire and disappointment: 'I miss sex when I'm not getting any, but I get nothing out of it when I am.' The content of the attraction that periodically leads them to break their vows of abstinence can vary greatly. It can be purely sexual, as it is for Salomé. It can reflect a more general desire to meet someone, as in the case of Elisa: 'Sexual activity non-existent, but a great need for tenderness.' It can also be a way of fleshing out the stories single women tell themselves, of spicing up their life stories and providing raw materials for their diaries and consoling daydreams. If the gap between the episodes is too long, the plot can become boring: 'It's always the same bad dream with only one character in it, and I'm bored with him: my last lover' (Katia).

Man-Hunters

Is there a link between arms, sex and the fairytale prince? Is there a link between these very different expectations, in which fragments of the male body can represent (either in reality or in the imaginary) just the need for company, wonderful dreams, the disappointing affairs in which it all comes down to sex, or the quiet pleasures of ordinary tenderness? Yes, there is a link. They organize the scattered fragments into an overall dream as best they can, but it is inevitably somewhat vague. It can also vary a great deal. The dream may be about a real Prince and a fairytale scenario, or about a more concrete 'ideal man' or 'Mr Right', should her criteria become more specific. But everything she does not have is furtively crammed into both versions: having someone there, attention, support, tenderness, eroticism. 'I love the wonderful dreams I tell myself in bed at night, and their surprise episodes. The man of my dreams comes and carries me off, just like in a fairytale. Everything is pink, and he is sweet and so gentle. I am his princess. And then, surprise, surprise, all sorts of things begin to happen. I can't tell you about some of them (it can get very, very daring). I had a problem with a leaking sink the other day. That night, I was rescued by a super-plumber' (Virginia).

One of the defining characteristics of the single life is that the future is always open. Although single women lead settled lives, their mode of existence and their way of managing everyday life are, in theory, provisional. A single woman might meet someone one day, and that might be the beginning of a whole new story. Waiting for that major event to happen can be an intense experience, but its intensity varies. If being alone means being dynamic and if the woman in question has come to terms with that fact, she does not expect a lot, but if a woman is on her own because she has no other option, she expects a great deal. Waiting makes her very unhappy. It is, on the other hand, unusual for a woman who is on her own to have no expectations at all: the idea that she might meet someone and have a different life is always there, and it preoccupies her mind when she is tired or having problems. In specific circumstances, waiting for something to happen can also follow a set pattern. It follows one pattern just before she goes out, for example (even on a banal trip to the shops). In the evening, it takes the form of a pleasant dream; when she wakes up in the morning, it adds a bit of excitement to the day that lies ahead. 'Almost as soon as I open my eyes, my heart is all of a flutter, and I say to myself: today's the day, or perhaps it will happen today. Every morning' (Virginie). 'Every day, I hope that I will meet the love of my life' (Marjorie).

Nothing, however, can rival the intensity of a real night out for the sole and definite purpose of finding a man or the Man. Now. The intensity is at its greatest at the beginning of the evening, between the moment when the decision to go out is taken, and actually going out, and it can inspire the most wonderful scenarios. It is increasingly likely that the dream, which is very uninhibited, will become a reality. It is no longer just a fantasy or just a form of compensation: it is becoming real. The emotion is at its height during this transition from the imaginary to reality. Because it can play on the uncertainties and ambiguities, there is a growing impression that the beginning of a new life story really is about to be written, that the wonderful scenarios are emerging from their limbo and are at last going to become part of reality. There is a feeling of living on another planet, a feeling that this is neither a dream life that is too unreal nor a real life that is too far removed from the dream. Babette takes her time to enjoy the happiness of getting ready to go out: 'When I say to myself that I'm going out, that tonight's the night I am going to meet him, my heart begins to beat very fast. Nothing else matters. I don't even put any music on.

I feel comfortable with both my body and my thoughts. I get pins and needles in my fingers as I put my make-up on.'

The pleasures of anticipation can be excessive. Because cultivating them means that what happens next is not nearly so nice: reality shatters the dream. Many of the letters describe the same pattern of behaviour: when she gets to where the action is going to take place, the woman takes a quick look around her and immediately realizes that the man of her dreams is not there. Is it possible to sum up a situation as quickly as this? Obviously not. Our first impressions of other people are no more than provisional indices and part of the long process of mutual type-casting (Berger and Luckmann 1967); it is not unusual for love to develop once it has overcome a disappointing first impression. But on occasions like this, it is as though the slightest negative signal provides an excuse for giving up at every stage in the attempt to establish a relationship. 'Whenever I meet someone I don't really like, I give up hope before I've even started and say to myself: what's the point, it wouldn't work out between us' (Olivia). Even worse, the disillusionment sometimes sets in even before she has noticed Mr Right is not there: there is an a priori conviction that he will not be. The illusion that the dream can merge with reality is gradually dispelled by the need to face facts, and the wonderful scenarios return to their imaginary world. And the idea gradually takes shape that there was something artificial about the heart that was beating so fast, that there is a price to be paid for using too much subterfuge. 'It looked like something that was meant to be, but it was just another disappointment' (Gaétanne). It is obvious that repeating the experiment eventually destroys the illusion that the dream can become part of reality and uses up all the potential emotion: the man-hunt degenerates into a sad but necessary routine. 'It's not that I want to. I'd be better off at home. But it's a question of life or death. A girl's gotta do what a girl's gotta do' (Brigitte).

Age Difference

'I try to go out because I hope to meet my one man in a million, but very often I come home in a very bad mood because he never shows his face. And as time goes by, there is less and less chance of my finding my soul-mate' (Marie-Christine). Why does she so often come home empty-handed? Partly because her anticipatory dreams are so extravagant: she spends so much time imagining what her Prince will look like that it becomes difficult to meet the man himself. It has to be said, on the other hand, that there is nothing arbitrary about this extremism: it prevents the encounter from taking place mainly because she does not really want it to take place. The internal conflict between the two halves of the Self is, however, much more significant. When a woman is on her own simply because she has no alternative, she will (whenever possible) quite sincerely make every effort to try to meet someone (which does not mean that it will be easy). When, on the contrary, a woman has come to terms with being on her own, the story of an alternative life is one of a number of wonderful scenarios, and it is very difficult to say how much credence should be given to it. The scenarios develop into parallel imaginary stories which can, in theory, intersect with reality. It is, on the other hand, highly unlikely that the dream will become a reality. It all depends on how she views the life she is currently leading: she may well be able to find a man, but she is not prepared to do so at any price. It is a case of either the Man who is absolutely perfect, or no man at all.

This explains why single women have the depressing impression that they are getting nowhere: as their expectations rise, the number of serious candidates falls, and they cannot find a man because they have ruled out those who might otherwise be acceptable. To some extent, this explains why they really are getting nowhere: in economic terms, there is an imbalance in the 'conjugal market'. 'I do go to the cinema and to cafés. I even go dancing. But I also have the impression of being out of step, of not being the right age, not coming from the right background, not having had the right education' (Gabrielle). The process is therefore as follows: because single women's dreams are so extravagant and because their expectations are so high, the imbalance between men and women becomes greater than it already was.

There are several structural reasons why this should be the case. The first has to do with the age difference between the men and women who do establish relationships. At the age of 30, there is a stable age difference of about two years: men marry younger women (Bozon 1990). And the later they marry, the greater the age gap: they want even younger women. Women who take time out to devote themselves to their autonomous lives (and especially to continue their studies and to make a success of their first jobs) may later discover that they have been marginalized without realizing what has happened to them. All at once, there are fewer men of their own age. The longer they go on leading autonomous lives and making their own way through the life cycle, the greater the age gap. They really are getting nowhere.

As Gabrielle explains so well, the second reason has to do with social status and standards of education. Like the age gap, the difference in the social status of couples is a constant: the man has higher status than the woman (Bozon and Héran 1987). The trajectories of autonomous women have, however, brought about a revolution: the more women devote themselves to the single life, the more successful they are at work. As a result, they reach such high positions and become so intimidating that they can no longer find potential partners who measure up to their standards. And still less can they find potential partners who are higher up the hierarchy. The trajectories of male and female autonomy are in fact very different: autonomous men tend to be at the bottom of the social scale, while autonomous women tend to be at the top. Their respective positions are obviously asymmetrical, and both men and women who have been on their own for some time find it difficult to form relationships. This is especially true if we cross match the social differences between them and the age difference: single men want younger women who are their social inferiors. But women are becoming more successful at work and devoting more time to asserting their autonomy.

The final reason is that men and women have different expectations. Men tend to emphasize sexuality and responsibility for domestic issues, whereas women tend to want support and intimacy. This is of course a traditional contrast, and it is usually overcome thanks to the careful management of the lack of satisfaction both parties experience in their relationships (Kaufmann 1992). But it becomes more pronounced and more specific as a woman waits longer and longer for a potential partner: from a woman's point of view, the last remaining candidates are disappointing. Hortense, who is 49, recently decided to give up waiting: 'I'm not going to be dragged into any more affairs. They are such a let down. The men are not interesting.' Inevitably, they begin to weigh men up: what can he give me, what could this or that candidate give me? And he usually pales into insignificance compared with the woman who is assessing his worth. Many of the letters spell out the fact that the men women meet are poorly educated and unsophisticated, rather as though they were straight out of another era. Autonomous women like and want different things, but the strength they have acquired leads them to relativize the qualities they do see: 'Why do so few of the men who are left come up to my standards?' (Albertine).

A Gloomy View of Life

There comes a time when women who have not succeeded in finding a man begin to make less effort and either abandon the hunt or relegate it to the realm of the imaginary. They retreat into themselves and deactivate the second part of the Self, which was once the source of so much excitement. Strangely enough, this admission of failure leads to an inner peace because the Self has once more become a whole. Now that the storm has passed, they are safely at anchor (see chapter 2). There is also less introspection and less need to write. There are few letters relating to this new sequence, and it is impossible for me to describe it with any accuracy.

The tranquil (and somewhat morose) calm of being at anchor is in contrast to the unstable aggressiveness of the period that went before it. The passages in the letters that complain about how difficult it is to meet someone and about the mediocrity of men are especially violent: they take a very gloomy view of life. Of course, not everything is rosy, and the age gap does make it difficult to meet someone. And the absence of any intimate support, of a shoulder to lean on and of arms to enfold them, to say nothing of other parts of the anatomy, makes everything worse. 'Whenever I meet someone who might be the right man for me, I very quickly become clingy: I'm living in such an emotional and sexual vacuum that I want the relationship to be a strong one from the very start' (Olivia). It is, however, striking to note how the descriptions of their frustrations tend to generalize and exaggerate, to see everything in terms of black and white rather than shades of grey.

Passionate love is another typical example. This is something else that is non-existent. There are flings and one-night stands that go no further than that, but there is never really any great passion. The picture is not in fact that gloomy. It is only when it is compared with a dream that the passion is mediocre. In fact, their hearts begin to pound on numerous occasions, if only during the early stages of the man-hunt. Reading some accounts suggests that some married women (six in all) were shocked by the way their single counterparts complained so much; they protested and felt compelled to write back to say that they – and only they – knew what it was really like to be in a loveless relationship, and that single women did not know how lucky they were. Although they asked not to be quoted (and I will of course respect their wishes), they wanted to share their secret pain and their secret wishes. Their married lives were very different from the models on display in the media: their experience is one of loneliness and loveless relationships, of the boredom of routine and the crushing weight of their domestic responsibilities. They too used to dream that their Prince would come, but their dreams never had the substance of dreams that might one day come true. It was too late for them: they had committed themselves to family life in all sincerity, but they had also ruled out all the other possibilities. When they did recall the periods they had spent on their own, they tried to revive the excitement and passion they felt at the time. The future was still open, unpredictable and full of promise. The letters all end in the same way: they advise single women to realize how lucky they are, and to make the best of their good fortune.

Married life is not always seen in such negative terms. In many cases, loving friendship and the team spirit makes up for the absence of passion without too many problems. The truth of the matter is that relationships can vary greatly and the truth usually lies between the two extremes: married life is neither the absolute horror described by certain married women, nor the wonderful dream some single women imagine it to be. The private-life model and its scenarios encourage the latter to idealize couples and families who make a show of how happy they are. They paint a gloomy picture of their own relational lives because of this *trompe l'oeil* effect and because the model forces them to do so: they put the emphasis on what they do not have, or on what they think they have less of. They sometimes forget (especially when their loneliness becomes oppressive) that they have something that other women do not have. Being single is in fact part of a very specific relational and emotional world. It deviates from the norms, but in general terms it cannot be described as being poorer. On the contrary, in many respects (the free and lively nature of their networks of contacts, their margin of freedom, their ability to write their own life stories, the potential to make their dreams come true, the emotions that are bound up with surprises, and so on) and in certain circumstances, 'single' women have no reason to be jealous of the sisters who have committed themselves to family life.

Married Men

There is, of course, still something missing, and there are specific problems. Close and regular emotional support is not much in evidence. There are few suitable potential partners. There are few potential partners, that is, for women who want a real relationship, but not for women who are interested in casual affairs. On the contrary, there seem to be hordes of these (or at least that is the impression the letters give). One type of man is especially well represented. It is time to talk about a new character who plays a far from negligible role in the lives of single women: the married man.

Married men traditionally have more adventurous sex lives than their wives. A single woman is the ideal prey. It is not only that she is free; she is also looking for affection and contact. In her eyes, a married man is a sort of indefinable individual who is at once attractive and repulsive. He is obviously a man, with all the vices and virtues that implies. Yet the adjective 'married' immediately imposes limits: he is not really a man. He has other commitments and cannot be used to write a complete story. And that is the real goal: finding Mr Right. So what can a single woman do with a man who is not really a man? Her need for warmth and her desire to make her dreams come true encourage her to go ahead with the experiment. All the more so in that cunning suitors can more or less succeed in looking like real Princes at first sight. They represent a fool's bargain that can give a single woman a rude awakening. 'I stagger from sordid affair to sordid affair' (Régine).

Sometimes however, real communications can be established. Sometimes, illicit relationships do last for a long time. They involve astonishing negotiations between two partners who do not have the same status. The married man lays down the rules that keep everything secret and ensure that exchanges do not go beyond strictly defined limits: his real life, or at least a major part of it, goes on elsewhere. Single women do, however, sometimes find that this secret contract works to their advantage. A married man is obviously far from being the Prince of her dreams, and her whole life is obviously not going to change because of him. But what seems to be a false response to an unspoken desire can prove useful. Precisely because it is no more than a partial response, it allows the two halves of the divided Self to strike a balance: the woman commits herself to a sexual relationship, but retains her autonomy and goes on organizing her day-to-day life as though she were single. 'It gives me a sort of emotional and sexual security. I know it won't last. But it means that I can go on waiting for a new Prince to come along and rescue me from my loneliness.' For Odile, it is no more than a minimum contract. The temporary 'Prince' in question is in fact a 'fairly elderly gentleman' she has been seeing two or three times a month for the last three years. He is no more committed to their relationship than she is. Pascale sees her married lover even less frequently. The emotional content of their exchanges is different every time. 'I have a male friend I see once a month. He is not free, but I've experienced some very intense moments with him in a way that I've never done before.' Carmen experiences very similar emotions when she meets her lover. 'Whenever we meet again, it is very intense. It never becomes stale or routine. I have all the good things, and none of the bad things. My heart remembers the moments together that we wanted so much. It makes it so much easier to put up with everything else.' So is everything perfect? No. Pascale always needs 'constant reassurance. Being so far away from each other is not ideal.' Carmen also complains about being far apart. 'I spend too little time with the man I love and never see him often enough. Holidays with him are grim. And then there's the waiting.' There is also the strangely unsettling nature of the situation, 'the guilt I feel at knowing that I should not be making love with him in a hotel room'. So what would make it feel legitimate? Why the feeling of guilt? Unlike her partner, a single woman has nothing to hide. But the accusing finger is already pointing at her, and the clandestine nature of the affair increases her feeling of marginality. Things begin to get difficult when, instead of being something that unites the two halves of the divided Self, the relationship confuses things still further by introducing a third and very different life schema: there is an autonomous Self, the relationship she dreams of having, and the secret meetings she cannot talk about. She has no autonomous Self, and she is not in a real relationship.

It is therefore quite unusual for a single woman to succeed in getting 'all the good things and none of the bad things' from a married man. A single woman who is fully committed to her autonomous life can sometimes do so. If, on the other hand, she is looking for a Prince or a husband, a married man cannot be anything more than a temporary and disappointing substitute. She also has to be very subtle about how she commits herself to such a relationship. And some aspects of it require delicate management. One of the (rather curious) characteristic features of such affairs is that they settle into a very fixed routine; the dates are set in advance, and the content of the activities is very repetitive. As is so often the case, the single woman is a woman divided. In a sense, the regular dates do meet one of her secret needs: they give her the support of a stable framework. But the affair becomes further and further removed from the dream, ceases to be a surprise and becomes less emotional, until it finally gives her the impression that she has ended up in the worst of all possible worlds. She is in a long-standing relationship, but enjoys none of the real benefits of being in a relationship. 'I had a passionate affair with a married man for five years. When I was with him I was free, I was loved and I was happy. But it became a habit and something routine.' Roseline immediately decided to break off the relationship. This is often an unavoidable decision to the extent that married men tend to forget how hard they tried to look like the Prince. Manon's lover very quickly reduced their relationship to a very basic sexual level. When she saw him turn up in a tracksuit and trainers, she could not stop herself from imagining that he had found an alternative form of exercise to the sport he was supposed to be playing. 'I didn't want any more secret dates once a week. They took place on the evenings when, for official purposes, he had football practice.'

Falling into a rut and reducing everything to a purely sexual level is not inevitable. The relationship can sometimes be full of surprises. It can be emotionally rich, and can thus go on being a real story that is worth telling. Paradoxically, this does not always make life any easier. The initial ambiguity (is this a real relationship or not?) was a positive factor that seemed to glue the divided Self back together, but it becomes a problem when it conceals what is really at stake and makes it difficult to reach a decision (should I break it off or not?). The Self becomes even more divided and even less capable of making a decision. It just lumbers along like some ramshackle contraption, 'I have two stabilizers on my bike to help me to ride through life. They are both called Didier. I can't bring myself to take them off. Even though they've made me fall off my bike so often, even though I've had my heart broken so many times, had so many scratches on my soul and so many plasters on my self-respect. Living a miserable life in order not to have no life at all is not really worth it. And even so I still don't have the strength' (Evelyne).

There is one card left, and it is often played: unilateral love. A relationship which, from her partner's point of view, does not in fact lend itself to such excesses, can be an intensely emotional experience for her. Pascale actually erected this principle into a 'rule to live by.' 'I decided to adopt a rule to live by: grabbing the good moments with both hands, savouring them for a long time as though they were sweets, and waiting for them to happen again.' She decided, in other words, to use reality to give more substance to her dream. Once again, danger lies in wait. There is a danger that a dream that acquires more substance will become a prison, and she has to remain in control of what she is manipulating. That is what Nadège failed to do, and that was her tragedy. Although she accepted that her lover (who left her four years ago and gave her no forwarding address) had never really been committed, she refuses not to believe in her wildest dreams: 'The Absolute was just out of reach, and I cannot resign myself to anything less than that. Love and Passion are the only things left for me.' She refuses to face up to facts, and when other men do make advances, she turns them down. Only two things matter to her: her dreams and the idea that there is life after death. At the age of 32, she is seriously contemplating death. 'I savour my nights, when my dreams bring him back to me. My dreams are the only things that make me happy. Without them, I would plunge into the void and take my secret with me. In the hope that we will be able to love in a different life, but in broad daylight this time.'

Dreams can easily spiral out of control because they play an important role in the lives of single women. But also because married men are not always as boorish as the two described above. While they may not represent the 'Absolute', their qualities and their thoughtfulness (which they can display all the more easily in that they do so in a particular context and for a limited amount of time) can make the few remaining men who are available pale into insignificance. Many women still cling, like Fabienne, to their impossible dreams: 'I have been living a marginal existence for the last eight years. I'm having a passionate affair with someone who is not free. And I have learned to live with a different kind of loneliness: the loneliness of a painful absence, full of doubts and jealousies.'

— 9 —

THE INTERNET REVOLUTION

A Sudden Change of Epoch

Something really did happen at the turn of the millennium. The atmosphere suddenly changed. Bestsellers like *Bridget Jones*, and cult series such as *Friends* and *Ally McBeal*, were unashamed celebrations of the single life, as were the trendy urban games based upon the 'search for a soul-mate' (speed-dating). At the same time, the number of computer dating sites, which first appeared in the mid-1990s in the United States (but which only developed slowly because of their technical limitations), literally exploded and increased their turnover tenfold in the space of three years (Online Publishers Association 2005). The world of dating suddenly changed. Was it the end of the 'accusing finger'? Was it the end of the dismal period when singles were torn between their desire to assert their autonomy and the desperate need for security? One might have thought so at the time, given the amount of energy that was unleashed by the 'Internet bubble': individuals were no longer the same. But the bubble burst and the energy was dissipated. Both the fears and the search for security were reactivated by 9/11. The change of atmosphere was no more than a (happy) parenthesis, and society's demons – anxiety and fatigue – have come back to haunt it. And yet the Internet revolution continued at the same rate once the parenthesis was closed. That is where the real mutation took place: the landscape of dating has completely changed. A date is now only a click away.

At the moment, the number of dating sites is increasing rapidly and they are generating considerable profits (they have an annual growth rate of 70 per cent in the United States: Belcher 2006), even though they face growing competition from free sites and even though a new trend has emerged, with sites that specialize by bringing together specific types of users (defined by race, religion, occupation, affinities and so on). They also face competition from messaging networks and blogs, which make it possible to talk openly and to become involved in someone else's life. The future will therefore probably look very different from what we are seeing today. But, whatever innovations the future might bring, the important thing is that dating via the intermediary of a computer screen has become not only widespread but commonplace in a very short space of time. The way in which it has become part of everyday life has been analysed by Robert Brym and Rhonda Lenton (2001), who demonstrate that the use of these sites is spreading rapidly and that news of them is passed on by word of mouth within networks of acquaintances. New users quickly overcome their inhibitions and criticisms and rapidly convince their new friends that they too should 'join the club'. Some even purchase computers for the specific purpose of accessing these sites. Online dating, whose image was once little better than that of marriage agencies, has, in the space of only a few years, become a normal and legitimate way of finding a soul-mate. It has become 'normal' and even rather 'trendy', which is not something that can be said of marriage agencies – these tend to appeal to a public that is rather traditional, rural and mature, and are a last resort for those who are desperate to find a partner. Those who visit dating sites, by contrast, tend to be young, highly educated people who live in the cities and take part in a lot of social and leisure activities (Brym and Lenton 2001). They are open-minded about change and are, for example, more likely than most to be in favour of women's rights and sensitive to anti-homosexual discrimination (Madden and Lenhart 2006). They are by no means as lonely and desperate as we sometimes imagine them to be. The other reason why computer dating has spread so quickly is that it has been imposed from the top down as a model for youth and modernity.

The popularization of online dating has been so obvious and so smooth that it makes the Internet revolution look like no more than a peaceful, superficial and essentially technological change that is far removed from 'real life', which appears to go on as it always has done. The change is in fact much more radical than that: even though the basic problems (commitment) remain the same, the Internet has ushered in a very different age of dating. Dating is now easy and intoxicating, but it is full of hidden traps that can make it more difficult than ever to find love.

Love Is Just a Click Away

All it takes now is one click. It takes only one click to see a succession of men, and more men – hundreds of them. They are smiling, pleasant and available. They put their attractive masculinity on display, tensing their muscles in their swimming trunks or proudly showing off their leathers as they pose on their bikes. A click is all it takes to choose one. Welcome to the consumerist illusion, which suggests that we can choose a man (or a woman) in the same way that we choose a yoghurt in the supermarket. But that is not how love works. Love is not reducible to consumerism, and that is probably a good thing. The difference between a yoghurt and a man is that a woman cannot introduce a man into her life and expect everything to remain the same. A man will turn everything upside down, and things will never be the same again. And nor will he, for that matter. Meeting a partner causes two identities to undergo a metamorphosis, and that is what is both irresistibly attractive and frightening about it.

The Internet gives the opposite impression. For a woman who is sitting quietly at home in her old socks and with no make-up on (if there is no webcam), making contact on the net is first and foremost a source of boundless reassurance. She can log on with one click, and log off with another. With one click, she can look at a 'profile' and then close the page with another click. She can send an email with one click, and, if the message she gets in return does not appeal, she does not even have to reply. An individual armed with a mouse imagines that she is in complete and absolute control of her social connections. She does not realize that she is becoming caught up in something and will not emerge unscathed. When she begins, it is all very exciting. All the usual obstacles appear to have vanished, and a world of infinite possibilities opens up. It is as though all she had to do is pick and choose between all the delights that are on offer in this magical wonderland. A Net surfer is a Pinocchio who is filled with wonder.

And yet the first difficulties appear very quickly. The first have to do with search methods. The techniques that guide the neophyte through the sites are very effective. But one question remains unanswered: how does love work? Is a soul-mate in some sense a manifestation of Fate? Will she intuitively know when she has found her soul-mate? Better still, does her heart skip a beat to prove that she has at last found the man Love has chosen for her? Paradoxically, the Internet reactivates the idea that 'somewhere, it is written'. Jennifer, also known as 'Cinderella 69' (she was born in 1969) dreams aloud in her blog: 'I'm telling you, this is Year Zero of Love, True Love, the Real Thing. It can't not work. You've been waiting and waiting for your Prince to come, and you still had a long wait ahead of you! Because he didn't know, poor thing! Now you've gone on the Net and everyone knows it. If it is written somewhere, you are destined to meet him. No more excuses; it has to work. All you have to do is look around you a bit.' In the old, pre-Internet society of the twentieth century, women also dreamed that Love would appear from out of nowhere and suddenly sweep them off their feet. Hence the widespread belief that they would meet their Prince in some open, public space. In reality, 72 per cent of us meet our future partners at school or university, at work or in our networks of family and friends (Madden and Lenhart 2006). In that sense, the Internet does represent a revolution, because it makes it so easy to come into contact with strangers. For some singles who live far away from the big urban centres or who have been marginalized for one reason or another, it represents an unhoped-for tool and a truly magical opening onto the outside world. The Net already has its stock of wonderful legends, like the story of the disabled couple who would never have met without it.

But let us reread very carefully what Cinderella 69 told us. Although she is firmly convinced that she is destined to meet someone, she ends by saying: 'All you have to do is look around you a bit.' Fate needs a helping hand. It is a truism to say that the Internet only works if we make active use of it. And it is, of course, when she begins to look around that things start to go wrong. The reversal is spectacular: the very thing that was so exciting (the vast numbers of men) is now mentally exhausting. There are too many of them, and too much choice makes it impossible to choose. Christelle, who calls herself 'Channelchris',[1] feels that her head is spinning: 'In any case, when you look at their profiles, they're all the same. Charming, sporty, honest, generous, funny, "no mind games", good looking, sensual. . . . They practically guarantee you'll be on cloud nine. Everyone's a winner. Oh, come on!' Like everyone else, she has to define the product she is looking for with more precision. Half Prince Charming (in terms of physical appearance and emotional attitude), half a clone of herself. Leisure activities, affinities: the idea is to find a man who is just like her. That is the basic principle behind Internet contacts: 'and possibly more . . .' But someone who is just like her really means someone who does not upset anything, who does not turn her life upside down,

[1] The comments from Cinderella 69, Channelchris, Q-tip, Elfie, Anadema and Banana Thong are taken from their blogs; those from Teddy Bear 88 are from a chat room.

who does not change its rhythms or upset her little habits. The man reverts to being a pot of yoghurt.

The Dark Side of the Web

Computer dating is irresistibly attractive for two reasons. The possibilities are endless (everything is possible and easy). It is also a source of psychological reassurance, at least while she stays in front of the screen. The reassurance is in fact relative, as the Internet is not as virtual as it is often said to be. Once contact is established, the relationship is real, and the distance only changes its modalities. It is, of course, easier to back down (either by making an excuse or by saying nothing), which also makes very intimate exchanges easier, but doing so is not without its repercussions for the man or woman who is on the receiving end. Many people prefer to meet on the Net because they are afraid of being rejected 'in real life'. Unfortunately, they are rejected even more frequently on the Net, and they often get more badly hurt too. The man or woman who does not know how to break things off quickly enough is immediately trapped. Christelle learned this to her cost. 'Before, I used to reply to everyone out of politeness. It seems that doesn't happen very often on dating sites. You have to learn to zap them quickly. Now I understand why they wouldn't let me go and sang my praises. "Thanks for replying. It's unusual for a woman to reply. Thanks, many thanks. Someone nice at last. Let's get to know each other better. We can't leave things at that" (And on and on and on. "No", I said. "No")'. Some people are overwhelmed with offers, and others are suddenly dumped. The Internet is like everywhere else: you can be slapped in the face.

The anonymity is relative too. Everyone chooses a user name and some play with their identity and try out all sorts of virtual lives by, for example, changing their sex to see what it feels like. But, with the exception of married men who claim to be single, most of these manipulations and lies do not go very far (a few years, a few centimetres or a few kilos). Indeed those who are guilty of telling lies are not even aware of what they are doing. Only one quarter admit to cheating (Brym and Lenton 2001). The rest do not have the impression that they are being dishonest when, for example, they post a photograph that was taken five to ten years ago (the viewer may take a very different view of the matter). They do not cheat too much because they really are looking for someone who suits them and, in order to do that, they have to be honest about how they describe themselves. Everyone

119

is rapidly identified on the Net, and then pigeonholed. It takes only a little experience to learn the verbal codes that indicate specific requirements. For example, a man who does not want 'to get too deeply involved' is in fact primarily interested in sex. Christelle reacts immediately: 'The alarm bell goes off.' She also reacts when she comes across those she calls her 'exes'. They were no more than online acquaintances, but she thought it was a case of 'perhaps more . . .'. 'Three months later. They're all present and correct. "Summersun". "Hope62". "Bond-008". "Homerus". "Aceofhearts". "F-sharp". So it can't have worked out the way they wanted it to. Obviously not. It didn't work out for me either.' These fruitless quests are a mirror reflection of her own failures. 'Click . . . Oh no, not him again. F-sharp (Oh No! Still signed up. That's a bit much coming from someone who always refused "dating to order"). I could have done without that. That will teach me to be curious. Mind you, it's just like passing an ex in the street. It has the same effect. Except that, on a dating site, it's there in black and white that he's still single. And except that he doesn't want to go on being single.' The Internet has a long memory, and every click leaves traces, even when we try to delete them. 'Breaking news: "Hope62" is single again. He's back. Not a comma in his profile has been changed. Fancy that, I'd forgotten he claimed to be "shy" (That's one way of putting it). For the benefit of new readers: this was the famous date on 8 October. Not something you forget. So, the thing with his Girl from Toulouse went into a tailspin, and so he signed up again' (Christelle).

The single man who thinks he is anonymous in front of his screen is in fact recording his changing opinions and behaviour on a database. And those changes can be identified and remembered both by those he talks to directly and by more discreet observers. Some of them have very good memories. Some surfers, who may or may not be known to him, quickly get an idea of who he really is, shape his reputation and judge him all the more harshly because they are not face to face with him. The most surprising thing about all this is that staying online too long to pursue a fruitless search proves to be a particularly damning stigma. Despite the pretence of freedom and tolerance, and despite the trendy technology, the old accusing finger is back, and it is sometimes worse than ever. The traitors are now within. The finger is pointed by other singles, and in a world that is reserved for singles. 'Q-tip' is convinced of this. 'Being single is like being unemployed. The longer you stay unemployed, the more reluctant employers are to give you a job. Oh yes, being unemployed for too long really is something to be worried about. Being single is the same. The longer you stay single, the fewer guys you attract. Because there's something fishy about a man or woman who has been on their own for a long time.'

Real Life

Once the excitement of the first months, and the urge to spend hours in front of the screen, is over, disillusionment and saturation set in. We become sick of virtual reality. It is all too rare for the men women meet on the Net to become real partners, and truly exciting relationships are even rarer. The infinite number of possibilities loses its charm, and the vast number of partners on offer becomes mentally exhausting. But it is still impossible to log off. The attraction is too strong. Even though it becomes nauseating, virtual reality proves to be less virtual than one might think because thousands of tiny threads irresistibly attach us to the screen, give us the feeling that we exist and are recognized as existing, and even that we can expand our horizons to infinity. How could anyone turn down such an intensification of the Self? Meeting people online quickly becomes a drug, and we can no longer do without it. Increasingly, we live in a world of addictions. This is because autonomous individuals who are doomed to construct their own lives need to be supported, to have people around them, to have cuddles and to be swept off their feet (Kaufmann 2004). Cocaine, alcohol and tobacco can all be misused and taken as drugs. So can sex, work and television. For some people, being connected to dating sites is a drug, and there is nothing soft about it. The exasperated Christelle, who dreams of 'getting back to real life', 'staying in bed all Sunday morning' and 'making lots of chocolate cakes', has taken drastic measures. 'My computer is on holiday too. Complete rest. I've uninstalled MSN, and that's saying something. . . . I've even put a sheet over it, so that it looks like a cage where the budgie has gone to sleep. That way, I'm not tempted. *Vade retro Satanas.*' Two days later, the computer was back on again.

There are two stages to Internet dating. The first is the endless sea of data and the countless contacts in cyberspace. Becoming intimate with someone with a click of the mouse button is a strange and novel experience; the feeling of intoxication is more intense than it has ever been, and so too is the unbearable lightness of being. The second stage is a face-to-face date 'in real life'. It is the Net surfers themselves who erect the barrier that radically divides the two stages and the two worlds from one another. Because they grow sick of virtual reality, they tend to contrast it with 'real life' and to idealize the latter. The transition from one stage in the dating process to the other is a fearful ordeal and a very problematic transition, but one that cannot be avoided. With traditional dating, that gap existed only to a limited extent. A first date could be a very emotional experience, but it was a date with someone who was both unique and someone already known to us (to a greater or lesser extent). We learn how to get to know one another on the Net, and we often get to know each other better and more intimately than if we were actually to meet. But the really strange thing about the first face-to-face date is that it is with someone who is not the same as the person we met on the Net. Once we actually meet, a very different story begins, and it really does involve someone different.

The self-image we put on display now plays an increasingly decisive role in many domains. Self-image is, obviously enough, even more important for anyone who is trying to find a lover. The sight of the face and body of the other triggers sudden infatuations, which are the modern equivalent of love at first sight. The tyranny of the image is unbearable for all those who have, or imagine that they have, some slight flaw or who do not meet the canons of fashion, or, in other words, the vast majority of us. For them, the Internet is a marvellous form of revenge. So let's hear it for 'inner beauty', which is a real cliché in all the stories and crops up over and over again. 'Last night, "Pompidou34" confided in me: "I am not a playboy, but it seems that it's what's inside that counts. That suits me." I'm quite prepared to believe him. I guessed that from his photo' (Christelle). Unfortunately, physical appearance does very quickly come to matter a great deal, sometimes to an obsessional extent, because it is masked (some men prefer not to post photographs) or seems to be made up (lots of people post flattering photographs).

Meeting someone after making contact on the Internet represents a new rite of passage. Sometimes, it can be brutal and it is always emotionally intense. This is because the biographical stakes (possible commitment) and psychological stakes (being found lacking and turned down) are so high. It is also because we have to manage the transition from the person we knew on the Net to the different person we meet face to face. We form an immediate impression at first sight. The identification is instantaneous, global, totalizing and categorical. We either like or dislike the person we see. The old secrets, which could be very intimate, warm or sincere, and the old complicities suddenly count for nothing. A single glance is all it takes to destroy everything. In some cases, we are sorry we gave so much away. We want to fade into the background, forget or run away. We feel uncomfortable. There is a great temptation to accuse the other person of cheating: he was lying when he described himself. As I have already said, there are in fact limits to the number of disguises that can be worn and the deceit is minimal. It is the context that is different, and that changes the way we see things. We are always very quick to form an opinion of the person we are talking to. And chatting to someone on the Net and face-to-face meetings lead us to form two different opinions of the same person. Neither tells us everything about the individual concerned. Neither tells the whole truth, and especially not the impression we get when we see someone and instantly forget about their 'inner beauty'.

There must be ways around this. Many people try to overcome the problem by being cautious and taking one step at a time. Two-thirds send photographs, and 86 per cent phone. A smaller number set up web cams (Brym and Lenton 2001). There is also a growing tendency to plan ahead without telling the other person, and find out who he or she really is (Madden and Lenhart 2006). How? By getting onto the Net, of course, and using search engines to follow up the clues he leaves behind. He leaves countless clues. They extend far beyond the dating sites, and make it possible to reconstruct a trajectory and to discover facets of his personality. Some people prefer to wait for a week or two before arranging a date because they realize how much is at stake and want to avoid committing themselves without giving the matter proper consideration. Conversely, a minority take no such precautions. They arrange lots of dates as though they were so many exciting experiments, and make no special preparations for them. They are usually men.

Men and Women: Sex and Commitment

More and more women are visiting dating sites, but they are not always looking for the same thing as men. Although many men are more in touch with their feelings than they used to be and are looking for romance, they are still obsessed with sex. This is especially true of the small group of predators who have few scruples and see the Internet as prime hunting ground. Pleasure is all they are interested in. Christelle was almost tempted by 'Fireblade11', for instance (a bit of sex from time to time can't do any harm). ' "I like briefs or Y-fronts, but never boxers. I hate clothes that are loose-fitting: I've nothing to hide, and I don't need to cheat." He's got some nerve, this

"Fireblade11" . . . Hmm . . . Calm down. This is a dating site, after all. Of course it is, but there's no need to rush things. I suppose some women must like that sort of thing. Fortunately, the photo is just soft porn. He's fully dressed. And on his bike! But I think that I only have to ask if I want a photo of him in his boxers. He's probably got loads of them.' Five days later, Christelle is less keen to meet him (there's more to life than sex). '" So, you like my profile, do you? Let's get to know each other better. If you don't like me, I've lots of friends who are single." Oh no, he wants to tell everyone in the neighbourhood! Careful, he doesn't live that far away from where I live. One click, and I've got it all: email, MSN address and mobile number. Slow down! I'm not sure that I want to. Puts it about a bit too much for my liking.' After a few disappointing experiences when the early promises were quickly forgotten about, Q-tip is now openly on her guard. 'When "Serial Pick-Up Artist" asks me where I get my pretty smile from, or when "Ridiculous Seducer" pretends to be interested in what I do for a living, I quickly realize that all the "Man with Balls" I have on screen is interested in is a shag.'

As always, the married men are the worst. The Internet has given them their second wind. For official purposes, they claim to be single but they regularly visit dating sites. It's all fantasy . . . and possibly more. A Canadian survey (Brym and Lenton 2001) estimates that 19 per cent of the men who visit these sites are married; an American study (Madden and Lenhart 2006) puts the figure at 23 per cent. As for the women they meet, they imagine the figure to be higher than that and state that almost 50 per cent of the men are married. Having learned from experience, Christelle is actually worried about the stability of their marriages and has issued a stern warning to married women:

We've got the Internet now. Even if you live in a village in the middle of nowhere, you're not safe. It's going on under your roof. Don't trust him. There are lots of warning signs. If your husband rushes off to his computer as soon as he's had his evening meal, ask yourself why. If he's still on his computer at 2 in the morning and panics when you go into the room, you've had it. If he spends whole weekends on it, you know what I think. I know what I'm talking about. I spent two months trying out the married men who go on the Net. Put yourself in his place. He chooses a nice user name, takes a few years off his age, makes himself a few centimetres taller, takes up sport again, takes a photo of himself in the garden and off he goes. He has all the little chicks in the world chasing after him. Each more beautiful than the last. They all want to get to know him. And possibly more. They'll even come to the house to find him. Him. Your husband. You ought to know that he's set up a personal in-box just to meet them. Husbands who use the Net are clever. So you'll never know anything about it. Unless you make the effort to catch him out.

And it is becoming less and less unusual for wives to make the effort to catch him out. In fact, it seems that spying on husbands is an economic sector with a great future ahead of it (Chatelain and Roche 2005). Especially as there is a real danger that men who met their partners through dating sites (which is now quite normal) and who have tried the drug of anonymous, safe chats in cyberspace will find it very difficult not to go back to it. They have also become used to the 'zapping reflex' (zapping him immediately if he does not live up to her expectations), and it is difficult to get rid of that reflex. This is probably just the beginning of the liquid love that Zygmunt Bauman (2003) talks about. Using the Internet is a very good way to liquefy conjugal and emotional ties. Falling in love has become very easy, if not too easy. It makes Christelle feel sick: 'At the moment, the site is offering a "love guarantee". "Sign up for six months. If you do not fall in love within six months, Match.com will give you six more months for free." It's a pure con. Of course you will fall in love during the six months' period! That's not the problem. Falling in love is easy. It's staying together that's difficult. Personally, I've never met anything but ghosts. I did fall in love. Deeply. But another six months? No thanks!'

'Don't Give Up!'

The liquefaction of love makes commitment even more difficult, especially for men. Christelle gave herself 30 days. 'Meet Mr Right on the Internet in 30 days? Meeting a man is easy. I can do that whenever I like. I can meet dozens of men, thousands of men. I really could have my pick of them. It's a lot to think about. Even if I do have 30 days. Meeting Mr Right is one thing. Keeping him is another. It's difficult to keep a man you've found on the Net. You've been warned.' Now that women have become suspicious, they too are reluctant to commit themselves. From that point of view, as from many others, the Net is full of contradictions. Men and women are apparently on an equal footing, especially when they first meet. They share information, secrets and emotions. But the old divisions soon reappear. Men are mainly interested in sex and having a fling, whilst women dream of true love and serious commitment. They put more and more warning notices at the end of their profiles: 'No time-wasters!' (Lardellier

2004). Unfortunately, there are a lot of time-wasters out there, and women (more so than men) meet with a lot of disappointments. Elfie has reached the point where she believes that all men are like that: 'Before I visited sites like Match.com, I had never realized what cowards men can be. Never. They promise you the moon. You are the most beautiful, the most attractive girl in the world. And once they've "consumed" you, they always swear "we'll see each other again", and then, if you're lucky, you might get a little SMS, and then . . . nothing . . . radio silence.'

Like that of many other men, the example of Teddy Bear 88 proves that this is, however, no more than one trend and that it is a mistake to make generalizations. He refuses to venture into the international market, which is full of disturbing temptations (see the appendix below). 'Because we want to keep a clear head, we 50-something-year-olds don't visit the profiles of those gorgeous "Russian dolls" and beautiful Colombians too often.' But, having learned from experience, he can confirm that there is nothing marginal about this trend. 'Some women do get really disappointed by the cheating and the lying, by all the womanizing, by the hurried seductions for purely sexual purposes and the complete lack of any kind form of emotion.' And Teddy Bear 88 sympathizes with their emotional distress. Unfortunately, not all men are so sympathetic. There are, however, those who, like Anadema and Indianajil, find that their distress takes some of the fun out of the game. Banana Thong was somewhat shocked by their comments, and hurls the accusation back in their faces: 'I've noticed recently that some of the men who use Meetic, like Anadema and Indianajil, are a bit disappointed, or even bitter. They are disappointed with the women they meet and say that they are indecisive, lacking in self-confidence, in love with their exes, depressed . . . and that's the least of it. Let me reassure you, gentlemen, there are also men like that, the only difference being that the main complaint against them is that all they think about is tits and bums.'

There is a lot of cheerful frivolity on the Internet, but there is also a lot of pain. That much is obvious from the way people who are looking for love encourage one another so often. Especially the women. The comments sent to the authors of blogs often end with an exclamatory 'Don't give up!'. It is a rather intriguing expression, when applied to the domain of love. It is as though love had become hard labour. These are some of the messages sent to Christelle: 'Don't give up!' Janna tells her, 'You will find happiness!' 'Don't give up!' adds the aptly named Sisyphus. 'Love is often where you least expect it. You'll find love eventually, I promise you.' 'Don't give up hope!' concludes

Cindy, 'Leave this artificial world behind you. Look around you: you might pass your Prince on the stairs or at the traffic lights.' These words of encouragement often refer to 'real life', which suddenly acquires all the virtues. It is striking how many of the comments refer to Love's imponderable riddles. After the supermarket phase, in which men were reduced to the status of yoghurts to be chosen on the rational basis of carefully researched criteria, they suddenly revert to being Princes who appear out of nowhere like some enchanting surprise. That wonderful belief is our modern religion (Beck-Gernsheim 2002).

An Experience in its Own Right

The Net makes a life that is already divided worse than ever: there is much more laughter, but there are many more tears. It eventually makes virtual reality even more sickening, makes one despair of ever meeting someone and leads to mental exhaustion. So much for the tears, and maybe I have said too much about them. The divided life also has its bright side. There is the joy of being free, and the feeling of lightness that comes with it. The Net is easy to use, and that allows us to break out of our loneliness, easily and at no risk to ourselves, when we wish and as we wish. And it can introduce us to a lot of new pleasures.

There is in fact almost only one problem with the Internet, and all the difficulties it poses come down to the same thing: it does not make commitment any easier. Anyone who does think it makes commitment easier is unlikely to find someone. If, on the other hand, we put aside the question of commitment, of really meeting someone and of life-long love, the Net can be a treasure house. It is an experience in itself, a life that is more intense. It puts us in touch with a lot of people, and it is only a click away. Its links immerse us in a vast network of acquaintances. We can identify some, but not all, of them. Some are close to home, while others are far away. We can form fleeting friendships and get close to someone for just a short time. We can share our emotions – lots of emotions – and exchange tokens of affection. Christelle fears that she will not find Mr Right: 'But leaving him aside, I get virtual kisses from all over the place and it never ends.' There is an obvious desire for closeness and tenderness on the Net, and the cruelty of the zapping is in sharp contrast with the underlying search for humanity and kindness, and the sensitivity. Hence the inflationary use of smiley faces: chatting on the Net can make us happy.

127

The profusion of smiley faces, which 'express as much emotion as possible with as few signs as possible' (Lardellier 2004: 185), is also a clear indication that we don't always really know what to say to each other. Little signs that express feelings are therefore a very useful way of establishing a shared intimacy without having to make too much effort. But there are also a lot of aspiring writers on the Net. Poets and all kinds of artists see it as a way of finding a voice and expressing their emotions. Astonishingly, love letters, which we thought had gone forever, are making a comeback after 100 years of oblivion. And, as at the height of the Romantic period, some people are happy to keep things on a verbal level. Which does not stop them from having a really good time. Witness Q-tip: 'I spent yesterday evening with Rainbow Scarf: his poems left me all of a quiver.'

All forms and all kinds of friendly and erotic exchange are possible. They can range from platonic exchanges of letters to a compulsively bulimic over-indulgence in dates that lead nowhere. An intermediary modality tends to become the established pattern: online flirting. There are none of the risks, stakes or disappointments that are inherent in face-to-face meetings, and the content can become 'very hot when you click with someone' (Banana Thong). Some 24 per cent of those who visit dating sites never go out on a real date (Brym and Lenton 2001), and online flirting is the most popular form of erotic activity. There are more people flirting than there are looking for a date. As for actual dates, it is really the prospect of commitment that makes them problematic, and it is as simple as that. Surfers have no worries about commitment, and their dates are an experience in their own right. The experience can be very vivid and emotionally powerful. This is especially true of men. They are certainly interested in sex, but that is not the only thing they are looking for. Even though he is vilified by Banana Thong, Andema is certainly not under the impression that he is a predator. He has his flings, and they are certainly sexual, but they are also emotional and relational (even though he never commits himself too far). He is surprised by the comments he gets on his blog. That the misunderstandings are mutual is quite obvious.

Oh really . . . about my relationship with Lila . . . I've heard it all before: 'Just another of his sexual exploits' . . . 'It was just physical' . . . 'All he was interested in was the sex' . . . 'he just wanted to get her on her back'. . . 'a fuck buddy'. Sex, sex and more sex. Anyone who thinks that there was nothing more to my relationship with Lila than sex is in for a big disappointment because we did all sorts of other things: meals, drinks, went for walks, watched films, read each other stories, smoked rare plants, chatted over a drink . . . and what's more, we respected each other. The emotional intensity varies, depending on the relationship, on the pleasure we get from being with someone else. It is up to us to decide when we want to call it love. When it comes to love, we all have our own standards. My relationship with Oona lasted for eight months, and you could say it was a loving relationship, if you compare it with the relationships a lot of couples are in. Conversely, just because you decide not to call it love doesn't mean that there isn't a bit of love involved, or that there are no feelings involved. There is an infinite range of nuances on the indifference/love spectrum, all kinds of degrees of affection, and we shouldn't forget that. So why does it seem to me that so many people find it so difficult to understand that? We have to stop trying systematically to put everything into two categories, like nice and nasty, good and bad, love and sex. When the only thing the guy is interested in is the sex, he has no respect for the woman. She is reduced to the status of an object. The expression is pejorative, and rightly so. It's a scathing attack on a 'relationship degree zero'. But when you describe what you see as a loveless relationship as being 'just sex', you reduce a relationship to a series of sexual encounters, leave out everything else and suggest that sexuality is something dirty and something to be ashamed of.

Making contact with someone online is an experience in itself in a lot of other senses too. Surfers go online in the hope of finding a soul-mate, but they in fact make all sorts of contacts and become involved in all sorts of things. They think they are going online to find love, but they discover many other things too. They join virtual communities which create whole worlds and, at the same time, reshape the identities of those involved in them (Rheingold 2000). The Internet is an unrivalled way of playing with your identity. But it is not just a game: surfers experiment with possible variations and try to find out what it feels like to be someone else. The Net is a tool for individual creativity.

This also explains why dating sites are now coming up against certain limitations, and why the future of the on-line search for love may not be restricted to such sites. The self-presentation is too conventional and formulaic, and every surfer is always trying to find more informal ways of meeting people, often by using chat rooms and messaging services. Most of them, however, do so by visiting blogs, which allow them to be more honest about themselves, to try to see themselves through the eyes of others. Blogs allow them to immerse themselves in the intimate details of someone else's day-to-day life. Blogs can be very vivid. People react to them and get close to the blogger. The paradox is that, because they are not hidden away in the bottom of a drawer like the notebooks of old, these modern diaries tend to create more links than any of the other tools that are available on the net, precisely because their starting point is a Self that is revealed in all its details and all its depth. Can it also be revealed in all its truth? We need to be somewhat cautious about this. It should not be forgotten that the Internet also gives us the ultimate and very modern freedom of being able to play with our identity. And that reminds me: Banana Thong has decided to put an end to her 'Banana Thong' identity and move on to a new life, and has therefore closed down her blog. 'I'd like to make a new start and cut myself loose from my Banana Thong identity. I'm in charge of my blog, and I have the power of life and death over it.' But, there again, having thought about it, she might not close it down completely. 'I put a lot of myself into what I've written here. Bringing a blog to life is a real drug. And I won't be able to wean myself off it that easily. I might write here from time to time, and I'll probably do the same in another blog. I have several projects in mind.' Four months later, Banana Thong is still dreaming of love and of finding the truth about herself. It is not that easy to change one's identity.

Part III

The Autonomy Trajectory

The private life model urges women to find a partner and to become part of a couple. But some mysterious force takes them in the opposite direction: perhaps living alone is the best way of making the dream of being a sovereign individual come true and of being the sole masters of our destiny.

The truth is that this force can produce very different life trajectories. Until now, we have been looking at an average portrait. We are now about to discover the existence of two very different sub-worlds. The dark side is terribly dark. But there is also a strange bright side where lives are constructed in the course of a headlong pursuit of more and more light. And the women who take that course get burned.

—10—

BEING ONESELF

Concepts have a history, and it might be worth recounting it. When they are used as tools to make the facts speak, concepts are at once stable and subject to a constant reworking. They are stable and collectively recognized because it is only when they display those characteristics that they can be embodied as clearly defined concepts that can be classified in dictionaries. They are also variable and adapted for specific purposes because, in the secrecy of the laboratory, every researcher uses them in his or her own way and for his or her purposes of the moment.

The Trajectory

The concept 'trajectory' is a good illustration of this ambiguity; it gives the impression of having a single meaning but is used in various different ways. Much of its power derives from the 'ballistic metaphor' (Passeron 1991: 205). A trajectory is a force which draws an individual into a life history that unfolds in accordance with its own logic. But when it comes to characterizing that force, the analyses vary. Claude Dubar (1998) identifies two main tendencies. There are theories that privilege the 'objective trajectory', or a sequence of social positions whose rules transcend and construct individuals. And there are theories that emphasize how 'subjective trajectories' are inscribed in individual stories based upon indigenous categories. He suggests that we combine the two theories, as that would allow us to look at both sides of the process of identity-construction. And in order to do that, he synthesizes the findings of the various theories of a 'trajectory'.

I have no ambition to follow Dubar's example, but will simply use the tool in my own way. It is, for example, impossible to sum up in just a few lines the critical contribution made by Pierre Bourdieu and his ingenious analysis of 'the specific effect of trajectory' (Bourdieu 1984: 453). It does, however, seem to me that Bourdieu's theoretical intention has an internal therapeutic function (it makes his over-rigid 'habitus' more flexible). Concentrating on the objective pole, he defines a biographical trajectory as a sequence of internalizations of a probable trajectory that is so clear that Jean-Claude Passeron (1991: 205) finds it 'too beautiful for the fabric that social facts are made from'. By plunging into the concrete profusion of social interaction, the sociologists of the Chicago School, in contrast, allow us to feel that fabric and to discover a very different vision of trajectories (Strauss 1992), which they more usually describe as 'careers' (Becker 1985). Their objective is to understand the biographical process as an intersection between subjective processes and the social frameworks that shape lives: 'The concept of career . . . allows one to move back and forth between the personal and the public, between the self and its significant society' (Goffman 1968: 119).

The conceptual tool they define is, however, ill-suited to our current research, because 'the social' is restricted to meaning 'interaction' and, what is more important, because there is no historical dimension: the social genesis of the context is not explained (Terrail 1995). Yet history does play a central role in the subject that concerns us. History irresistibly sweeps along individuals who do not always understand what is happening to them. It makes people social innovators even though they have not deliberately chosen to be in that position. It is therefore individuals who make history because what they do and say speeds up the processes that put them in the vanguard of history. Despite themselves.

Although the concept of trajectory used here is grounded in the sociological tradition, it gives a central importance to this historical impetus. The concept is therefore much broader than and incommensurable with a mere biographical itinerary: the autonomy trajectory is a force that transcends individual lives. It is part of both the day-to-day minutiae of individual lives and the *longue durée* of historical trends.

The Irrepressible Injunction to be Oneself

The same obsessive question keeps coming up: why am I leading this weird life? The most intriguing thing about the single life is the feeling of being both free – exceptionally free – and being irresistibly carried along by some enigmatic biographical trajectory. What is the key to the mystery? Who is pulling the strings that control my destiny? Neither mirrors, clairvoyants, diaries, blogs nor even girlfriends can ever provide an answer.

And yet the key to the mystery is simple. But, like all simple things, it is difficult to explain. It has a lot to do with the long trend towards the individualization of the social, which is now a major force for change: modern individuals want more and more control over their own lives. They want to define their own truth, choose their own morality and take responsibility for their own identities. They are of course much less autonomous than they might think. The important thing is, however, that they have an ever-greater choice in a wide variety of domains. The decision to live as a couple or not to do so is no more than one element in a broader process.

It is, however, an important element: few other choices involve such a commitment to the future. Giving up the single life in fact shatters individual identities in two senses. It means, first of all, sacrificing part of the Self to a new conjugal entity (how great the sacrifice is can vary). A couple cannot come into being unless part of the individual identities of the partners becomes fused: becoming 'us' means that we can go on being 'ourselves' only in a controlled fashion and only within certain limits. Becoming integrated into a family then deflects our trajectory in a new direction, which is clearly defined by a series of stages that unfold in accordance with a logical sequence (Kaufmann 1997): the unpredictable torrent of life becomes a calm river. From the point of view of the individual who is trying to remain in control of his or her destiny, two things have to be given up: part of his or her identity is collectivized, while the other part is delineated by limitations that can no longer be changed.

The most obvious solution is to drift into conjugal life without asking too many questions. The ideal version of that story involves True Love and Prince Charming. Unfortunately, the true Prince is often in no hurry to show his face, and as time goes by, women tend to begin to evaluate and compare the two life-hypotheses and the two trajectories. A woman's thoughts therefore begin to focus on this theme: 'Given that I can't find a man who is good enough for me, why shouldn't I go on being alone? What advantages does that option have to offer?' The letters describe at length women's attempts to answer that question, and they take the form of arguments that pile up one after the other. The strange thing is that these inventories constantly confuse two very different kinds of reason: the concrete details of everyday life (breakfast in bed, few domestic responsibilities, etc.) and abstract principles that are almost indescribable (being me, feeling free, etc.).

The details of how daily life is organized represent clearly identified reasons for remaining single, and their importance can be evaluated with some precision. It is as though they were purely subjective expressions of an innermost self, rather as though they were familiar elements of a strictly personal world: 'Reading whenever I feel like it, at any time of night or day, spending three hours in the bathroom, not sacrificing my life to a dreary round of making meals and doing housework. I wouldn't give that up for anything in the world' (Alexandra). The abstract principles, on the other hand, make the woman who formulates them part of a trend that transcends her and carries her away: 'I want to be happy, I want to express myself and I want to live my life to the full. I feel rich and light. It's a momentum, an energy. Why should anyone want to stop themselves from living a full life?' (Alexandra). The historical impulse is almost palpable: the irrepressible injunction to be herself propels her towards a destiny that cannot be defined. A multitude of ineffable and diffuse signs whisper that this momentum transcends the limits of the Self; a woman who is experimenting with autonomy is vaguely aware of being involved in a broader process. Her girlfriends have similar doubts and are living proof that the force that urges them to remain single is not purely subjective.

What is the dynamic she feels she is caught up in, and how can it be expressed? The letters betray a certain dissatisfaction with the answers single women are given, and alternate between day-to-day trivia and vague generalities. That is why the lists of complaints grow longer and longer. It also explains the obvious desire to do all they can to combine the two sets of reasons. It is as though they were trying to knead together specifics and generalities in order to discover the truth about the impetus that is propelling them. The same dissatisfaction is apparent in their attempts to decide whether their single status is something that has been forced on them or something they have chosen. Many letters put forward both a thesis and an antithesis in the space of only a few lines. Once again, it is difficult to express a truth that lies (in most cases) somewhere in between the two extremes. Autonomy is irresistibly attractive, and these women feel that they have been caught up in a process they do not understand. And yet the decision has to be made on an individual basis, and has to be based on concrete personal motifs. Their single status is both something that is forced upon them and something they choose. That is in fact the secret behind their trajectory, and the mystery that surrounds the force that drives them on: it takes shape at the point where deeply subjective feelings intersect with broader social trends.

The collective, dynamic aspect of a trajectory (its propulsive force) is no more than the result of personal micro-decisions taken by an infinite number of individuals. But they all perceive it as an external reality. This is true even when the individuals concerned are scarcely prepared for it: many single women are becoming more autonomous even though the preconditions that might allow them to make sense of their autonomy are not all present. There is an obvious discrepancy between their intuitive perception of their trajectory, and the difficulty they have in describing its content other than in terms of domestic details. It is as though the historical process began with the social, and forced individuals to become part of it without knowing what they are doing. Babette gets very annoyed about this lack of clarity: 'All that for the sake of this bloody independence. And what do I do with it when I've got it? What is this independence, at the end of the day?' When she asks herself these questions, she cannot grasp their deeper meaning but only a few pathetic symptoms. 'Does it mean that I've chosen to live like this just to be able to spend my Sundays under the duvet?' And yet, for a whole series of reasons she finds it difficult to express, she does not feel ready to deviate from her trajectory.

Widows

The injunction to be oneself is irresistible and it can lead women to embark upon the single trajectory. But it does so in very different contexts and very different ways.

Most of the women who are now living alone are widows. They represent the heritage of a recent past. They initiated the trend towards residential autonomy that could be observed all over Europe after the Second World War. This was obviously not a deliberate move on their part; many of them had lost their husbands. The new cohorts of widows living on their own aroused little curiosity: no one imagined (in the silence and discretion that surrounds mourning) that they were the harbingers of a future revolution in private life.

The reasons for the change lay in the fact that different generations no longer lived together. When one partner died, the other found him or herself living alone at home rather than being taken in by his or her family. This phenomenon was exacerbated by the different mortality rates for the two sexes, and by the age difference between the partners (and the effects of these two factors were cumulative): millions of old women suddenly had to learn how to live on their own. There could not be a better illustration of the supra-individual nature of certain trajectories. Their new domestic reality was a product of external forces: after the cruelty of death came the coldness of loneliness. And yet their new status resulted from the actions of a few individuals who really were motivated by a desire to be autonomous. I am not referring to the widows themselves, but to a generation of children who were trying to become more independent of the families in which they had grown up. Many observers stressed that kinship still played an essential role. Its continued importance went, however, hand in hand with a change of form: the bonds, which had a symbolic importance, were strongest when they worked at a distance, and on condition that each household was in control of its day-to-day affairs. The assertion of the sovereignty of small domestic groups was part of the general trend towards the individuation of the social. 'A kind of collective individualism . . . prepared people for the real individualism with which we are familiar' (Tocqueville 2004: 167).

This first wave of singledom has probably almost peaked in Europe: the number of old women living on their own is still rising, but it is now doing so more slowly (the increase, which is bound up with their improved state of health, is restricted to the eldest amongst them), and the real upheavals are taking place elsewhere. A few developments should, however, be noted. The most significant is that the number of widows, expressed as a proportion of the total number of old women living alone, is falling. These other women are on their own not because they have lost their partners, but because they took the decision to break off a relationship and find it impossible to embark on a new one. Couples find that one transition in particular requires very delicate handling: the transition to retirement (Caradec 1996). Even at this advanced age, the link between being single and the trend towards autonomy is becoming more direct.

Young People

The second wave was to be much less discreet. It began in Scandinavia from the 1960s onwards and is now beginning to spread to the countries of Southern Europe.

It was more visible because it was bound up with a tumultuous self-assertion on the part of young people, who were asserting their own style and their own socialization and rejecting those of adults. The most obvious aspects of their style are well known, and include modes of dress, styles of music and so on. At a deeper level, the specificity of socialization into youth revolved around a central axis: the refusal to be integrated into the family. Young people were beginning to inhabit a space midway between episodes: the time they spent with their families of origin (in which they played the part of children) and the time they spent with the families they themselves started (as partners and parents). In this intermediary space, the values they proclaimed rejected everything to do with domesticity: real life was elsewhere, and it was open and carefree. Like their friends, they were following a trend. But where was this trend leading? It is difficult to say. What was being rejected was, on the other hand, very clear: they were refusing to settle down to adult life too soon. Doing so was defining their identities for ever. Because they were young, they had complete freedom to invent themselves: the future was still open. In an intuitive attempt to protect that treasure, commitments – and especially family commitments – were deferred. It takes time to find oneself.

It takes a long time to learn how to define one's own identity: there is a danger that young people who are inadequately prepared for doing so will subsequently suffer from 'dependency in private relationships' (Singly 1998: 362). This phenomenon is characterized by a whole series of stages. Children are now taught at an early age that the Self is a work of art. They have to succeed in putting down their own markers (by relying on groups of friends rather than their families) while still remaining faithful elements of the family unit. The process accelerates during adolescence, when the reformulation of identities becomes a very active process; they have to know their place in the bosom of the family, and at the same time manage a Self that is evolving and becoming increasingly independent. There is now a tendency for this phase of relative autonomy to last longer, as young people begin the task of self-definition earlier and earlier, and leave the parental home later and later. The division of labour is as follows: the family takes responsibility for their material well-being, whilst they concentrate on their own development. If they became immersed in domesticity, a form of socialization specific to young people would come to an end: they must remain free to experiment with alternative identities. Although they go on living in the parental home, they gradually become more autonomous as they grow older. After the age of 20–21, young people enjoy an almost total freedom of movement, and the time they spend socializing with their parents is reduced to a minimum (Roussel and Bourguignon 1979). In short, they are provided with board and lodging but they have also constructed the basic

139

framework that makes them autonomous. So why do they leave home? They do so for various reasons. There are geographical factors that are beyond their control (they go off to study or work in a different city). They grow tired of living with their parents. They itch to be completely independent, and to have their own homes. The latter factor, which has a lot to do with their headstrong nature, is more pronounced amongst girls; worried parents keep a closer eye on their daughters than on their sons. Residential autonomy allows them to escape that (Bozon and Villeneuve-Gokalp 1994). And then it is time for them to live on their own.

It is a strange experience, and it is rarely thought of as a real project: one fine day, they suddenly find themselves alone in a modestly furnished flat. Emilienne did not really know what she was doing. It was as though it was happening to someone else and her new life still feels strange. While she was a student, she went on living with her parents. She moved out to take up her first job, which she started a week ago: 'This is the eighth evening in a row that I've spent alone in front of the telly. It feels funny. I'm not sure what is happening to me. I'm not used to this.' Who can say what will happen next? Entering the adult world increasingly involves spending a period of time on one's own. How long it will last is hard to predict. In some cases it lasts for only a short time. In others, it may last for a very long time, or even for ever. It is often followed by a whole series of other sequences: conjugal experiments, going back to live with one's parents, or another period of time on one's own. The main factor that determines how long someone will remain on their own is a reluctance to make a definite commitment to adulthood and to close the parenthesis of youth. Settling down with a partner means that the parenthesis is closed forever.

Young people experience their residential autonomy by spending periods of time on their own. Some of them do not do this for long, but their numbers are rising. A cross section of the census data, which shows the number of people who are living alone at any given moment, reveals a spectacular rise in the number of people in this position. In the developed countries, the rise has, in recent years, been steepest in the group aged between 25 and 35.

Women Who Have Broken Off Relationships

The third wave, which was fuelled by the break-up of relationships, did not follow any specific timetable. Although there have been some historical variations, the number of women who are living alone after

140

the break-up of a relationship has been rising gradually but inexorably over the last 30 years or so. In recent years, the number of divorces has begun to rise more slowly (because people think more before getting married). That downturn is, however, more than compensated for by the growing number of unmarried couples who split up. In general terms, relationships are becoming more fragile, and fewer of the break-ups result in the establishment of new ones (Toulemon 1996).

In two out of three cases, it is the woman who decides to break off the relationship. Women invest more of themselves than men in their families and, because of this, their lives are more dependent on them. The choice between remaining single and living as part of a couple allows them to choose between two very different identity trajectories. Because it frees them from family responsibilities, their autonomy gives them more flexibility, which is an incomparable advantage when it comes to having a successful career (single men, by contrast, are at a slight disadvantage, compared with married men). Rejecting the possibility of autonomy and opting for integration into a family therefore demands compensation. Although they are always consciously aware of it, the possibility of having an alternative identity does encourage women to take a critical view of commitment to a conjugal partner. There is no reason why they should not marry. But they do not do so at any price, and have no qualms about asking for a divorce if the marriage proves to be disappointing. Falling in love with a new man is no longer the only thing that results in the break-up of an established relationship: a lack of satisfaction is all it takes. Charlene's case is a good example. She lived with a man for four years. 'It was all wild passion to start with.' And then she began to feel that their relationship was falling into a rut. 'Our little studio flat, our little car, and our little bills.' She wanted 'a carefree life, an intense, crazy life' and therefore had no qualms about breaking off the relationship. Simply because her ideal was to find someone who would 'thrill her', and because the thrill had gone. The separation raised no problems: 'I discovered that I was free, and that my life was my own.' In contrast, being on her own again is a real breath of fresh air. And yet she has absolutely no intention of remaining single for any length of time.

'I'm waiting to meet Mr Right'. Spending some time on her own is no more than a way of managing her identity trajectory: she will remain on her own until she finds a better partner.

Separating is obviously not always as easy as that, and its financial and psychological effects can be devastating, especially for women. The rule is as follows: if her married life was characterized by a lack

141

of autonomy and by dependency, the post-separation period will be more problematic. Should her marriage break down, a financially dependent woman who has over-exclusively devoted herself to her family, who has no job, or only a part-time job, will pay a very high price for having opted for family life (Singly 1987; Cardia-Vonèche and Bastard 1991). A married woman may experience a relational dependency: there is a danger that a woman who is too attached to a group that is close, closed and dominated by the family will not be able to establish a new support network and will shut herself away (Kaufmann 1994b). A married woman's identity can be defined by others, and a woman who expected more of her partner than of herself will sink into depression (Francescato 1992). Then there is the issue of social dependency: a woman from a modest background who is dependent in all these senses will sink into poverty after the break-up of her marriage (Martin 1997).

And yet when it is the woman who decides to leave, there is always a feeling of liberation (things are obviously very different for women who are abandoned). 'When my life as a single woman began, it was heaven, despite all the worries' (Gisèle). It can be so heavenly that the project of forming a new relationship leads nowhere, in which case she is quite happy to be on her own. Manon, who recently found herself in this situation after the break-up of her relationship, even claims that she will be true to her new values for the rest of her life: 'I will never again put my trust in a guy. I believe very strongly that living on my own is better.' This is, however, probably a provisional statement, as all she dreams about is love. Besides, the way ideas about marriage vary is very closely tied up with the biographical trajectory of the individual concerned: the more a woman devoted herself to her family before the separation, the longer it will take her to contemplate embarking upon a new relationship (Villeneuve-Gokalp 1991). She needs a sort of personal breathing space. Manon is at just that stage.

Women are usually alone for limited periods of time. It is unusual for women consciously to rule out the possibility of a relationship in the long term, which is what Marie-Laure says she has done: 'So I've rarely spent a whole night with a man. No weekends and no holidays. I like being alone in my cocoon at night. I take a shower, take my make up off, and I have my evening to myself.' In most cases, some ordinary prince will come along and upset her daily routine. A new phase in her life will begin. The phases of the life cycle always follow, however, a characteristic pattern: the periods of time she spends on her own will become longer (Festy 1990). For young women, the transition from being single to being married is smooth and rapid. Older women may have children from a first marriage; they demand attention, and the women concerned therefore have less time on their hands, in both material and emotional terms. Women between 50 and 55 very quickly reach the point when the group of potential candidates becomes smaller. It is not just that they spend longer periods of time on their own; they will not find new partners.

Predisposing Factors

The injunction to be oneself leads a growing number of individuals to experiment with spending time on their own, and that is how the majority of them now take their first steps towards adulthood. This irresistible and indefinable urge to be alone is often stronger than the will of the individual concerned. Some people, however, are affected more than others and settle down to living on their own on a long-term basis (while others quickly close the parenthesis). Who are they and why do they do this?

This question allows us to emphasize once more the complexity of the mechanisms behind identity trajectories, which are a combination of internal and external, subjective and objective, individual and social factors. The overall historical trend is inexorable. The dynamics of autonomy therefore affects a growing number of individuals. But at the same time, the trend is powerful only because it affects more and more people: it is because some individuals decide to live alone that others follow their example. Each individual is drawn into it for specific reasons, and it is, in theory, possible to list those reasons. Doing so might, however, result in some mistaken interpretations. When individuals explain why they are on their own, the reasons are in fact often no more than excuses: there is an obvious discrepancy between the original motive (which is often of minor importance) and its biographical effects (which are often major). A grain of sand can be all it takes to encourage more and more people to live on their own.

A few examples are, however, needed to illustrate the wide variety of reasons why individuals become autonomous. They are deliberately given in no particular order. Some may be too deeply involved in their studies (and have an immoderate enthusiasm for French or maths), whilst others may devote too much of their energies to their brilliant careers. Such preoccupations can distract a woman from even thinking about looking for a partner; as time goes by, there are fewer and fewer men available and it then becomes difficult for her to embark upon a relationship. Two or three rather pernickety domestic habits, which may seem inconsequential to begin with, can become the start-ing point for a perverse spiral: the longer she stays single, the more engrained these habits become and, the more engrained they become, the more the conjugal hypothesis becomes unlikely. What common sense calls 'bachelor habits' are often the products of the trajectory effect rather than of an individual predisposition. Individuals who are sexually precocious tend, for example, to develop a particular rela-tional style that subsequently leads them to have a great number of partners (Bozon 1993), and that inevitably implies that they will spend more and more time between partners. The latter example applies mainly to men. So too does the tendency to hypertrophy sexuality and to place such a high value on making conquests, which is quite normal during adolescence, that it becomes an adult characteristic. As the individuals concerned grow older, the disillusionment turns to bitter-ness, and the bitterness is all the greater in that such ideas are no longer age-appropriate.

Common sense is quick to define a few typical examples that define the situation: the incorrigible seducer, the crazy old maid, the shrink-ing violet, the embittered asocial individual, the calculating egoist, and so on. The analysis is, in a word, reduced to character traits. Such traits do have a role to play, to a greater or lesser extent. We need, however, to understand that these psychological factors never inter-vene on their own; they become causes (reasons why people are on their own) only when the context works in their favour. They predis-pose, but they are not in themselves sufficient causes (Vexilard, cited in Mucchielli 1998). Chance and the context are in some cases the only things that do intervene. Look at the sad story of Gabrielle. Bursting with life and eager to establish relations, she always took the initiative and came into contact with lots of people. Her job has, alas, taken her to a town that is both conformist and conservative, and her lifestyle does not fit in. She is too eccentric and too warm. Elsewhere, she would have been a queen; here, she is nobody.

Predisposing character traits are not always mutually consistent and cluster around two contrasting poles. Shyness, anxieties about others and about life, introversion, dependency and low self-esteem (all of which are often bound up with inadequate social and cultural resources) make it difficult to enter into relationships and to be assertive: it is not that they do not want to, but that there is no possi-bility of doing so. Having an assertive character, grandiose plans and a high level of self-esteem (which has a lot to do with having a good income) makes individuals reluctant to commit themselves to rela-tionships: it is not that there is no possibility of doing so, but that they do not want to. Strangely enough, the 'too much' and 'too little' aspects of the problematic of being oneself lead, by different paths, to the same outcome: people are left on their own.

Angéla clearly comes into the 'too much' category. As she herself says, 'I'm not easy to live with.' She cannot imagine being able to sacrifice some of this inner ferment: she refuses to compromise. She wants to make her way through life on her own terms in order to be her own woman. It does not always take such conviction. Françoise is more reasonable and lucid, but keeps asking herself why she wants to go on being single: 'Perhaps, deep down inside me, I don't want to give myself to someone completely.' The impetus to be autonomous does not have to be strong for it to have major effects. Even when it is weak, the personal injunction to be oneself is in phase with a deep-rooted social trend.

The Impulse to Remain Single

The impulse to remain single comes both from deep within the self and from an indefinable social injunction, and it is as though it came from nowhere. 'The search that keeps us on tenterhooks sometimes gives us wings and puts an end to the grim conformism of not being able to do anything' (Carmen). The divided lives of single women mean that the impulse comes and goes in fits and starts. 'Waiting, hoping, believing, coming very close to the dream that escapes us, stopping for a moment, and then going on looking. It's like a never-ending pendulum movement that drives us on' (Carmen).

Certain aspects can be more clearly identified. Especially when the autonomy trajectory begins with a rejection of the private life model. 'All those little couples who are set in their ways . . . it's enough to make you sick' (Virginia). 'Being trapped into a framework is not what I call being alive. Being alive means doing what I like, with who I like, and when I like' (Hélène). The dynamics of flight are obviously clearer after a break up. 'I'm finally living the life I was meant to live. I feel free, and I have no obligations and no exhausting domestic tasks' (Jeanine). Even when the decision to break off the relationship was not bound up with any particular horror of marriage: 'After 25 years of being in a relationship, I plucked up the courage to leave my cosy cocoon. Not for what most people would see as a serious reason. Just to be me, to be fully and authentically me.'

One other aspect is quite clearly identified in the case of women: the question of equality. The greatest injustice of all probably relates to the issue of being in control of one's own identity (more so than to the issue of sharing domestic tasks or being able to take on public responsibilities). Once a woman commits herself to her family, she loses some of her potential for self-realization (much more so than a man), because the construction of her personal identity is to a large extent mediated through the family collective. Carmen is fully aware of the fact that she is experiencing what is in historical terms a new possibility. 'What freedom gives us, and the possibilities it opens up, is amazing. It opens doors that women never dared to open because they were held back by their husbands and because they had full-time responsibility for their children.' This is also the point over which male and female autonomy trajectories diverge so much. Women are much more likely to be motivated by a desire to be themselves and, while financial autonomy is a precondition for independence, it does not necessarily mean giving up the idea of love. 'That's the absolute dream: being loved without becoming dependent on a man' (Carmen).

Although it is the antithesis of having family commitments, being single is not pure freedom. The implications of being single are quite predictable (see Part II above). Not being part of the private life model is conducive to introspection. Being outside the family institution undermines the discipline of routine and is (for better or worse) conducive to a more carefree and open lifestyle. Compartmentalizing a network of relations and having control over its individual parts means that there are fewer social constraints (Burt 1992). All these elements are conducive to one particular quality: creativity. It is therefore no surprise to learn that many writers and artists, including some of the greatest, were single. Anthony Storr has analysed (1988) how the decision to remain single can be the essential factor that makes the inner world more meaningful, and can be a prerequisite for creativity. Norbert Elias (1993) cites the example of Mozart. Having been deprived of the company of friends of his own age as a child, his isolation led him to develop the power of his imagination, and that became a lifelong character trait. According to Elias, the structure of his personality made him a man who wanted to pursue his dream. Rejecting the normalization that was on offer (composing when asked to do so by a patron), he refused to abandon his own vision of what music and its social role should be: music should be written by composers who were in the direct pay of audiences that appreciated their work. He therefore brought his private unhappiness and social failure upon himself, but he freed his creative potential at the musical level and redefined the social role of the artist.

146

Unfortunately, not everyone can become a Mozart, and loneliness does not always produce such brilliant results. And that is the problem: being on their own provides millions of people with the ideal conditions for creativity, but not the concrete opportunities that would allow them to give it a substantial content. On the contrary, single people very often speak of the discrepancy between the potential they feel they have within them and their lack of real achievements and the emptiness of their lives. It is as though the creative machine was in neutral and producing only more mental fatigue. Hence the indefinable nature of the impetus to remain single: the 'search for the impossible' (Carmen) never reaches its goal. Yet it does seem that the issue of creativity is central to the autonomy trajectory. It is quite obvious that it is creativity that is its full meaning, as we can see from some of the life histories analysed by Erika Flahault (1996). Provided, of course, that we define creativity and the notion of a work of art in very broad terms: there are thousands of ways of being inventive and of leaving behind some permanent achievement in stone or fabric, in texts and drawings, or in hearts and minds. This does not necessarily mean that we have to be successful in media terms. Surely a beautiful love affair can also be regarded as a work of art. It seems paradoxical to claim that only the long-dead affairs that have been turned into novels or films can be works of art.

The problem lies in the discrepancy between creativity and the status of single people. It is quite possible that we are, in historical terms, seeing an increase in individual creativity. That would be quite in keeping with the growing tendency for identities to be self-defined, as the two things are closely related. There is, however, a disproportionate tendency for individuals to remain single. Although many single women do lead miserable lives because they have no alternative, others cannot really express their potential even though their experience of autonomy is more positive. This is a major feature of the autonomy trajectory: it affects many individuals, even though they do not want it to. They are by no means all members of the small group that deliberately chooses to be single and who are able to benefit from all the advantages it has to offer.

The Lesser of Two Evils

The propulsive force is essentially indefinable, and the arguments come down to a few minor details to do with everyday life. Why go on living this way? Singles find it difficult to answer that question.

They do, on the other hand, have a very definite idea of what living with a partner would be like. This explains why they constantly observe and evaluate family life: the flaws in the alternative hypothesis reassure them and provide them with an answer (in the negative) that their single status itself cannot provide. As with many other aspects of their lives, their views are, however, contradictory. Family life often appears in an idealized form in their secret dreams. But for the purposes of the arguments that justify their choice of identity, they look for and exaggerate its flaws.

'The very idea of being in a settled relationship makes me shudder' (Joanna). Its most obvious flaw, which has already been pointed out, is that the narrow framework of socialization marks the end of the ability to invent the Self, and the end of youth. It is not so much the family as such that they reject, as a mode of existence, a way of 'living on a small scale' (Joanna) and of vanishing into a suffocating normality. 'When I look at my girlfriends who are stuck at home with children, I really do not envy them at all. When I look at the couples I see around me, the way they live their lives gives me the shivers: an old-fashioned night out, a night in front of the telly, screaming matches. It's so confined, so petty. If that's what it's all about, quite frankly . . .' (Olivia). If that's what it's all about, the minor disadvantages of being single seem preferable.

There is still the hope of finding the one man in a million who won't put her in a cage: a real Prince with whom she can have a relationship that is free and open. Unfortunately, the familiar hypothesis is flawed in another way too: 'It has to be said straight out: the problem is that most men aren't up to it' (Babette). Angéla has reached the end of her tether. She is tired of 'the show-offs', the 'male chauvinists', the 'tortured artists' and all the other 'infantile men': 'What could be more natural than wanting to have nothing to do with all that mediocrity and preferring to be on one's own?' Laurence is not so extreme or, to be more accurate, has become less extreme. At the age of 35, she is now ready (or more ready than she used to be) to compromise in order to find the right man. She goes out on a lot of dates, and always tries in very concrete terms to project herself into a future relationship with the man she is with at the moment. The verdict is immediate, and it is always the same. 'I've nothing against couples, but I've never met the right man. I can't see myself spending my whole life with any of them.' Why are men so mediocre (or why are they perceived as being so mediocre)? Certain reasons have already been given: the social difference (the positions of single men and single women are not symmetrical) and their different expectations (men do not share the same view of relationships). It is this that leads Hortense to say: 'Men are of no interest.' Then there are single women's sources of information: because of their position, they tend to hear more negative versions of the story. Of course they meet men who, at first sight, look like real Princes, but before long they see the carriages turning back into pumpkins. They also meet a lot of married men who have a great deal to say about the horrors and misery of their conjugal lives, and about couples in general. Their situation has two effects: they are led to believe that married life is a private hell, and they know from experience that many husbands are unfaithful. Sometimes, they even have to reject the advances of a friend's husband. That is what happened to Odette: 'It makes me sick and it's enough to put me off marriage for life. The fact that I am still single has a lot to do with the fact that I know so few couples who get along.' And to clinch the argument, the former girlfriends who are now married, and who feel vaguely guilty about having betrayed the group, have no qualms about seeking forgiveness by emphasizing the slightest difficulties and problems of married life. The overall picture that emerges from all this information is both coherent and very gloomy. And it is all the more gloomy in that the selective listeners who gather it are looking for arguments that justify their decision to remain single.

'If that's what it's all about, quite frankly . . .' – Ingrid seems to complete Olivia's sentence for her – '. . . if the only alternative is being unhappy with someone, I'd rather be unhappy on my own.' It is unusual for a woman to take a deliberate decision to remain single, or to be unreservedly completely enthusiastic about doing so. But single women have only to compare their decision with the alternative hypothesis about private life to bring out its positive features. The contrast between the two is striking. 'Living with a man? An assault course! Living on my own? A delightful assault course!' (Geneviève). The most widespread reason for remaining single is a rejection of marriage. When they have a choice, they choose to be single for want of anything better. 'Fitting in with the classic schema does not suit me; so I have to learn to come to terms with the fact that I'm different.' Like many other women, Evelyne was reluctant to embark upon this strange life trajectory. And then she gradually learned to understand its intrinsic logic: it is an expression of autonomy and self-realization. 'I am now learning to come to terms with my loneliness (which I used to find so frightening), and I'm learning to discover myself (I never used to take much interest in myself). In any case, I have no choice: I'm on my own.'

The longer a woman remains single, the more difficult it becomes to escape that trajectory. 'I've grown too fond of my freedom'

(Laurence). For a woman who has reached a certain age, this is because there are fewer potential partners. It is also because they have become settled in their habits. The final reason is that they become extremely demanding. The alternative hypothesis is seen through the prism of their current situation. When single women are in control of their lives, the disadvantages of family life are even more obvious. 'When you enjoy being on your own, you become very demanding. That's the problem' (Angéla). 'Coming to terms with being all on your own makes you become terribly demanding: I'm not prepared to give up my stable life for just anyone' (Olivia). A woman who has settled into the autonomy trajectory tends to evaluate what she might or might not get out of a man she meets in very concrete terms. There are often two columns to the balance sheet. There tends to be a long list on the debit side. There are few nice surprises on the credit side. 'I already have a complete list of all the things I would lose, and it's a long list: my freedom, my little treats to myself, not having to share my pigsty with anyone, my dreams of being a writer. I scream as soon as someone treads on my toes. It would therefore take a big "plus" to make me give up all that. And the few sad men who do come along are regularly sent packing inside three minutes. Of course this one could fix my car, and of course that one is nice. And this one is drop-dead gorgeous (and a bloody fool). But there's always something missing, something badly missing. I still half believe that it will happen, but I'm always so disappointed that I'm beginning to wonder if Mr Right will ever come along' (Yasmine).

Two Trajectories, Two Identities

Common sense (which insists on believing in the substantiality of being) notwithstanding, we have to accept that an individual is an open structure and is constantly being reshaped. Embarking on one particular trajectory does more than change the external trappings of our lives; it changes us profoundly. Even more so when we are able to choose between two very different trajectories. This is particularly true of single women, and there are several reasons why that should be the case.

The first is that they are women and that, when it comes to defining their identities as women, society's injunctions are contradictory: they must go on being 'real women' and at the same time they must be men's equals. They cannot become men's equals unless they achieve financial independence, and that implies a commitment to work. But a commitment to family life makes it more difficult to focus on work. And some major bridges are burned when a woman has a second or third child. There is no easy solution to this problem. Although a lot of imagination has gone into them, the various measures that have been implemented in an attempt to reconcile women's work with family life have had no more than a limited impact (Fagnani 1998). Women are therefore torn between possible identities, and are constantly obliged to choose between the two and to define compromise strategies (Commaille 1992).

The final, and much more serious, reason is that they are single women. Every day, a married woman has to make choices relating to a thousand and one day-to-day decisions (how much time for herself, and how much for the family?) and has to try to integrate these minor variations into a single, coherent trajectory. A single woman, by contrast, is faced with a choice between two very distinct trajectories which differ in almost every respect: a settled existence and the burden of housework versus freedom and the lightness of being – two lives and two different personalities. They have to choose between devoting themselves to another and remaining autonomous.

The first trajectory is that of devotion, which draws upon the traditional model for constructing a female identity. It is a very simple model: a woman is someone who can transcend her personal interests by devoting herself to the family she loves. She becomes its irreplaceable mainspring. She is the angel in the house. Her identity is defined by that love and that function; her individuality merges into the whole she has created.

The second trajectory – autonomy – propels her into the unknown, and it is not easy to tell where it will lead her. This model is ill-defined but irresistibly attractive: a woman steps down from the old pedestal and begins to invent her life as she sees fit. Her identity is defined by her reflexivity and her dreams. This is such an intense revolution that few dare to look it in the face; women become autonomous by feeling their way.

151

—11—

WAITING

Dinosaurs of Love and Galloping Horses

I noted in the previous chapter that it is, paradoxically, possible to embark upon the autonomy trajectory by starting out from two very different ways of defining a personal identity. Women who are lacking in self-confidence and who have become socially dependent tend not to have the skills that they now need to construct a relationship ('It's not that I don't want to – I've just never had the opportunity'), whereas the spirit of initiative and high self-esteem make women reluctant to commit themselves ('It's not that I haven't had the opportunity – I just don't want to'). The outcome, however, is not quite the same, as the course of the autonomy trajectory depends upon how they embark upon it.

Part II of this book allowed us to look at portraits of women who are living on their own. We looked at their inner conflicts and the way they are permanently torn between tears and laughter, between the dark side and the light. They all experience this combination of the two sides of life, but not all of them experience it to the same extent. If their identities are fragile, the balance tips towards tears; self-definition gives them more energy and the ability to develop positive self-representations. Without wishing to be systematic or mechanical, there is an obvious link between this and their levels of income: women who are poor tend to be uncomfortable with their single status, whereas rich women tend to be quite comfortable with it. And singles are not evenly distributed across the social hierarchy. The average figures are deceptive: on the whole, the income of a one-person household is similar to that of other households. But we arrive at that figure by adding together the incomes of two very

152

different sub-groups; singles are either poorer or richer than the average household.

This new breakdown by no means invalidates the portrait that emerges from Part II. Women who live on their own tend, because of their social position, to display the same character traits: the warm/cold bed and the recourse to fortune-tellers can be observed in all social milieus. Every level of analysis of the social produces a specific and complementary body of knowledge (Desjeux 1996; Lahire 1998). While the overall view provides a cross-section, we begin to study two different worlds when we take these two sub-groups into consideration.

The relationship with the social bond is one example. Those who are single because they have no alternative tend to be part of a typical relational structure. It is narrow, local, stable and closed. They do not go out often, are in search of supportive and protective relationships and want to be supported by a familiar outside world. Those who choose to be single, in contrast, actively animate networks that are broad, open and subject to change. They dominate and manipulate their networks without becoming dependent upon them, and are self-sufficient. These two positions, which articulate identity and the social bond in different ways (either it is the basis of their identity or it is used instrumentally), define two different psychological types. Donata Francescato (1992) defines them in poetic terms as 'dinosaurs of love' and 'galloping horses'. The 'dinosaurs of love' are nothing without the social environment that makes them what they are; they expect everything from the other to whom they give themselves. When her husband left her, Odette thought for a moment that she would not survive: 'I have never been as unhappy as I was during those years. Learning to be on my own, suffering because of it and hating it was unbearable. It was awful: first the pain and anguish when the love of my life left me, and then that dizzying emptiness!' When they break up, part of their world collapses around them. They are still the same, but they have been diminished. They huddle up with what they have left, and seek refuge in the idea of the love they have lost. The 'galloping horses', by contrast, continue their headlong flight. Driven on by the sound of their own hooves, they smash through the obstacles that come up if need be, and constantly fling themselves into new projects. We will look at their surprising journey in the next chapter. For the moment, we will enter into the gloomy depths of the world of the 'dinosaurs'.

The Ravages of Love

The dinosaurs dream of being completely contained, but their dream is far removed from the modern trend towards individual autonomy. They are spokespersons for a world that is facing extinction. They are the dinosaurs of love because their holistic quest revolves around love. Love must sweep all before it and rule their lives. There must be no doubts. Love should not be calculated and it should require no effort. The way they view that emotion is therefore archaic too: Love is absolute and Love will save them. It is heaven-sent and they will immediately know it when they see it. So all they have to do is wait. Wait! They are very familiar with that stance, and they are still waiting. They expect a familiar environment to give them support and protection. And because they think Love is heaven-sent, they are still waiting for their unlikely Prince to come. The more they believe love to be something that is heaven-sent, the stronger the tendency to wait for him, and that traps them into their loneliness even more. The paradox is as follows: if they wait too long, it makes it even more unlikely that their Prince will ever come because they make no effort to meet him. Maggy never takes the initiative with men because she refuses to interfere with the workings of fate: fate must decide everything for her. 'We all have our fate, and if we are destined to find love, our day will come of its own accord.'

Maggy is 25, has her whole life ahead of her and has time to revise her views. Girls must be given time to dream. The problem is, in fact, not so much the dream itself as the way it clashes with reality. It is out of step with reality and the only solution is to adapt it to fit in with the real world, and that takes careful management. The process is exactly the same as that involved in looking for a first job. Continuing our education also makes us dream, but a brutal encounter with the world of work quickly brings us back to earth. I am not suggesting that we have to give up our dreams too early: working in a job for which we are over-qualified might result in too low a professional trajectory. But we also have to learn to lower our ambitions if we wish to enter the world of work at street level, just as we have to learn to enter the world of ordinary love at street level: without giving up our dreams too quickly, but without believing in them too blindly. Take the examples of Judith and Ingrid. If they really wanted to be on their own, everything would be fine, but they obviously want to be in a relationship. And because they have an idealized vision of love, the way they manage the discrepancy between dream and reality appears to frustrate their plans. 'The men I see around me are so conventional. So if it's not going to be a wonderful romance, it's not worth the risk.' Judith is 42, so shouldn't she be lowering her ambitions and taking a few risks rather than passively waiting? 'It has to be Him. It's Him or nobody!' Ingrid is out of work, distraught and in urgent need of support. Is she really in a position to gamble everything on fate?

For Want of an Alternative

Waiting automatically turns the present into a void. The true Self becomes the Self that inhabits the parallel imaginary universe into which the woman projects herself. At the same time, the flesh-and-blood Self is experienced only in the form of a temporary substitute: life loses all its meaning and substance, 'It must be just a phase I'm going through. I'm deeply afraid that one day I will look back at my life and see nothing: just a void and nothingness.' The idealization of Love makes the experience of waiting acute because it gives Love a face; the exaggerated dream of the Prince undermines the foundations of what is already a fragile concrete identity. The process is gradual. When the waiting does not last long or is a transient experience (which is very common), it is not problematic: what would life be like if we had no dreams? When the waiting becomes indefinite and when they deny the reality of what is happening to them, single women are plunged into an abyss of extreme isolation. It can even destroy their personalities. 'All this waiting is destroying me' (Maria).

There is an indissoluble link between waiting indefinitely and defining one's identity by default. Being on a low income encourages that tendency: the present is full of absences. This is particularly common in working-class milieus where access to a certain normality is the only possible basis for a positive identity (Schwartz 1990). 'No job, no husband, no kids, and everybody must be thinking "So what's left?"' (Flora). The norm of private life ('Husband, baby, house') asserts itself with all its devastating power because it reinforces the negative aspects of her actual life. 'The more I go on doing nothing, the less I can do anything. Sometimes, when I'm still in bed at midday, I have the impression that I'm nothing. I mean nothing to myself, I mean nothing to other people, and I no longer exist. I'm just me, and no one looks at me, and there is no one waiting for me. I can't even get out of bed!' (Betty).

'Husband, baby, house': the dream becomes an obsession. Once a woman has reached a certain point, the indefinite wait seems to be a source of comfort (which is in fact very deceptive). It is as though she

155

were leading two completely separate lives: her present misery and the very different life that might suddenly begin and which depends upon a mere whim of fate. All she has to do is wait. Her deepest thoughts reveal that her ideal is to be dispossessed of her identity; she dreams of being completely taken care of, of throwing the last vestiges of her autonomy out of the window, of giving up all responsibility for herself and of vanishing into 'the anonymity of normality' (Flahault 1996: 299). 'I dream that the nightmare is over, that I can rely on someone who will take care of me. It would be so nice to hear someone say: "Do this! Do that!" All Betty wants is to obey someone' (Betty).

The woman who waits indefinitely lives in an empty present tense. The waiting affects every moment and every detail of that present tense. Take the story of Raphaëlle and her condoms. Everything seems to get off to a good start: she takes the initiative in an attempt to meet someone, goes out a lot and has everything she needs in her handbag. Unfortunately, that is all she does. She waits, and nothing happens. The packet of condoms takes on a cruel dimension because it crystallizes her failure and symbolizes her lack. Just looking at that useless encumbrance reminds her of the 'painful emptiness'. Raphaëlle's life is beginning to be ruled by the logic of indefinite waiting. 'The condoms are always there. I never go out without them. I wait and wait and wait. And then there's the disappointment, the painful absence of love and the feeling of being incomplete.'

Sentenced to Hard Labour

'It's hard to meet people these days, either men or women; no one knows what to do about it' (Bérangère). 'I do try, but I just can't find a man' (Ida). Meeting someone and starting a relationship now takes specific skills, and developing those skills is a lot easier for someone who has more social and cultural resources at their disposal. This explains why poverty is increasingly defined by having narrow relational networks: those who have big portfolios of social relations are rich (Héran 1988). Making contacts and starting a relationship also requires a certain effort, especially for singles. 'If you are on your own, you have to try harder if you want to have any kind of social life. You have to take the initiative' (Amélia).

Never resting on one's laurels, always forcing oneself and taking new initiatives: once again, this stance is the complete antithesis to being integrated into a family, which provides, by definition, peace and regularity. The single life is a fitful life and a life that is perpetual

156

motion: inside–outside, recuperation–effort. Single women often make an effort just for the sake of it, in order to feel the impetus, and with no definite prospect of change. Because it is only by making an effort that you can 'furnish a life', as Claudia puts it so well. 'It's horrible having a TV dinner every night, and furnishing your life by going out for a meal with the girls, having Club Med holidays and spending evenings at Mum and Dad's.' 'You have to pretend you're happy. It never ends and you have to keep busy. I often think of those films where the hero is on a glacier and cannot go to sleep for fear of being frozen to death. You have to keep on the move' – Elodie, who is 'terribly lonely', unemployed and afraid that the cold will get to her. 'Always making an effort' in order to 'furnish your life'.

Inside–outside and recuperation–effort are not part of the same movement, and it may be helpful to take a quick look at the subtle links between the two. We have already seen that 'inside' provides the deepest rest. Being inside the inside is even better. It is even better to be inside a regressive and intimate envelope (bed, a bath). The hardest thing of all is the effort it takes to force oneself to go out in order to try to meet new people. On the basis of a rapid descriptive analysis (which, at a superficial level, might not be inaccurate), it is therefore tempting to equate 'inside' with rest, and 'outside' with effort. If, however, we take an in-depth look at the precise mechanisms behind the process that is at work here, it transpires that what seem to be the most obvious mechanisms are not always the most important in structural terms: we have to be wary of details and minor discrepancies that might mask a very different reality (Kaufmann 1996).

Comforting Habits

In the present case, taking into account the least obvious factors (the long-term effects of making an effort) turns the whole analysis upside down. Making a subjective effort and making an effort in the outside world have very different implications. We will look first at the latter. Either the efforts are directed towards the most sublime goal, which is also the most difficult to achieve (meeting Prince Charming at last), and are therefore almost always doomed to failure; or they consist in furnishing a life, usually with the help of girlfriends, in which case they last for only a short time because the girlfriends will turn traitor. In both cases, we are talking about transient activities which will soon give way to other activities, and which will leave few marks on the future frameworks that are used to structure everyday life. Matters are very different when the effort is subjective even though it seems to be more discreet. The goal is usually to overcome the exaggerated tendency to let things go and to regress (which, when it becomes a habit, leads to a disorganized personality) by forcing oneself to accept a minimal day-to-day discipline, especially in the domestic domain. It is, in other words, necessary to limit the excesses of the revolt against domesticity, even though it is an essential way of emphasizing the pleasures of the single life. This brings us back to the way a single woman's life is divided into two, as the importance that is accorded to domesticity is subverted by that permanent tension. While the pleasures of the revolt against domesticity can become problematic if it makes life too carefree, the discipline of domesticity can be a way of stabilizing and furnishing a life. A single woman who has reached this particular point in her trajectory (stricter domestic discipline) may (at last) find a sort of equilibrium and tranquillity: she can overcome the conflicts inherent in her single status thanks to set routines that stabilize her life in much the same way that a family would stabilize it. But in her case, there is, by definition, no family involved. She never asks herself why she goes through the same routines day after day.

This explains the famous 'funny little ways' of single women. They obviously stem from certain character traits, but the real reason why they become so pronounced is that they are defence mechanisms and are bound up with the social position of single women: in some contexts, imposing stricter domestic constraints on themselves is the only way they can stabilize their identity. It is the only lifebelt they can find in a stormy sea. Hence the feeling of relief or even comfort that can come from being trapped at home, once they have finally abandoned all hope of meeting Prince Charming. The idea that they might meet him was part of a different life. 'There was a time when I wasn't like this. I was living on my nerves, and my head was spinning. Every day was an ordeal: I was on my own and I desperately wanted to meet someone. Then I got used to it, organized my little life and my habits, and discovered something like an inner wisdom. Not complicating the issue is the most important thing of all' (Yvonne).

Habits are so comforting that they make it possible at last to find peace and quiet, and a certain equilibrium. But there is a high price to be paid: this wisdom is based upon a withdrawal from society and a retreat into the isolation of one's own little world. It is in fact the withdrawal that provides most of the comfort; the 'accusing finger' no longer has anything to point at. Public defeat creates the preconditions for a private victory. The tactic used by the dinosaurs of Love is always the same: they cling onto what they have. When, by some quirk of fate (a break-up, a death), their world becomes even smaller, they double their investment in what they have left. They therefore often find themselves staring at their own four walls (though a pet may also be involved).

The calm and the inner equilibrium they experience stem from their surrender to the constraints of domesticity and their total acceptance that they are confined to their own little world. There therefore has to be a ban on outside adventures and wild expectations, which might destroy the fragile edifice that structures these women's personalities. The mental exhaustion of the divided life has gone, but the hopes have to go too. In order to live in the present tense, they have to learn to stop expecting a different life.

But how can a woman who is on her own stop dreaming of having a different life when the telly and the magazines talk of nothing but love? She cannot help herself, and Prince Charming comes back to haunt her dreams. It is then, and only then, that disaster really strikes. When she was living a tumultuous divided life that forced her to get out and 'always make an effort', Prince Charming could cause only limited damage. Sometimes he could even help her to find a date or give her the strength to face up to the difficulties of her life. When in contrast, her lonely little flat is her whole world, going on waiting for him and living alone for want of any alternative drains her day-to-day existence of all substance. Waiting on her own does not end in tragedy so long as she is leading an open and active life. Nor does retreating into her own little world, so long as she is happy to live her life in the present tense. But a combination of waiting and withdrawal inevitably plunges her into extreme isolation.

Extreme Isolation

Extreme isolation is indissolubly bound up with the idea that there is no alternative, and that makes the emptiness of the life she is living even emptier. 'Emptiness, nothing, nowhere and no one: those are the ingredients of my life.' Salomé spontaneously draws a parallel with 'my girlfriends from the old days': 'almost all of them have a man, or even a husband and children to keep their minds occupied'. It is because she has no children, no husband and not even a man that she is 'empty', 'nothing' and 'no one'. Because she thinks she has no alternative, she waits passively and believes that fate alone will decide her future. If her Prince does come along one day to rescue her from this unbearable life that is no life, it will be because 'it is written somewhere' (Salomé). This fatalistic view of life is often extended to a woman's current situation: 'My loneliness is just there; it's an illness that has taken hold of me' (Adrienne). As a result, her philosophy of life becomes tangled up in knots and becomes Manichean: it is either nothingness and loneliness as a form of illness, or Prince Charming and deliverance. But if she waits too long and idealizes him too much, he becomes inaccessible. The emptiness becomes even emptier, and the 'disease' gets worse.

The loss of self-esteem that results from this descent into hell inevitably has an effect at the organic level. 'The outcome is tragic: I can't come to terms with it. I find it very hard to love myself. I feel that I've reached a dead end. I'm finished' (Dorothée). Salomé feels that she is living in 'some kind of time warp'. Her birth certificate tells her that she is 21, but she feels 'old and worn out.' It is as though she no longer inhabits her body and as though her identity has become uncertain and volatile. It is not just that she is 'old', or just that she is 'nothing'; her 'nothing' is also 'nowhere'. Ten or so of the letters seriously evoke the possibility of suicide.

Life can also become empty if a woman waits too long and shuts herself away in her lonely flat. But a flat can also provide a minimal degree of protection, even when the absence of domestic constraints does little to support her identity. The most serious collapses do not in fact occur when she is trapped in her own home, or when the Self's different territories disappear: no home, no job and no family. 'I'm in between temping jobs. So I've gone back to live with Mum and Dad, and it's another day on my own with the classified ads. It's a load of laughs' (Dorothée).

The loneliness that creates the inner void is rarely the result of purely relational factors, and the mechanism behind this destructive isolation is largely social in nature. The first blow often results from the loss of one's job, especially in the case of men. There is then one last hope of protection, especially for women: they can turn to their families. When they have neither a job nor a family, they can easily embark upon a negative trajectory, and slide into social exclusion and disintegration (and they can go a long way down). The loss of the last protective bonds is now the main criterion that defines social exclusion. 'Not being able to rely on close family is one form of what we now understand by living in great poverty: the poverty of those who have become disaffiliated and who become down and outs with no source of income and no family' (Commaille and Martin 1998: 99). Negative trajectories are experienced as histories in which poverty is closely associated with loneliness. Take Ingrid's sad story. When she was an adolescent, it seemed to her that she had a normal future ahead of her: 'I had friends, and I can even remember having a laugh.' And then it was one casual job after another, one failure after another, and she lost her self-confidence. She eventually became resigned to being unemployed and disillusioned. Because she could not afford a place of her own, she had to go back to live with her parents and, when her father became seriously ill, had to devote most of her time to caring for him. 'I have nothing. I have a roof [*toit*] over my head [Ingrid writes *toi*: 'you']. But I have no autonomy. Not even a corner to call my own. I don't really eat properly. Anorexia. I've not had my period for a year now. I've lost interest in a lot of things.' She is paying a very high price for the negative side of her lonely life but she does not have the usual compensation of being autonomous. And she is very aware of the fact that this is unfair. And her unhappy story helps us to understand that being trapped in the home is usually not the worst of all possible outcomes, provided that there are still some shreds of autonomy. The worst of all possible outcomes is having to devote oneself to others without getting anything in return, of ceasing to exist as an individual and still being lonely. 'My whole life has been a series of gloomy episodes: an unhappy childhood, a job that drove me mad and a non-existent private life. I have the impression that I've always been someone's servant and that I've never looked after myself. I feel myself being invaded by an enormous void' (Donatienne).

We have discussed the feeling of being trapped at home and the perverse spiral of exclusion, but there is also a third type of negative trajectory: there can, for all sorts of different reasons, be a sudden disaster. There are not necessarily any warning signs, and neither the individual's social environment nor her relational habits appear to be predisposing factors. From that point of view, Marie-Line's story is typical. 'I'd been living with the love of my life for 12 years. Of course we had never really been in love, but we were so close and needed each other so much that the symbiosis was perfect, and we were as close as could be. And then, all at once, I met Him, my lovely man.' For the first time in her life, she had fallen head over heels in love. She went to see an analyst who advised her to give free rein to her desire. And so she resolved, with rage in her heart, systematically to wreck what was, all things considered, a family that worked well, and to face up to 'his pain, my daughters' pain, telling my parents about what had changed, all those painful moments'. There was no stopping her. She acted out her love scenario, and it showed her how empty her previous life had been. Unfortunately, the Prince Charming who had seduced her soon proved to be very different from what he had seemed to be. He was distant and unavailable. And she suddenly found herself alone, without really understanding why, 'and with my career in ruins on top of all that'. 'I'm on my own, out of step with the rest of the world, not a penny to my name, so miserable and so sad.' She is so tormented by the lack of love that it is now impossible for her to go back to her old life. 'I'm very afraid that I won't find someone to love me before I get old.' So she dreams of Prince Charming, and plays a waiting game. But who is Prince Charming? Sometimes he is a handsome man with no name. And sometimes he is 'the man I love'. In the evening, late in the evening before she goes to sleep, she spends a long time looking at his photo and wondering about the future and watching the clock tick.

Negative Individualism

Robert Castel writes (1995: 462) that his 'chronicle of the wage-system' can be read as 'the story of the rise of individualism, and of the difficulties and dangers involved in living as an individual'. At centre-stage, we see a triumphant individual who is in control of what he is doing but who masks a parallel form that 'associates the complete independence of the individual with his complete absence of consistency'. Castel calls this 'negative individualism' and it can be defined in terms of what it lacks. Its paradigmatic form is the vagabond. The vagabond is defined by the 'fact that he has no place to call his own, which puts him on the other side of the mirror of social relations' (p. 465). The vagabond is a 'pure individual' who is 'completely destitute'. Vagabonds are 'the useless weight of the earth' (p. 464).

During the metamorphosis that took place at the end of the eighteenth century, triumphant individualism became a model for the whole of society, and assimilated negative individualism: 'Destitute individuals were asked or required to act as though they were autonomous individuals' (p. 465). Carried away by a trend they could not control, these people who were 'of no use to anyone' (Geremek 1976) had no alternative but to sink into anomie while still being under the impression that they were fully involved in the dynamic of autonomization.

Exactly the same process is at work in the very specific expression of individualism that is known as the single life. Those who are single because they have no alternative are drawn, despite themselves, into a trajectory that is meaningful only at the opposite extreme, of when it leads to a positive autonomy. Their social exclusion, the fact that they are of no use to anyone and the way their lives are defined by a series of absences propel them into an anomie that takes the form of an inability to act, low self-esteem and the unbearable feeling of emptiness that is so often evoked in the most pessimistic of the letters.

Even when, at the lowest point in her life, Dorothée feels she has 'reached a dead end' and is 'finished'; even the 'old and shop-soiled' Salomé and the Ingrid who has become anorexic: for them all, their irrepressible desire for autonomy reveals that they are still part of a major historical trend. In its own way, and despite the suffering it causes, negative individualism is (to some extent) an expression of a new aspiration towards self-definition. Remember Ingrid who, in the midst of the tragedy that is her day-to-day existence, still dreams of leading a more autonomous life and of having 'at least a corner to call my own'. Or think of the deeply depressed Chloé, who has just lost her last girlfriend to a husband ('Now, I really do have no one'), and who is sinking into an isolation that leaves her more alone than ever ('the worst thing of all is knowing that things won't get any better'), but who can still see a ray of hope: 'My life is so empty that I am learning to appreciate my independence, and to rely on no one but myself.'

'WOMEN CAN DO ANYTHING!'

Flight as Therapy

Unlike family life, which can prove to be a daily burden but which does stabilize identities, the day-to-day existence of a single woman is her own, but that can make it difficult for her to manage her identity. Retreating into the comfort of habits does have a soothing effect, provided that she completely forgets that her life could be different. Forgetting about that masks the fact that the single life is a life divided. If, however, that division is not forgotten, she must, on the contrary, learn to live with the fact that she is constantly coming and going between the inside and the outside. When she feels a sudden impulse to go out, it is actually a way of running away. Whatever form the flight takes, one half of the Self is always running after the other half. Life becomes unstable when it is lived in this in-between space.

This is most obvious when it becomes impossible for a single woman to construct a coherent and positive 'inside' identity; she feels ill at ease and becomes self-critical. 'If you stay shut up at home, you get bored and feel very down. In order to forget how lonely you are, you have to keep busy, keep on the go' (Maggy). Flight then has an immediate therapeutic effect, as it removes her doubts and restores her inner equilibrium. 'It comes over me all at once when things are doing my head in. So I put my seven-league boots on and off I go! Paris belongs to me!' Virginia suddenly turns herself into someone else, rather as though she had waved a magic wand. Therapeutic flight does, however, require a minimum level of energy and will power. Sabine, for instance, does not feel up to it tonight. 'I don't want to play the usual game tonight. I'm not going to the cinema or the theatre. I'm not going out with my single girlfriends to feel good about myself, and

164

I'm not going to try to get off with some will-of-the-wisp of a man. Tonight, I'm staying in by myself.' She is too tired, and needs a rest so badly that the fact that she will be on her own is of secondary importance. And yet, day-to-day experience has taught her that it is helpful to develop this energy so as to experience a more positive identity for a while. Despite the tiredness and the effort it takes, we have to 'force ourselves'. 'Sometimes it takes a huge effort to go out, even with girlfriends who are keen and begging you to do so' (Frédérique). 'I know full well that it's a way of hiding the fact that I am lonely, but I force myself to go out and I lead a hectic life' (Gwenaëlle). Forcing herself: the ethical imperative gradually becomes part of the mental schema that governs her actions. 'Whether you want to or not, you have to force yourself, force yourself to go out. You have no choice about it' (Albertine). Going out represents an elementary discipline and becomes the plinth on which her personality stands: she has to go out in the same way that she has to eat, wash, get dressed and go to work. The therapeutic effect is then forgotten, and all that remains is a compulsive habit. The sequence is as follows. At first, she goes out in order to feel better about herself (which immediately wards off her feeling of being ill at ease). Then she goes out for the sake of going out (the therapeutic effect is transformed into a code of behaviour). And finally she goes out because she has to go out (it becomes a categorical injunction). Nathalie often no longer has the energy it takes. But the obvious ethical need to go out, which has now become incorporated into a categorical injunction, makes her doubly critical of herself ('I hate myself when I spend an evening alone in front of the telly'). And Frédérique's nights out are almost a painful obligation: the only satisfaction comes from having done her duty. 'Often, after a night out that hasn't been that much of a success, you still go to sleep satisfied and tell yourself "I can cope with anything".'

These more or less compulsory nights out and sudden impulses to go out (because we feel uncomfortable in the comfort of our own homes) can take many different forms. The impulse to go out can be a positive response to its stated goal (rather than a way of warding off an inner feeling of unease) and can trigger a real desire, in which case it is neither a form of flight nor a compulsion. 'My nights out are my little treats to myself. I improvise. It's a kind of freedom' (Babette). But it is usually a response to some negative capture. Something is wrong, or she is finding difficulty in constructing an identity. For Monique, going out has become a minor compulsive reflex: 'Whenever I'm feeling down, I go out to buy clothes.' Salomé's impulses are much more violent: 'I try to cheer myself up with different kinds of fixes.

I overdose on nights out when I smoke and drink. I overdose on work. I've recently started to go for country walks at night.' That the reasons why she goes out like this vary is of secondary importance. No matter what the starting point may be, the important thing is that going out is a determinant element that gives a new impetus to the trajectory that results in active autonomy. It triggers, often unwittingly, a series of mechanisms that helps to intensify the logic of the single life. We will now look at that series of mechanisms.

The Logic of the Shell

Experience does not just teach us that we have to force ourselves to go out. It also teaches us that the therapeutic effect works on one condition: the woman who goes out must become someone else. Above all, she must not show that she has her doubts or feels ill at ease. On the contrary, she must make a show of being together, radiant and positive. And she must be able to show it. 'The one thing I've learned is that, if you want to keep a man, you have to play at being a woman who is happy, totally fulfilled and sure of herself. If you don't, they're off because men don't like whiners' (Brigitte). 'When I show myself for what I really am, in a mess, tipsy or sad, I can see other people avoiding me because they feel uncomfortable. So I pretend. I put on my mask and pretend to be the kind of girl who'll do anything for a laugh. I lay it on thick with the cynicism and the irony. So long as it makes them laugh, so long as they go on asking me out, so long as they keep on phoning' (Salomé).

The main purpose of going out is to meet people: friends, girlfriends and perhaps a man. To feel the warmth of being part of a social network, and of existing in the eyes of others. And the others in question hate any hint of trouble or problems. A single woman therefore has to make an effort to show herself in a positive light, and to look happy (even though she desperately wants to talk about her problems).

In order to do so, she has to hide half her life and show only the bright side of the single life. She lies only by omission. And yet the feeling of living a double life is intense; it is an almost caricatural version of the divided life. And the Self that is shown in its best light eventually comes to look like something alien. Hence the impression that she really is lying, which is heightened by the very real little lies she tells. 'I lie. I make up stories about the friends I have to go to see, and that reassures everyone. It's all an act' (Roseline). 'Why should I tell the truth when all it does is make me feel ill at ease and lonelier than ever?' (Dorothée). Katia watches the other Katia she puts on display in surprise, and is no longer sure that she can recognize herself in what she sees. 'They tell me I'm fantastic, that I'm in fine form. It sounds funny.' The splitting becomes worse when her friends or family join in the game of 'Let's pretend' more than she would like them to. Marie-Christine, who always dreams of getting married and having a baby, feels she is caught in a trap of her own making. 'If only they knew the effort I make not to explode when my family tell me – ever so kindly – not to saddle myself with a husband!'

She would like to be able to revert to a more coherent and sincere self-presentation: the image she is projecting really is a deceptive mask. It's a lie. The expressions 'mask' and 'lie' often figure in the writings of women whose dreams conform to the norms of private life ('Husband, baby, home') and who are single only because they have no alternative. 'I pretend to be the kind of woman who'll do anything for a laugh', says Salomé, who speaks of her own cynicism and sees her disguise as an imposture. When, in contrast, a woman takes a positive view of her single status, the mask is no longer seen as a lie but as part of a divided Self. Its function then becomes clearer: it is protective. Rather than speaking of a mask, Adeline finds just the right word: 'I've developed a shell.'

Although this protective mechanism is meant to be intimate and personal (supporting identity), its workings are relational; it is the mirror supplied by the gaze of others that raises Adeline's self-esteem. The construction of an identity is the result of a permanent transaction between 'identity-for-oneself' and 'identity-for-others' because the way we see our own lives is out of step with the ways those around us see it (Dubar 1991: 116). 'Identity for oneself' does not play the dominant role in this complex and changeable transaction: it intervenes in the definition of our identity in the same way that the gaze of other intervenes (to a greater or lesser extent). Our shell, just like the little movies we project inside our heads, is central to the process of constructing a self.

The principle is simple: a single woman lets us see the positive side of her divided life. Those around her hate scenes and are only too happy to accept this 'offer of a possible identity' (Dubar 1991: 117). And when the transaction goes on for a long time, repeating this exchange becomes a habit: her positive identity becomes a reality within the network of interaction. 'So I pretend, and I must be very good at it because my colleagues never stop telling me that I'm totally fulfilled, that I'm happy in myself, and that I have no problems'

167

(Marie-Christine). According to her, this is a lie. She is convinced that 'the real Marie-Christine' is very different. The real Marie-Christine is sad and helpless. The logic of the shell works slowly and, given her position, Marie-Christine does not feel its full effect. When a single woman is on her own because she thinks she has no alternative and experiences the utter dejection of extreme isolation, her shell becomes a complete lie: it is a mask that deceives. The mechanism that reinforces her identity has yet to be triggered. It comes into play only when the image she puts on display seems to her to be a possible part of a composite identity rather than a complete lie. The logic of the shell, which will subsequently take on a positive meaning, begins, then, in pain and sorrow because it splits the personality still further. The mask is no longer purely deceptive; it reveals remnants of part of a shattered Self. The Self is so shattered and so volatile that our 'identity-for-others', which has been stabilized in the course of our interactions, gradually becomes the major point of reference for our identifications. Because we put it on display so often and because it looks so natural, the shell becomes, thanks to a contamination effect, the pole that unifies the Self. What was initially no more than an illusion, or an appearance that we invented in order to protect ourselves, is not simply transformed into a part of the Self; it becomes the most authentic part of the Self, and the rest of the Self tries to organize itself around it.

A number of factors intervene before this shift occurs: the specific influence of interactions, the role the social bond plays in the way our identity is defined, and so on. Some, and especially the most physical aspects of our self-presentation, have a very direct impact. When a woman wears a mask in order to act out a part, the illusion has to be complete. 'You have to fill in the gaps and hide anything that might scare people off' (Katia). Doing this means making a permanent effort, both in psychological terms (trying to look happy rather than heartbroken) and in physical terms (trying to look fit, relaxed and, ideally, irresistibly beautiful and bursting with energy). 'Seen from the outside, I attract admirers. Seen from the inside, it feels like hard labour' (Marcelline). It may well be hard labour, but it gets results. Thanks to the shell effect, the most active single women really do laugh more, and really do become more beautiful and more dynamic. They put more time into looking after their bodies and their self-presentation, and spend more than most women on hairdressers, beauty products, clothes and going to the gym. 'My own solution is to feel that I am both beautiful and desired' (Olivia). The logic of the shell does not just transform their idea of their identity, which centres on the most positive aspects of the image they project. It actually changes their bodies:

they undergo physical changes and the rhythm of their lives and personal activities is restructured. When she divorced after 30 years of marriage, Marcelline was not in the habit of thinking and acting for herself. Learning to do so meant that she had to reorganize her inner life, which was now ruled by the image she wanted to project. 'Looking after yourself is not that easy, and nothing in my education had taught me how to do so. I'm always pushing myself, always on the go.' 'You see women with partners becoming flabby, vanishing body and soul into their pots and pans, and their children. Single women are instantly recognizable. They are spruce and tidy. We are condemned to being beautiful' (Babette).

The Paradox of Appearance

Once the mechanism that supports and reinforces our identity has been established, it becomes difficult to escape it. It propels us, whether we like it or not, into a much more radical autonomy trajectory. The critical shift involves what we might call the paradox of appearance. Let me briefly recall the previous episodes. Embarking on the single life encourages her to 'cope' rather than to 'wait'. It is a way of making her day-to-day existence look more positive. When a woman who can cope goes out, she projects a positive image, and it becomes her public identity. When her shell is so firmly in place that it becomes the essential pole with which she identifies, everything seems to be fine. Carried away by this dynamic, the single woman is less tormented, even in subjective terms. Her positive image makes her more successful at work. She expands her circle of friends. Her good health reassures her family (who would be even more reassured if she got married). Ultimately, even her girlfriends prefer this radiant vision, which makes them look good too, even though they do accept the darker version.

And then what? Could it be that someone is missing from this idyllic panorama? Yes. There is, in fact, only one person missing, but he is very important: a man. An autonomous woman (and at this point it becomes possible to describe her as such, rather than as a single woman) looks so beautiful, so strong and so sure of herself that she is both impressive and intimidating. Such is the paradox of appearances: when the image is too positive (and especially when it is associated with professional success), it becomes difficult to meet the man she wants so much to meet (and it is often because she wants to meet him that she makes such an effort to look good). 'I have a job with a lot of

169

responsibility, and many people envy me that. I make a show of being very strong and have male tendencies, and people also find me pretty. In a word, these trump cards do not always work to my advantage: men are overawed, not to say intimidated' (Bérangère). 'Some guys have told me that I scare them off' (Charlène). Marlène takes the analysis further 'I definitely feel that I am both attractive to men and repel them, at the same time.' An autonomous woman is so free and so radiant that she is indeed attractive. But the counterpart to her attractiveness is a countervailing force: she appears to be inaccessible. The same words appear again and again in the letters: 'barriers', 'coldness'. 'Is it because I'm afraid that others will see what's going on inside my head that I appear to be so cold?' (Charlène). 'Despite myself, I look unapproachable, even like an ice queen, whereas, deep inside me, I desperately want to find someone. I'll have to learn to let my defences down' (Jeanne).

What is a woman to do? There is no way out of the trap. 'It seems that I look unapproachable. In my case, it's actually shyness. But I'm not going to walk around with a sign around my neck saying "Shy"!' (Annie). Revealing one's fragility is indeed a delicate business, as it might disrupt the logic of the shell. The best way to pretend is not to pretend too much, but that is a difficult art to master, and it is often not enough.

'Women Can Do Anything!'

Carried away by the positive image they exhibit, the galloping horses construct, despite themselves, a biographical world in which everything centres coherently on their self-assertion. Embarking upon a relationship is the only thing that remains problematic. And their self-assertion makes that still more problematic.

We perceive the coherent identities of the most active autonomy trajectories intuitively: if the horses gallop even faster, we cannot even see that the single life is a divided life. But an infinite number of invisible ties tends to rein them in. Where are they heading? They do not seem to be going in any particular direction. On the contrary, there is a lot of pressure to remember the norms of private life. But their headlong flight is taking them in quite the opposite direction, and into the unknown: their ultimate goal is neither a husband, nor a baby, nor a home, but the absolute Self.

When a vision is too radical, it becomes frightening. Many autonomous women therefore try to find a compromise. Coming to terms with the intrinsic logic of their trajectory (and saying farewell to the conjugal hypothesis) allows them to lead better lives. If they are too assertive, they may find themselves becoming involved in some dubious adventures. The answer lies in a subtle equilibrium: finding a way to cling to the logic of autonomy while still maintaining links with a more traditional identity and with 'normal' society. There are various different ways of doing this.

Things can be bracketed out. The logic of autonomy is experienced with great intensity, but it is seen as something that will not last. This is common amongst young women. 'I'm quite comfortable with myself; living the free life is extraordinary, and my career promises to be fascinating. So I've decided to put my love life on the back burner for the moment. Once I've found a job and somewhere to live, then I'll start looking for "my" man' (Delphine, 28). 'The day I meet Mr Right is the day when my professional life will be no more important than it deserves to be. We'll automatically find the right balance' (Annabelle, 25).

A tightly controlled inner division can be maintained. 'I'm living a double life. In the outside world, I am super-chick and I let nothing stand in my way. Being "superwoman" is wonderful, and I don't want to come back down to earth for anything in the world. And then there's my secret garden, where I'm a little girl who dreams of meeting her Prince Charming' (Babette).

A woman's commitment to the logic of autonomy may be limited: she may just get on with a life without making a great show of her autonomy and without shouting about it from the rooftops. Mature women often do this and adopt an intermediate position; they neither assert themselves in a radical sense nor lapse back into their comfortable habits. This is autonomy as a last resort. 'I've become used to accepting it and organizing my own little life. I've become hard-hearted and I've learned to be self-reliant; which doesn't leave much room for a partner, should one come along' (Olivia). They take a fatalistic view of their autonomy. 'I don't expect anything from anyone, and I know that I have to be self-reliant. Too bad. That's the story of my life. You have to take people as you find them, love them for what they are, and without too many illusions. That way, you won't be disappointed' (Aurore).

Women who are enjoying a provisional, limited or controlled autonomy still feel, however, that something is missing. There is always the possibility of greater self-assertion, or the intuitive feeling that their trajectory is propelling them forward. It is as though the virtual framework for their resocialization were already in place; all they have to do is go with the flow. The temptation is all the greater in that embarking on a very active trajectory can be a way of redefining their identity: the virtual framework that will resocialize them is more coherent than the lives they are currently leading. One force draws them towards that ideal, which is both strong and clear. But another force holds them back: the norm of private life. The more they assert themselves, the more they feel they are being profoundly revolutionary and subversive, and it is that that makes them afraid to go any further. They are revolutionary when it comes to sexual equality. Although equality is problematic within the family model (Kaufmann 1992), autonomy makes it easy to achieve it rapidly. They are revolutionary when it comes to the basic structures of society. Women and their domestic skills (devotion) are still the cornerstone of the family, which is itself an essential basic element of society. Simply replacing the values of devotion with those of autonomy might bring down the whole edifice. The increasing number of women who are living on their own, especially when they are at their most assertive, is a harbinger of unthinkable social upheavals.

It is difficult to describe the internal development of trajectories, because they are products of two contradictory tendencies. In terms of the life cycle, it is common for women to be very self-assertive when they first find themselves alone, or until such time as they revise their views (or embark on relationships). The possibility of radical autonomy comes to look like just a youthful illusion, and they will fall back into line. But in historical terms, it is becoming more and more common for women to spend periods on their own. They are doing so later in life, are being more assertive about it, and this upsets the family order still further. The outcome is that their life cycles become inverted, and this is a new phenomenon: a life that began quietly and respected the family order as she waited for her Prince gradually evolves into an assertively autonomous life. 'I used to be like that once upon a time. I was waiting, as though my life had been put on hold. And then I discovered my freedom and the possibility of choice. Being on your own gives you the opportunity to really live, to think about things and to grow up' (Karen).

A woman in Karen's position is about to reach the most advanced stage of this strange female trajectory in which the Self is the centre of the universe. The autonomous woman has turned her back on conjugality, and her goal is to 'construct herself as a subject'. Such women often put a lot of their energies into their studies, into one or another of the intellectual professions or some form of artistic creativity. They are surrounded by their works in progress. 'I tell myself that I've had a lucky escape; I'm not stuck in the domestic hell of a little life with a little husband in a little house: death by a thousand cuts. I've always had my dreams about the freedom, writing, being in the movies. OK, so the results have not been fantastic, but my life is exciting, and I wouldn't change it for anything in the world. I have endless discussions with my friends and set the world to rights. There are also nights when I have encounters of a very different kind, and mornings that are full of promise: what shall I try next in my attempts to make a real success of something? I have an insatiable appetite for the future' (Céline). Marlène has no plans to write books or to be in films. But she too has embarked upon a radical autonomy trajectory. She is perfectly happy, very independent in material terms (plumbing holds no secrets for her), is very involved in her job as a manager, has a wide network of friends and is actively involved in community life. She runs a football club (a male club), and has become a local celebrity. So what about men? She is so busy and sure of herself that there is little room for them in her life. 'After a couple of days, I can't handle it any more.' Especially as she is very demanding. 'So if I do have to live with someone, he really has to have something extra. . . . All right, so it's not easy. I won't put up with mediocrity. It's all or nothing. I want to live out my dreams.'

Autonomy with Company

It is unusual for anyone to adopt such an extreme position with such clarity. Even the most assertive autonomy trajectories come up against the man question: a whole life without a companion is too hard to contemplate. As in many other domains, a compromise has to be found. Unable to have long-term conjugal relationships because they are in such a hurry that relationships are unfeasible, many autonomous women find ways of drawing up rules for limited partnerships. They are neither really in relationships nor really on their own. Some 8 per cent of women aged between 20 and 50 state that they are in loving relationships but are not part of a couple, and that figure is rising (de Guibert et al. 1994).

These relationships take different forms, but they are all based upon a partial commitment and are characterized by sustained periods when the partners are on their own. The relationship is no more than hinted at. Jeanine (who divorced her husband because she was disillusioned with marriage) is thinking along these lines and dreaming of what is now the classic structure of non-cohabiting conjugality.

173

'There's no law that says you have to be part of a couple. When I was married, I felt as though I was being invaded, and it was often disappointing. Wouldn't the ideal solution be to have a lover but to live apart, and share only the best things in life?' Gabrielle, who is also divorced, is looking not so much for sex as for tenderness and someone to talk to, someone who is supportive and who will listen to her. She therefore tries to imagine a new type of relationship that would be more flexible: long-term but not too serious, a sort of enhanced friendship. 'I don't want a casual relationship or a night of wild, dangerous sex. I want someone I can share things with, talk to and enjoy life with.' For her part, Gisèle has different ambitions, and her version of long-distance conjugality is different too. Her children take up a lot of her time and she does not feel the same need for just a warm presence. On the other hand, and at the age of 45, she still behaves as though she was 18; she falls madly in love and is always having affairs: 'I've always got a man somewhere in my life, sometimes two. Being in love when you're over 40 is wonderful.' She keeps her two lives strictly separate. 'Never under my roof.' No Prince ever comes to the house where her children live. They always meet somewhere else, as though in an enchanted land.

The idea is to experience all the excitement of being autonomous while still being part of a couple in some sense. The trajectory of self-assertion therefore appears to be slightly less radical. If, however, we look at it more closely, the effects of 'autonomy with a companion' are just as revolutionary. The concessions that are made to coupledom are offset by the subversive nature of the new conjugal model that is on offer. It is no longer based upon stability. And nor is it based upon sharing the same territory. There is not even any complete or exclusive commitment. This is an 'à la carte' relational and emotional life (Saint-Laurent 1993: 158). It is truly innovative, a 'living laboratory in which everyone is experimenting with a shared solitude' (p. 159). The private life model ('husband, baby, home') does not come under direct attack so long as the trajectories of even the most radical autonomy are completely outside it, and far removed from it. 'Autonomy with company', by contrast, makes a direct assault on the model because it offers a concrete alternative that can become an immediate reality.

In the interests of futurology, it would be worth listening more closely to the pillow talk of these couples who are half friends and half lovers. An important part of our future may be being decided here. They may not know it, but these autonomous women (and men) with companions are inventing the future.

CONCLUSION

An analysis of the statistics on the make-up of households leads to one inescapable conclusion: the number of people living on their own is rising inexorably. The social position of these autonomous singles is also changing. Once relegated to the margins, they are now present in the centre of the most innovatory entities: they live in the big cities, they are young and they are well educated. And yet the logic behind this development remains invisible, and no one has thought it through. Not the least paradoxical thing about it is that singles themselves can neither see it nor think it through.

This is because it is quite unthinkable and subversive. So long as the rise in the number of people living alone is described in descriptive, anecdotal or moral terms, the revolutionary nature of the phenomenon will remain obscure because the actors are not aware of the historical trend that is influencing their behaviour. Once the logic behind the trend is revealed, everything looks very different. It enables us to see current debates about the family in a new light.

These debates are frustrated by the adoption of ideological positions (Martin 1996), and are constantly reduced to mental categories that cannot be questioned and that slow down the advance of knowledge. 'It is obviously difficult for sociology to "denaturalize" the family' completely (Queiroz 1997: 122). The debates are often dominated by the deceptive illusion (which derives from opinion polls) that the family is, despite the destabilization of its structures, still not only a central value but also the main axis around which private socialization revolves. Society in fact clings to the family only because it is losing its pivotal role (and is losing ground to the individual). And it clings to it all the more tightly in that the shift is obvious. Hence the optical illusion: the strengthening of the family is in fact no more than a defence mechanism or a knee-jerk reaction in the face of what appears to be nothing more than anarchy and chaos.

The family is now at a crossroads. To restrict the argument to the couple, it is now founded on an insoluble contradiction: 'The ideal of authenticity, which lies at the heart of individualist culture, insists that we have to be in phase with ourselves; we are under an inescapable obligation to act in accordance with our own desires, and that makes the question of the Other eminently problematic' (Chalvon-Demersay 1996: 87). As for the family as a whole, the upheavals that are going on open up possibilities that have to do with our collective inability to reinsure the symbolic order of kinship for everyone. Irène Théry believes that it is, despite everything, still possible to undertake that Sisyphean task. Yet she still concludes that the tensions we are now experiencing 'make it impossible to predict the future of the family institution. . . . This has very far-reaching implications. We have entered a period of uncertainty' (1996: 14).

The family is certainly not dying. Far from it. On the contrary, it has succeeded in revolutionizing itself and doing all it can to coexist along-side the aspiration towards autonomy, so much so that it has become 'central to the construction of an individualized identity' (Singly 1996: 14). François de Singly emphasizes how and to what extent it is now our close relatives (partners, parents) who tell us what we really are and show us our most intimate selves. But although this reshaping of the family is profound and real, it is not enough to express the full potential of autonomy; the assertions of a more radically individualized Self are expressed in all sorts of ways. The new attention that is being paid to autonomy within the family is only one aspect of a broader trend that goes far beyond it and which, in some cases, represents a challenge to it.

Two trends are beginning to converge. Outside the family, the irresistible rise in the number of single trajectories results in the invention of new and supple forms of limited conjugality. Inside the family, the emphasis is increasingly on the individual: the need to listen to one's partner (Singly 2000), respect for personal territories (even on the part of elderly couples) and the emergence of forms of education centred upon learning to be autonomous (Singly 1996). This is even true of the memory of the dead, which now takes a more personalized form (Déchaux 1997). Both trends converge on the same goal: reconstructing emotional bonds around individuals who are in control of their own destinies. Non-cohabiting couples are, for example, the point where the two trends meet. They can be seen from outside just as easily as they can be seen from inside, and can be defined both as individuals with friends and people in long-distance relationships. The family is obviously not reducible to emotional bonds. It also inscribes its members in the *longue durée* of kinship, which is a private inter-dependence system and an institution that defines a moral commit-ment. But this vast conglomerate, which also has considerable historical weight (and which is therefore very slow to change), is also lurching in the direction of the same enigmatic goal, even though it is never clear just where it lies.

The characteristic feature of this trend is that practice is outstrip-ping theory; practices are becoming established before we have any clear picture of just what they are. The norm of private life is out of step with the times, and is evolving very slowly. While the simplistic slogan, 'husband, baby, house', remains the same, its content has to be more clearly specified. The statutory and unbudgeable husband is giving way to a companion, or a friend-lover who is the privileged partner in a closely knit team. The house itself is becoming more attractive, but it now represents a more personalized investment. Which leaves the baby, who is now the supreme value. It is without any doubt the baby who is blocking a more rapid reformulation of the norm. It is often for the sake of her baby that a woman is on the look-out for a family-oriented husband/dad and a real family home (the three terms are mutually reinforcing). The issue of children prevents us from inventing a new type of conjugality that makes more room for individual autonomy, and the traditional definition of the norm is therefore reinforced.

We continue to stumble on without knowing where we are going, and nothing can stop us. We are spurred on by one decisive element: the changing position of women in society (EPHESIA 1995). A woman is not an individual like any other (Mossuz-Lavau and Kervasdoué 1997). In historical terms, women's starting point was a situation in which their role (devotion) made them the lynchpin of the family and the private realm (Héritier 1996), whereas most men had already begun to assert their autonomy, especially in the public sphere (Lefaucheur and Schwartz 1995; Bihr and Pfefferkorn 1996). Because it is at a disadvantage from the outset and calls into ques-tion the basis of social organization, the dynamic behind women's new assertiveness (and the demand for equality is no more than one aspect of it) is, in comparative terms, much broader and more sub-versive than its male counterpart (Duby and Perrot 1992–4). All the more so in that the change, which inevitably has the support of all states that aspire to being modern (Schultheis 1991), has been very rapid.

A moderate assertion of women's autonomy can be reconciled with commitment-devotion to the family thanks to the support of the state and an internal reform of the domestic institution. But a more radical assertion inevitably leads to a social logic that is incompatible with the promotion of 'family values' (Commaille 1992) because it is a subversive logic. Women who resolutely embark on the autonomy trajectory (by flaunting a positive identity without the help of men or by inventing new forms of limited conjugality) are the most threatening of all agents of revolution.

They would, however, be very surprised to learn that. They are still under the impression that they are not actually part of a real trend. Many of the letters adopt, for instance, a self-critical tone and apologize for ascribing such importance to their trivial lives; the writers have no idea that they are moving mountains. The main point is that private life is changing in this way because there is no alternative. There will be a lot of tears shed along the way. Even the most active autonomous women are not very sure what they are doing. They are in the eye of the cyclone of individualization, but they have no desire to be there and do not understand the whirlwind that is sweeping them away. They form an unwitting avant-garde, and are footing the bill for a transitional period which has yet to identify where the new boundaries of private life lie (and which is a long way from doing so). They are condemned to live in a conflict-ridden and unstable in-between period. Most of them are uncomfortable about this. Stigmatized by the 'accusing finger', they huddle in their regressive envelopes, and are, for a while, comforted by their girlfriends. As they wait hopelessly, they become terribly lonely. No matter whether they opt for the therapy of flight or the logic of the shell, headlong flight is the only way they have of coping with this strange life.

But the further they advance (and therefore reinforce the overall trend which will influence others), the less clear these autonomous women are about where they are going.

EPILOGUE

And what if I were wrong about the Prince? The story can't end like that.

Will anyone believe me? I had not foreseen that there would be a story, or that there would be an end to it. Still less a happy ending, as in a fairytale. I have always loathed fairytales. When I was a little boy, they made me feel very ill at ease. I needed to keep my feet on the ground, and I wanted some straightforward answers. My vision of life was too chaotic as it was, and the last thing I wanted was more uncertainty.

That gives you some idea of how I was reluctant to get involved with this Prince Charming business. I took a dim view of that character right from the start (sociologists very rarely succeed in being totally neutral). But I became carried away by the logic of my research, and the letters constantly evoked that ridiculous archaism (despite their emotions, sociologists do, despite everything, try take an honest view of their raw materials). To begin with, everything was fine: although he played far too important a role, I felt quite justified in taking a poor view of the Prince. He was far, far removed from reality. When the letters talked about a white horse, it was obviously no more than an image, and I was not taken in. Indeed, it was no more than an image that took a literary form. As for real dreams, I knew perfectly well that the Prince adopted more fashionable disguises. Be that as it may, he was far removed from reality, and quite unlike the flesh-and-blood men that women had to deal with if they wanted someone to share their lives with. As I quietly got on with my research, I therefore collected stories about the horrors of waiting for him to come and about how it made women so terribly lonely. He was the source of all their ills. It was all grist to the mill.

And then, little by little, I had to come to terms with the facts. I went back to my file-cards, looked at the lives I thought I had understood in a new light and plunged myself (reluctantly and for the first time) into a reading of *Cinderella* and various other fairytales in order to complete my documentation. A different Prince – or rather the same Prince, because he was just as unreal and unworldly – began to intervene in a different way, and played an unexpected role in the story I was telling. As I wrote about and analysed the single life, a story really did begin to take shape. And what is worse, it was a fairytale. A modern fairy tale! ('The Single Woman and the Fairytale Prince'). But it was not the story everyone expected to hear ('They got married and lived happily ever after'). And, as it happens, it cannot be told in just a few words; we have to go back to the analysis in order to glimpse a happier ending.

*

* *

The alliance between the autonomous woman and the fairytale prince appears to be unnatural. They live in completely different worlds. She lives in a concrete world, and he lives in a dream world. She is very much part of the most modern trends of her day and is trying to take control of her own future all by herself. In order to do that, she has to make decisions and choose. She has to take stock of everything, including love. He, in contrast, has yet to shrug off his medieval finery, and expects her patiently to await her fate. He tells her she should be dazzled and swept off her feet by Love without looking too closely at what is happening to her.

This book has, however, shown us that dreams and reality can be closely intermingled. As for a mismatch between the autonomous woman and the fairytale prince, our analysis of coupledom has shown us that couples are not symmetrical. Being part of a couple does not mean being two of a kind. In a sense, it is, on the other hand, possible to live as a couple only if differences, or even opposites, become complementaries. Every conjugal story is a particular (and often very complex) combination of both tendencies. The alliance between the autonomous woman and the fairytale is basically nothing more than an extreme variation (opposition) on an ordinary exchange.

It is, on the other hand, a variation that requires some intellectual effort if we are to understand it. Let us go back to courtly love for a moment, as it can provide us with a few clues. For our purposes, there are, it seems to me, two important points to remember. First, in the chivalrous ideal, there is a very close link between prowess and love. Courtly love is an invitation to undertake a creative act, to transcend the Self. So much so that we might wonder which is more important: the love or the prowess? Then there is another element: the 'chivalry of love' is an 'ideal society' that is 'far removed from the world of the living' and in which 'everything comes together in perfect harmony to guide humanity's actions' (Markale 1987: 65).

Love is an extraordinarily complex reality, and it has by no means revealed all its secrets. On the one hand (and this is something we are not really in the habit of thinking about), it is a process that changes identities. In normal circumstance, our identity is grounded in every-day life, and can only be transformed slowly and to a limited extent (Kaufmann 1977). When we fall in love, by contrast, the old Self sud-denly emerges, and then there is a moment of uncertainty and indeci-sion. Extreme emotions undermine identities. And the emotions are extreme for the very good reason that identities become uncertain at such moments.

Strangely enough, the most active autonomy trajectories have a lot in common with this uncertainty as to our identity. Both are impulsive movements that constantly attempt to reshape the Self. And they are therefore emotionally charged: there are secret pleasures and there are secret tears. The impulse to become more autonomous is less intense, but its effects are more permanent. Whereas passionate love lasts for only a short time and then relapses into the calm feelings of the new identity that comes from being part of a family, the Self that is released by autonomy trajectories always feeds on reflexivity and emotionalism.

Which brings us back to the Prince. As in the ideal society of the chivalry of love, the real Prince is so handsome and so perfect that we can never meet him in the society of the living. He is therefore in an ideal position to ensure that the impulse never weakens. Love and the impulse to be autonomous fuse and become confused. They merge into a bid for self-transcendence. Love does indeed allow us to perform great feats, and it does make the autonomy trajectory more dynamic. It must therefore be used very carefully. The Prince, in par-ticular, has to conform to a specific figure. He is an intimate compan-ion who must remain distant. He must be a virtual figure who is a member of an ideal society that is apart from the world of the living. The woman has to succeed in believing in him without really believ-ing in him; what she thinks and what she does must, so to speak, run on parallel lines. If she believed in him too literally, she would go on waiting for him to come. Her life would be even more divided than it already is, and would take her back to the negative pole of her trajectory.

To put it bluntly, the Prince is not an unconditional ally of the autonomy trajectory. His role is more neutral. He reinforces the existing structures of socialization. If used properly, he can support the dynamics of the single woman's autonomy. By the same criterion, he can also ensure that it is the family that really socializes married women. He then ceases to be the ally who helps the married woman to transcend herself, because constructing an identity is an exhausting task, and becomes the figure who consoles her for the other lives she has not had, and who helps her to escape the boredom of an identity that has become too stable. 'After 20 years, there is nothing to do. You get worn down, and it becomes monotonous: 20 years of going through the same motions, with the same person, and in the same bed. Fortunately, I can still dream. He carries me off on his white horse. I can't reconcile myself to the fact that I will never relive the magical moment when we met, the initial thrill, the first glance, the first kiss. But I'm a loyal wife. So I make do with my dreams, and they are full of mad desires and frustration. That's my other life. With my red-hot lovers and my Prince Charming' (Maïté).

Just like the married woman, the autonomous woman has to succeed in living out her dreams, believing in them as though they were real (part of the time) and making a clear distinction between her dreams and the real world (the rest of the time). The exercise is all the more complex and subtle in that, in some cases, the dream can begin to fuse with (carefully selected) fragments of reality. Not in the expectation that a heaven-sent Love will suddenly take the concrete form of a real Prince who suddenly comes down from heaven to live the ordinary life of the society of the living. On the contrary, the starting point has to be the Self she constructs and the real world in which she lives. In the right conditions, 'autonomy with a companion' does give love many (brief) opportunities to spread its wings. 'If it doesn't last with Thibaud, that's too bad. I'll have enjoyed what's best about love. Happiness means being able to join together little bits of nice moments, both sane and insane' (Karen). Real passion (unlike the Prince who exists only in dreams) does not (unlike the meeting with Mr Right) allow her identity to be defined solely by her family. All the preconditions for an enduring passion appear to be there. They are created by the dream but they are still grounded in concrete reality. The only problem is that, quite apart from the fact that it is hard to construct, the real world is rarely radiant enough to give the dream a purchase. The trick is knowing how to strike gold in places where, at first sight, there was only glitter. Once more, this vision is very similar to the courtly definition of love: it takes work to produce the emotion. It has always been this way: we have to work at it. The dynamics of autonomy makes us more autonomous in every domain; the trajectory leads to the invention of a new code of love.

*

* *

The word 'fairy' derives from the Latin *fatum*. In the stories, they are the hand of destiny. Cinderella is happy to wait; it is the fairies who open the door to happiness for her. The modern Cinderella is uncertain what to do. A lot of women find themselves in the same position. But a new Cinderella is emerging. She is not willing to let anyone take control of her life, and has resolutely embarked upon the autonomy trajectory. It is therefore impossible to write the epilogue to the classic story, precisely because the future remains open, and it is still possible that the effort she is making will bear fruit.

Cinderella is no longer content to wait. She no longer stares transfixed at the palace. She is becoming a Princess. She can stand on her own two feet. She can go where she likes, and love is not the only thing she is interested in. And (just like the Prince in the old story, who was dazzled by the poor servant girl), she is from time to time touched by the grace of an ordinary but handsome man who crosses her path.

APPENDIX
THE GLOBALIZATION OF SINGLEDOM:
THE FIGURES

The rise in the number of people who are living alone is part of an unstoppable, large-scale and steady historical trend. It is also a global trend. Globalization is not simply an economic process; it also affects the most personal aspects of our lifestyles. There are obviously great differences between one continent and the next when it comes to family behaviours. But the desire to invent a Self (which explains the rise in the number of people who are living alone) affects the entire world, or most of it, and adapts itself to the cultural and historical features of each particular country. The diversity of its forms and rhythms must not conceal the fact that this is now a global trend, and that it is emerging simultaneously (albeit in different forms) all over the world. Some of the figures that follow might suggest that countries should be classified on the basis of how much progress they have made towards individual autonomy. That would be a misreading induced by indicators that reveal only one aspect of what is happening. Social mutations in fact occur often much more suddenly in countries that make the transition from a family world governed by traditions to certain forms of individual autonomy in only a few decades, than in countries that have been part of this trend for over a century. The figures (which sometimes have to be put in perspective) are, however, essential if we wish to understand the scale of the phenomenon.

The Unstoppable Rise in the Number of One-Person Households

A number of convergent developments have to be emphasized (it is becoming more unusual for grandparents to live with their children;

fertility rates are falling). They are occurring all over the world and they all have the same outcome: the size of households is decreasing, and it is doing so rapidly. It is, on the other hand, more difficult to understand, on the basis of the statistics, why so many people are living as couples. Whereas people presumably dream of love more than ever before, individual demands make it more and more difficult for them to share their lives; they are spending less time in conjugal relationships, and more time living on their own. It is not easy to make a clear distinction between singles and couples, as a growing number of intermediary forms (short relationships, non-cohabiting couples) make it possible to combine autonomy with a relative or temporary commitment. Nor is it easy to give clear figures for the number of singles. This is for three reasons. First, the General Register has become an unreliable way of defining them: old distinctions, such as that between 'single' and 'divorced', no longer mean that the individual concerned is not living as part of a couple (many serious errors are now made when estimates of the number of singles are based on figures from the General Register). Second, the boundaries of the new conjugality are both porous and unstable. Finally, relational alternatives (family ties, flat-sharing) mean that it is now possible to live with other people and share accommodation without being part of a couple. Most surveys are made on a household basis (rather than on an individual basis, because it is more difficult to quantify how many people are living alone), and the usual practice is to count the number of people living in the same 'household'. This form of calculation produces one startling finding: 'one-person households', the overwhelming majority of which are undoubtedly singles (some loosely defined conjugal forms slip through the statistical net), even though they are no more than one part of the broader picture. The figures for one-person households make it possible to measure the extent to which residential autonomy has steadily become more common over the past 50 years in the Western world. Here, for purposes of illustration, are the figures for the United States.

This type of change can be observed throughout the Western world, though not all countries began to undergo this demographic mutation at the same time. It always develops in the same way. It begins with an increase in the number of senior citizens who are living alone; this results from the fact that the different generations no longer live together. The figures then peak amongst young people, especially in the most highly educated milieus. The trend then spreads to all age groups as a result of the rising divorce rate.

In Europe, the trend began in Scandinavia (and especially Sweden)

Table 1 One-person households as proportion of all households in USA (1,000s)

Year	All households	One-person households	% of total
2004	112,000	29,586	26.4
2003	111,278	29,431	26.4
2002	109,297	28,775	26.3
2001	108,209	28,207	26.1
2000	104,705	26,724	25.5
1999	103,874	26,606	25.6
1998	102,528	26,327	25.7
1997	101,018	25,402	25.1
1996	99,627	24,900	25.0
1995	98,990	24,732	25.0
1994	97,107	23,611	24.3
1993	96,426	23,558	24.4
1992	95,669	23,974	25.1
1991	94,312	23,590	25.0
1990	93,347	22,999	24.6
1989	92,830	22,708	24.5
1988	91,066	21,889	24.0
1987	89,479	21,128	23.6
1986	88,458	21,178	23.9
1985	86,789	20,602	23.7
1984	85,407	19,954	23.4
1983	83,918	19,250	22.9
1982	83,527	19,354	23.2
1981	82,368	18,936	23.0
1980	80,776	18,296	22.7
1979	77,330	28,296	22.7
1978	76,030	16,715	22.0
1977	74,142	15,532	20.9
1976	72,867	14,983	20.6
1975	71,120	13,939	19.6
1974	69,859	13,368	19.1
1973	68,251	12,635	18.5
1972	66,676	12,189	18.3
1971	64,778	11,446	17.7
1970	63,401	10,851	17.1
1969	62,214	10,401	16.7
1968	60,813	9,802	16.1
1967	59,236	9,200	15.5
1966	58,406	9,093	15.6
1965	57,436	8,631	15.0
1964	56,149	7,821	13.9
1963	55,270	7,501	13.6

1962	54,764	7,473	13.6
1961	53,557	7,112	13.3
1960	52,799	6,917	13.1

Source: US Census Bureau
Legend: In 2004, there were 19.5 million one-person households in the USA. Whereas the total number of households has doubled since 1960, the number of one-person households has quadrupled.

Table 2 One-person households and single parents as percentage of all households in 2001 (EU)

	One-person households	*Single parents*
Belgium	25	3
Denmark	26	2
Germany	39	2
Greece	19	2
Spain	17	1
France	25	3
Ireland	24	3
Italy	21	1
Luxemburg	27	1
Netherlands	35	3
Austria	33	3
Portugal	12	2
Finland	40	2
Sweden	42	7
UK	31	5
EU-15	29	3

Source: EUROSTAT 2003
Legend: In Belgium, 25% of households consist of a single person living alone, and 3% of a single parent bringing up children on their own. It should be noted that modes of calculation vary from one institute to another. Eurostat uses rather narrow margins to count the number of one-person households. Other sources therefore give a much higher percentage for Denmark. French national census data for 1999 and 2004 give 31% and 32.8% one person-households, respectively.

and then spread from north to south. Table 2 gives the number of one-person households as a percentage of all households, and the percentage of parents who are bringing up children on their own. The trend is so regular and so constant across the whole of Europe that it is possible to make credible forecasts. Eurostat has developed three different scenarios for EU-15. The first 'individualist' scenario estimates that there will be 71 million one-person households in 2025, while the intermediary or 'reference' scenario gives an

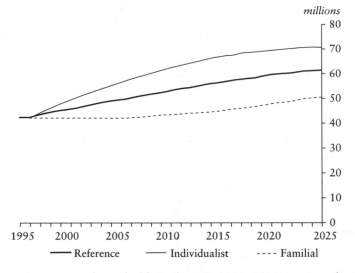

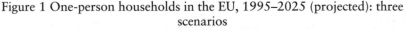

Figure 1 One-person households in the EU, 1995–2025 (projected): three
scenarios
Source: 'Evolution des ménages dans l'Union européenne: 1995–2025',
Statistiques en bref, Eurostat, 2003

estimate of 61 million, and the 'family' scenario an estimate of 51 million (see figure 1). Table 3 (absolute figures in millions) and figure 2 (one-person households as a percentage of the population as a whole) give the intermediary scenario's estimates for individual countries.

Although the demographic shift began earlier in Scandinavia and now affects large numbers of people (one in two households in Sweden consists of a single person, with or without children), it is now Southern Europe that is seeing the biggest rise in the number of one-person households, and experts predict that the gap will narrow. A similar trend is observable on a world scale, and especially in the urban metropolises of Asia: those countries that were rather slow to join the trend for the rising number of one-person households now have the highest growth rates and are narrowing the gap. In the case of Japan, their number rose from 11 to 30 million in the space of only five years (1995–2000).[1] This develop-

---

[1] Population Census of Japan, Statistics Bureau, Ministry of Internal Affairs and Communications.

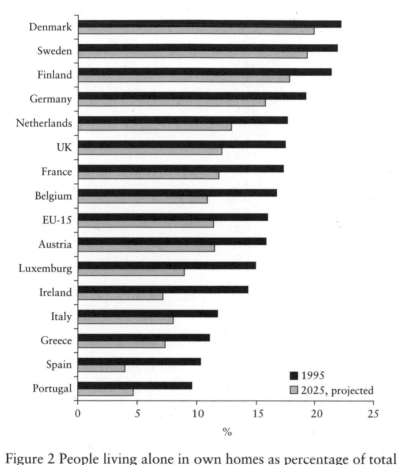

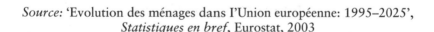

Figure 2 People living alone in own homes as percentage of total
population: 1995 and 2025 (projected)

Source: 'Evolution des ménages dans l'Union européenne: 1995–2025',
Statistiques en bref, Eurostat, 2003

ment is all the more remarkable in that it affects the young, despite
the obstacles created by the cost of housing and the importance of
family traditions.

Countries where this demographic mutation began earlier continue,
for their part, to see the proportion of single-person households
increasing, and there is no indication that the trend might weaken. In
Canada, for example, their number rose by 30.4 per cent between

189

Table 3 Projected number of one-person households (millions)

	1995	2010	2025
EU-15	41.9	53.1	61.9
Belgium	1.1	1.5	1.8
Denmark	1.0	1.1	1.2
Germany	12.8	14.8	16.1
Greece	0.8	1.1	1.3
Spain	1.5	3.0	4.1
France	6.8	9.1	10.9
Ireland	0.3	0.4	0.6
Italy	4.6	5.7	6.5
Luxemburg	0.04	0.06	0.08
Netherlands	2.0	2.4	3.1
Austria	0.9	1.1	1.3
Portugal	0.5	0.7	1.0
Finland	0.9	1.0	1.1
Sweden	1.7	1.9	2.1
UK	7.0	9.0	10.7

Source: 'Evolution des ménages dans l'Union Européenne: 1995–2025', *Statistiques en bref*, EUROSTAT 2003

1991 and 2001 (twice as fast as the total number of households).[2] In Australia, where the number of 20–29-year-olds living on their own has doubled in 30 years, experts predict that the trend will continue for the next 20 years (with an annual increase of between 1.7 and 3.1 per cent).[3] It is this type of household that is experiencing the highest rate of growth.

Interpreting the Figures

The spectacular rise in the number of singles has, quite logically, stimulated curiosity and interest. The press regularly runs headlines about the phenomenon. Journalists look for figures, often find them very difficult to understand, and frequently make mistakes. The most serious mistakes arise when they use the General Register's categories (single/divorced), which no longer provide systematic proof that individuals are not part of a couple. Another widespread error is to confuse

[2] Census of Canada, Statistics Canada. The proportion of one-person households (as a percentage of all households) was 25.7 per cent in 2001.
[3] *Year Book Australia 2004*, Australian Bureau of Statistics.

people with households. The fact that 25 per cent of households consist of one person does not mean that 25 per cent of the population is single (in the remaining 75 per cent, there are at least two people in every household). In, for instance, the EU-15, 29 per cent of all households consisted of only one person in 2001, but these same one-person households represented 10 per cent[4] of the population as a whole.[5]

At first sight, this percentage may appear to be simpler and more realistic. It is in fact much too low, as it includes children in the total population; in order to arrive at a more satisfactory percentage, we would need figures that relate only to the adult population. Although percentage figures are useful when we are comparing different countries or measuring historical trends, they are difficult to use when we are trying to establish magnitudes.

This leaves us with the absolute figures (as shown in tables 1 and 3), which are not subject to the same errors of interpretation. While they do quantify single-person households, they do not, unfortunately, describe all the other ways single people live. Not living as part of a couple is not necessarily the same thing as living alone in one's own home. It could also mean living with one's parents, living alone with one's children, sharing accommodation or living in an institution. Although these forms are less visible, they are by no means marginal when taken as a whole. In 2001, for example, almost one million people were living in shared accommodation in Canada (as against the almost three million people who were living alone in their own homes).[6] The number of young people who go on living with their parents until the age of 30 or 35 continues to rise, and is now quite high, especially in countries that still see marriage as the classic mode of conjugality. When people marry later and when society finds it unacceptable for people to live alone in their own homes or to cohabit, living with their parents is often the only solution. In the countries of

---

[4] This average allows us to place certain countries that have recently joined the EU and some that have applied to join:

Estonia	12%
Cyprus	5% (2003)
Latvia	9% (2002)
Lithuania	10% (2002)
Hungary	9%
Poland	5%
Slovenia	7% (2002)
Slovakia	9% (2003)
Croatia	9% (2003)
Romania	8% (2002)

[5] Figure 1 refers to the population as a whole. This explains why the percentages are lower than those given in table 2.

[6] Census of Canada, Statistics Canada.

Mediterranean Europe, for example, these figures make it more obvious that many young people aspire to personal autonomy than the statistics on the number of one-person households.[7] Table 5 confirms the findings of table 4. In Portugal, for example, only 27 per cent of women aged between 24 and 29 are living with partners. This is the lowest figure in Europe (76 per cent of Danish women of the same age do so), but only 4 per cent of them live alone in their own homes.

The same indicators cannot be used to estimate the number of singles in different countries. As we shall see, for example, in the countries of the Maghreb, the assertion of women's autonomy usually takes the form of deferred marriage, but it is very unusual for a woman to live on her own in her own home. The age at which women marry and the percentage of single women in different age groups are therefore decisive factors. In countries where living on one's own or as part of an unmarried couple is commonplace, the most reliable method of calculation is to count the number of one-person households. If, however, we wish to obtain a more accurate picture of the total number of people living on their own, other categories have to be introduced. The three main categories are:

1 Young adults living in the parental home.
2 People in shared accommodation.
3 Parents bringing up children on their own.

Then there are other more marginal groups. There are 'children' of 40, 50 and even 60 who are still living with their parents on either a temporary basis (after a divorce, for example) or on a permanent basis. There are people living in various institutions (retirement homes, monasteries, etc). And there are the homeless who, in Western societies, often have no family. In most European countries, the sum total of these various groups gives a figure close to that for one-person households. If we wish to have a more accurate picture of the total number of single people and an absolute figure that allows us to avoid gross errors of interpretation, we therefore have to double their numbers. We still have to make a more accurate calculation. Doing so requires work, as the available indicators are complex to use. And we cannot under any circumstances arrive at the absolutely net figures that all statisticians dream of. This is because the indicators are

---

[7] The fact that they go on living in the parental home for longer can of course have other meanings. Especially when the economic crisis leaves no other choice, or when young people are afraid of committing themselves fully to adulthood. On the example of Italy, see Becker et al. 2005.

Table 4 Percentage of young single people living in parental home

	Men 20–24		Women 20–24		Men 25–29		Women 25–29	
	1986	1994	1986	1994	1986	1994	1986	1994
Spain	88.1	91.5	76.1	84.3	53.2	64.8	35.3	47.6
Greece	76.5	79.3	52.3	62.3	53.8	62.6	23.8	32.1
Italy	87.8	92.2	70.4	82.4	49.6	66.0	25.5	44.1

Source: Cordon and Antonio 1997
In 1994, 47.6% of Spanish women aged between 24 and 29 were living with their parents. Women marry younger than men and therefore leave the parental home earlier. But both men and women are marrying later, and more of them live with their parents when they are still single.

being used to measure something that is particularly elusive, and it will become increasingly elusive now that couples are more concerned about the authenticity of their feelings than the stability of institutions. We cannot quantify love, and nor can we divide it into categories.

Late Marriage

As we shall soon see, the growing assertion of women's autonomy takes many different forms in different parts of the world. It is therefore all the more important not to concentrate solely on one-person households. That is certainly a radical form of the single life, but it does not tell us everything. We also have to use other demographic indicators, which can be very eloquent in certain socio-cultural contexts. Divorce rates are one example. In countries where the family was solidly based upon the institution of marriage, becoming part of the historical trend towards individual autonomy was often signalled in spectacular fashion by a sudden increase in divorciality (annual number of divorces per 1,000 inhabitants). The highest rates are currently to be observed in the Czech Republic (3.2), Ukraine (3.7), Belarus (4.1) and, highest of all, Russia (5.3).[8] These are higher than the rates in the EU-15 countries.[9] All societies experience an initial phase in which marriage – the institution on which coupledom is based – has to break down if individuals are to assert their

[8] *Statistical Yearbook of the Economic Commission for Europe 2005*, UNECE.
[9] The USA is something of a special case, as there are both a lot of marriages and a lot of divorces (4.2 per 100,000).

autonomy. In a second phase, marriages break down because individuals experiment with non-institutionalized conjugality. Finally, they commit themselves when they feel ready to do so and are sure that they have found the right partner. The number of cohabiting couples who break up then rises steeply, while the number of divorces continues to rise but does so more slowly. Countries such as Estonia, Latvia and Lithuania, for example, saw their steepest rise between 1990 and 2000, but are now approaching the average European rate.

I have already said something about the deferral of marriage in connection with those young adults who are living with their parents for longer. This is an essential indicator, and in many countries it says as much about the growing desire for autonomy as the number of one-person households. The age at which women marry is rising steadily year by year all over the world, as is the age at which they have their first child. While this phenomenon is closely associated with the fact that women are now spending more time in education, it is also a first and unavoidable precondition for the assertion of their autonomy. This is obvious in societies in which women used to marry very young and were subordinate to their all-powerful husbands. It may appear less obvious in societies that have been part of the trend for several decades, especially as the fact of not being married does not prevent women from being in relationships or having children. Yet the age at which they marry continues to rise, even in Scandinavia,[10] and there are reasons for this. In these countries, marriage is increasingly becoming a symbolic act and, above all, coming to signal a change of identity (commitment to a family project). As a result, it is becoming more difficult for women to assert their autonomy, even in Sweden. When the age at which women marry rises in any type of society, it means that deferring marriage has become a way of prolonging that part of the life cycle that is most conducive to self-invention, be it in Stockholm, Tokyo, Caracas or Tripoli.

A Short World Tour

The dry, disembodied figures can give the impression that we are witnessing a linear trend towards ever-greater personal autonomy. Yet

[10] The average age for marriage rose from 30.8 years to 32.3 in Denmark between 1993 and 2003, from 28.5 to 30.4 in Finland, from 30.6 to 32.9 in Sweden and from 29.3 to 31.6 in Norway. Source: Eurostat.

although the main trend in societies all over the world is indeed moving in that direction, it takes specific forms in different countries. We are currently witnessing an unprecedented phenomenon; cultural globalization means that the whole world is caught up in the same process, even though different countries have very different histories and cultural points of reference. That is why it is basically a mistake to see things in terms of advances and retreats, and why it will be an even greater mistake to do so in the future. As cultural globalization depends upon interconnections between countries, the trend (which can take many different forms) is becoming simultaneous. We are not talking about a clash of civilizations, but about positional wars and an attempt to find answers to questions that are being asked all over the world.

The trend towards ever-greater personal autonomy is not, moreover, the only factor at work. The rise of autonomy and personal reflexivity (Giddens 1991) in fact inevitably also trigger quite the opposite trend, or a search for meaning and stable points of reference, which often take the form of beliefs, either 'soft' or totalizing. The thirst for spirituality and the temptations of fundamentalism are not archaisms. They are pure products of our advanced modernity. All over the world, people are going back to traditions, religions and cultures, and stimulating a demand for meaning and reassurance as to their identity on the part of individuals who have been undermined by their own self-doubts (Kaufmann 2004). The tensions between critical autonomy and the need to have one's identity confirmed are particularly acute in Muslim countries, especially when it comes to the issue of the position of women. The intensity of the debates and the struggles to grant Muslim women more autonomy is, as it happens, a perfect illustration of the erroneous nature of the linear vision of the trend towards individual autonomy. These women are not 'backward'; on the contrary, they are in the front line.

Taking only one-person households into account is tantamount to overlooking the extent to which Muslim societies are now being seriously undermined by the growing autonomy of women. The continued influence of the family means that there can be no cohabitation or conjugal life outside marriage. In Morocco, for instance, single mothers are still violently stigmatized (Naamane and Gessous 2005). At the same time, women are subverting the individual/family relationship from within by studying longer and marrying later. In countries such as Egypt or even Saudi Arabia, the reassertion of an Islamic identity that forces women to wear the veil must not conceal this underlying mutation. The revolution in behaviours is even more

195

obvious in the Maghreb. In 1965, women married at the age of 18 in Algeria and Morocco, and at 19 in Tunisia (Dumont 2005). In 2000, they married at 28 in all three countries, and they are now close to the average for European countries. Within the space of a single generation, they are remaining single for 10 more years: the change has been spectacular! Women want to choose their own husbands, and they are having considerably fewer children – 2.2 per woman in Tunisia in 2003 (Dumont 2005); in Lebanon, the fertility index has actually fallen to 1.9. Women are remaining single for longer, and marriage no longer means that they lose all their individuality (Samandi 2006). The same mutation can be observed in the passionate debates that are taking place over divorce. Islam has traditionally been more tolerant of divorce than Christianity, but it takes the form of repudiation, which gives the discretionary power to men. There are therefore two things at stake in these debates: making divorce easier and giving women greater rights. Tunisia enshrined equal rights in its Constitution as early as 1956.[11] Morocco's new family code of 2003 marked an important breakthrough. Although Algeria is somewhat behind Tunisia and Morocco, changes are quietly taking place; the grounds on which women can ask for a divorce have been defined more broadly (Hammadi 2004). These social forces are obviously not all converging in the same direction. The quest for identity, which is increasingly important, may reactivate aspects of tradition that will allow men to defend, or even re-establish, the power they are in danger of losing. In the West, the trend towards greater autonomy is leading us into the mists of existential uncertainty; in the Maghreb, it takes the form of a fight against enemies who can be clearly identified.

A similar analysis could be applied to Turkey, the difference being that in the big cities, and especially Istanbul, single-person households are becoming less and less of a marginal phenomenon. In 1988, they represented 3.3 per cent of all households; in 1998, they represented 4.9 per cent of the total (Ünalan 2002). As in all other countries, the trend began with the old. But in the last few years, significant numbers of young people in urban milieus have begun to live alone in their own homes.

Not all Muslim countries are experiencing the trend towards greater individual autonomy with the same intensity. The differences between them are not really a reflection of the degree to which religion retains

---

[11] Even so, women are not actually the equals of men, especially in terms of their ability to inherit property (Samandi 2003).

its hold, as even its most radical expressions can represent a very modern quest for an identity. The split has more to do with the preservation of traditions which confine women to subordinate roles. The two indicators we have already mentioned (women's level of education, and the deferral of marriage) are essential here. They allow us to conclude, for example, that Pakistan and Afghanistan have yet to become part of the trend, or have done so to only a limited extent (women marry very young and are poorly educated). And yet the signs are unmistakable in Bangladesh, despite the country's poverty: even though women still marry very young, the age at which they do has risen by several years (19 in 2003), and the number of girls attending school rose by 90 per cent between 1980 and 2000, though it is true that the country's schools are very basic (Dumont 2005). The same trends are even more clearly observable in Indonesia, and they are having the usual effect: on average, women are having fewer children.

The weight of the traditions that strictly control individual behaviour through the intermediary of the family institution also explains why India has yet to undergo this demographic and anthropological mutation, but there are in addition other reasons why it is making such slow progress. The trend towards greater personal autonomy, which is breaking the hold of the family, mainly affects women. Now, in both India and China, sexual discrimination at birth favours boys at the expense of girls: there are fewer women than men. This imbalance means that more men are looking for marriage partners. Women therefore find it difficult to resist their demands, and continue to commit themselves to marriage at a very young age, especially as they are poorly educated and as it is usually their families who take the decision. The situation is, however, changing very rapidly in the big cities, mainly because India now sees that education is a precondition for development. Besides, the vast majority of poorly educated women who are still subject to their families' decisions have succeeded in expressing their aspirations towards autonomy. They have done so in an astonishing and roundabout way: through fiction. During the great age of European romanticism, love poetry and romances were a tool for individual emancipation from the hold of the family. In modern India, the huge success of Bollywood movies serves the same function. Most of them tell the story of a boy and a girl who choose one another freely and in the name of love, notwithstanding the plans of their families.

Latin America paints a different picture of the question that concerns us. It is obviously impossible to sum up in a few lines the enormous complexity of a sub-continent in which there is a great contrast between the big cities, where the lifestyles of the middle classes are similar to those of Europeans, and the vast rural zones and impoverished urban areas where the situation is very different. On average, the indicators for girls' education and the age at which women marry show that there is a marked trend towards greater personal autonomy here too. But the trend is highly differentiated in social terms, and is creating two very different worlds. They do have one behavioural characteristic in common: conjugal mobility. Coming to terms with one's autonomy and experiencing it as something positive requires cultural and financial resources. In a situation of great poverty, individuals tend, in contrast, to become autonomous because there is no alternative, and that leads to social disruption. The data for Colombia and Venezuela reveal that conjugal unions are very unstable. In Argentina, many young men are candidates for emigration (Dumont 2005). In Brazil, girls from disadvantaged backgrounds find it difficult to gain access to contraception, and their educational prospects are poor (Heilborn et al. 2006).

In contrast, Asia, like the Muslim countries, is characterized by the continued – and strong – hold of the family.[12] Its hold is, however, coming into sharp conflict with a quest for autonomy that has been exacerbated by economic and urban development. I have already cited the example of Singapore. Countries such as South Korea and even Thailand are also moving in the direction of greater individualization, but that is because women are marrying later rather than because they are achieving residential autonomy. As for Japan, it should be the subject of a chapter in itself. Family values still have great influence, but marriage traps women into domestic roles that subordinate them to husbands who are never at home (Jolivet 2002). As in Southern Europe, the favourite tactic adopted by women who wish to expand their autonomous space is to put off getting married, while living alone in their own homes or with their parents. In 1999, the academic sociologist Masahiro Yamada published a polemical book denouncing the 'parasitic singles' who were living off the older generation, and claiming that they were undermining Japan's economic growth by reducing the birth rate, which is now one of the lowest in the world (Yamada 1999). The book was a great success and became the subject of passionate debates. A polemic about singles helped to reveal the social changes that Japan is experiencing.

---

[12] There are, however, exceptions, such as the Philippines. Although the majority of the population is Christian, celibacy, cohabitation and divorce are very common (Dumont 2005).

Although this world tour has been too rapid and remains incomplete, it is difficult to end it without saying a word about the United States. Given the extreme diversity of familial behaviours in the country's different ethnic groups (Blacks, for example, are still feeling the effects of the period of slavery which destroyed the structure of their families (Dumont 2005)), it is difficult to be concise. For once, it is not white America that is setting the fashion for the rest of the world when it comes to family lifestyles. As I have often remarked, the main influence comes from Northern Europe. The specificity of the United States is the continued importance of marriage (and the high divorce rate that goes with it), whereas Scandinavians tend to cohabit. It might be objected that there is little difference between a couple with a marriage certificate and a couple without one. That little difference does, however, put women in very different positions. At a time when the search for Mr Right was still a national sport that preoccupied the minds of American women, Scandinavian women were beginning to win their autonomy with the support of the welfare state (Daly and Rake 2003). The specificity of the USA has become less pronounced and everyone is now asking much the same question on both sides of the Atlantic: how can we live with someone and still be ourselves? No one has found the miracle cure that provides the perfect answer.

Mail-Order Brides

In the age of the Internet and satellite television, we increasingly live in a single world in which we all react in the same way when a major event takes place anywhere on the planet. We glean ideas, images and points of reference from the flow of data that inundates us as soon as we have the means to log on. It takes only one click to open up a world from which we can extract our culture or territory. With only one click, historical and cultural differences appear to be erased, as though by magic. The Internet is accelerating the globalization of lifestyles. The fact that the dating market is now organized on an international basis is, from that point of view, emblematic. Several hundred commercial sites now structure the new market in 'mail-order marriages'. They are expanding rapidly and are making considerable profits. At first sight, the most striking thing about this is the dizzying breakdown of old barriers that is facilitated by technological innovations. It allows large numbers of individuals to escape the local traps in which they used to be caught. Everyone seems to be able to find someone with whom he or she gets on. It is as though their interlocutor, who at least lives up to their expectations and is easily accessible, lived just down the street. But an analysis quickly reveals the extent to which the exchange is unbalanced and characterized by a North/South divide (and it has to be said that the South now includes Eastern Europe).[13] Nicole Constable (2003) paints a damning picture of exchanges between the United States and Asia, and the Philippines in particular.[14] American men (or at least white American men with good incomes) are looking for particular kinds of women, and have difficulty in finding them in their own country, which has, in their view, been poisoned by feminism. They want old-fashioned wives who are both good housekeepers[15] and obedient. And above all, they want wives who are young and beautiful.[16] Reverting to the old tradition of arranged marriages, the mail-order system gave the marriage agencies a new lease of life. Delighted men were shown catalogues of beautiful young women, and 'romantic tours' to the recruiting areas were organized. Being a little too visible or even shocking, the form soon came up against its own limitations and drew legislators' attention to the dangers of people-trafficking. A new form of mail-order marriage emerged; it uses the Internet in what appears to be a more open and fair way. In reality, the structure of the exchange between men and women remains almost exactly the same.[17] The phenomenon of 'long-distance marriages' emerged slightly later in Europe. It is now expanding rapidly, and centres on exchanges with Eastern Europe and Africa

[13] The categories of 'North' and 'South' are very approximate. It would be more accurate to speak of dominant and dominated countries. And besides, the position of these countries can be inverted (and inverted very rapidly), regardless of their geographical position. This is especially true of South-East Asia. In the space of only a few years, Taiwan, for example, has been transformed into a major centre for the market in mail-order brides. The young brides (who are both beautiful and docile) come mainly from Mainland China and Vietnam. Specific sub-markets are also being structured. Korean men, for example, prefer Chinese brides of Korean origin.

[14] American men have turned away from Asia in the last few years, and are increasingly interested in East European women. In 2001, the authorities delivered 8,000 'fiancée' visas for young Asian women and 5,000 for women from Russia, Ukraine and other East European countries. The visas are valid for 90 days. If the marriage goes ahead, the young woman is given permanent resident status; if it does not, she is sent back to her own country.

[15] Robert Scholes (2006) points to one significant fact. The young Philippino women who are looking for husbands in the United States have often had previous experience of immigration, as domestic servants.

[16] Nicole Constable stresses that many of these very young women come from rural backgrounds in the Philippines. The globalization of the marriage market is discouraging women in the dominated countries from late marriage (which was the usual way for them to win their autonomy), just as tradition used to do.

[17] Slightly better educated women from the South (and the East) are now becoming involved. The demand from men in the North remains constant.

(Draelants and Tatio Sah 2003). Certain geographical preferences are becoming apparent, and they overlap with linguistic affinities inherited from colonization or from racial similarities (some men like a hint of exoticism; others do not). But the principle behind the exchange remains the same: submissiveness, youth and beauty in exchange for access to the Western metropolises and money.

The prognosis for this new marriage market is very good, even though the promises that are made are rarely kept, and even though the misunderstandings are constant. Most of the young mail-order brides in the dominated countries are trying to escape from their poverty. They sometimes also dream of romance, and their dreams are fuelled by the Western media, but the reality of marital relations in their own countries is often still harsher than their poverty (Draelants and Tatio Sah 2003). Unfortunately, their cut-price Princes often turn into very ordinary frogs who are primarily interested in their own creature comforts. Once the dream has been shattered, the cultural differences that looked so attractive become so many sources of misunderstanding and conflict. But this painful experience can also be formative, and it can give rise to a new aspiration towards self-assertion. The poor husband then discovers that the wife he chose from a catalogue because she was so sweet and obedient has mutated into a self-confident woman who is demanding her autonomy. Take the example of the sad tale of Monty Wheeler, who is the hero of a graphic novel by Mark Kalesniko (2003). The young Asian bride he selected so carefully in order to have a quiet life turned into the very opposite of what he imagined her to be, and even went so far as to pose nude for a photographer. It is no accident that social issues have become common fictional themes. Books and television often signal major changes. It happened with singles (and the question of the commitment issue) a few years ago with cult series like *Friends* and *Ally McBeal*. And now it is happening with mail-order brides. That is no accident either.

Men and Women

In the long term, the globalization of the marriage market may greatly accentuate the imbalance between men and women. That is the likely scenario. Western women have difficulty in finding men who are 'good enough'. For their part, men may well find dynamic women attractive but they prefer them not to be too demanding because they want to be sure that the relationship will be problem-free. There is therefore a

201

danger that many more of them will turn to the international market than today in order to buy submissiveness, youth and beauty. Which means that there will be fewer potential partners for the highly educated and independent women of the big cities of the North; in the meantime, the poor men of the South will find it even harder to find wives.

This catastrophic scenario is all the more likely to prove accurate in that it simply accentuates the differences that already exist between men and women inside the national perimeters of the countries of the North. We have already seen that the age at which they embark upon relationships or get married is a major indicator of women's autonomy. There is also still an age difference between marriage partners, and this too is an indicator that the workings of marriage are not always truly egalitarian (Bozon and Héran 2006). There are therefore more and more single men, especially as they are looking for younger women. Being less autonomous than women in domestic terms, they often live with their parents, as we can see from table 5.

The age difference is inverted by about the age of 35–40,[18] and then becomes much more pronounced in old age (because of the difference between male and female mortality rates). Those men who are still single and in good health are able to choose from a growing cohort of available women. It is as though both men and women were putting more and more obstacles in their own way, and making it less and less likely that they will find a partner (not to mention the fact that they have different expectations). The numbers of men and women of the same age who are still single are never equal. They do not live in the same areas and do not move in the same social circles. Single women are, for example, over-represented in the big university towns, whereas men living in the countryside cannot find conjugal partners. When it comes to the occupations of men and women, the analysis is a little more complex. On the whole, women are lower down the hierarchy and earn less. There are therefore a lot of women on modest incomes, and even women who are in a difficult position, especially if they are bringing up children. But single women under 60

---

[18] Although there is a surplus of young men, older men find that there are growing numbers of women who could, in theory, live up to their expectations. This is because, whereas young men of 18 are likely only to marry girls of their own age, men of 40 might marry women aged anywhere between 18 and 40. After the ages of 35–40, a perverse and self-perpetuating mechanism comes into play: the more men are spoiled for choice (because there are large numbers of younger women), the fewer opportunities there are for women (especially as there are fewer of the older men they want). As women have a greater propensity to remain single than men, men therefore have more choice.

Table 5 Men and women aged 25–29 living with partner, alone and with parents (as percentage of age group)

	Men living with partner	Women living with partner	Men living with parents	Women living with parents	Men living alone	Women living alone
Belgium	37	65	50	24	13	11
Germany	30	50	46	26	24	24
Denmark	61	76	3	4	36	20
Greece	18	43	77	52	5	5
Spain	16	32	80	63	4	5
France	43	53	52	31	16	16
Ireland	22	34	65	58	13	8
Italy	12	34	84	61	5	5
Netherlands	57	75	15	4	28	21
Austria	33	48	49	32	18	20
Portugal	17	27	79	69	4	4
Finland	58	66	13	5	30	29
UK	59	65	31	15	10	21
EU-15	40	55	43	31	16	15

Source: *La Vie des femmes et des hommes en Europe. Un Portrait statistique. Données 1980–2000.* EUROSTAT, 2002 (1998 figures)
In Belgium, 37% of men aged between 24 and 29 are living with a partner, 50% with their parents, and 13% are living alone in their own homes.

who have no children are in a better position than most women in their age group, whereas the opposite tends to be true of men (Hall et al. 1997). The fact that women are relatively over-represented at the top of the social hierarchy, while men are under-represented at the bottom, is enough to ensure that women have difficulty in finding men who are 'good enough'. They have not totally abandoned the idea that a man can have higher status (and at the same time be their equal), whereas men want, even though they are not keen to admit it, to reproduce the archaic level that allows them to make less effort than their partners.

This is why men are turning to the new globalized market. Once more, we find that it may have multiple effects. I have already said a little about its effects on the countries of the South. It also poses a threat to the women of the North. In an ideal scenario, it is possible to imagine the viewpoints of men and women converging, as they are currently doing in so many domains, and that they could fight side by side and gradually replace the old unequal conjugal model, especially in terms of age difference. But the Internet's globalization of the marriage market provides some men with a way out.[19] They are certainly in the minority, but they are openly making demands that could not be expressed elsewhere (an age difference of 15–20 years is not uncommon). It is obvious that if this trend continues, there is a danger that it will become an obstacle to progress towards a more egalitarian model and that the number of single women in the West will increase. One thing is certain: although national dating sites put men and women in contact with one another on an equal footing, the international market is a one-way street: men seek and choose, and women put themselves on show and try to sell themselves to the highest bidder. The catastrophic scenario is especially catastrophic for women.

---

[19] Most of the American men who are in search of mail-order brides are white, and the vast majority of them have a high social status and are politically conservative (Glodava and Onizuka 1994).

A NOTE ON METHODOLOGY

Stages in the Research

I began working on the theme of singledom in the early 1990s. I did so at the request of the European Commission, which wanted an overview of the growing number of one-person households and a better understanding of the question of loneliness in Europe. I therefore synthesized the existing data by reading, analysing and classifying 280 pieces of research on history, demography, sociology and psychology (Kaufmann 1993).

A researcher who is faced with this kind of task has two main methodological options. The first is to organize the data around a central argument. That means, by definition, that the researcher is very selective and that he inevitably organizes his material around his own problematization. The documentation (including the theoretical documentation) is there to be analysed at a higher level and to be used as a basis for further theorization. The only alternative is to remain at the level of a documentary or descriptive logic, to classify and explain the data and then synthesize it on the basis of thematic and problematic similarities. My personal preference has always been to take the 'argument' line, and to leave it to others (who have a taste for such things and whose competence is greater than mine) to expound and classify the data on a systematic basis. In the present case, it proved impossible to go too far in that direction because I had been asked to make a real synthesis, but also and mainly because the documentation that had been collected proved to be an obstacle to its problematization. It was characterized by a quite exceptional confusion at the level of definitions and by an autistic disciplinary compartmentalization of the production of knowledge. Everyone stayed within their own domain and had their own ideas about the question; unfortunately, lots of little ideas do not add up to make one big idea. The situation therefore made it imperative to begin with an elementary clarification and classification in order to have a solid basis for subsequent work.

While these very different pieces of research were being synthesized, an analysis was made of household consumption-budgets, using the statistical tables compiled by EUROSTAT (Kaufmann 1993). That analysis provided much of the basis for the 'portrait' of the single women painted in Part I. Readers who would like more detailed information or European comparisons can consult the research report. A number of articles were subsequently published in scientific journals. The references are given in the References (Kaufmann 1994a; 1994b; 1994c; 1994d; 1995b; 1995c).

All these texts could have been collected and published as a book and a documentary-style dossier. For a while, I did think of publishing them in that form. But something was missing. The book would have had no heart, if I can put it that way. I had great difficulty in committing myself to a book which had no strong central argument or which did not give an insider's view of the question under discussion. And I had neither an argument nor an insider's view. The accumulated erudition seemed to me to be rather dry and disjointed. So it languished in a drawer for about a year. And I waited.

I did not have to wait for long. Because the data was so scattered, I could not bring myself to undertake a qualitative study, as I usually do; the subject was taking me in all kinds of directions, and they were all of interest. And then something unexpected broke the deadlock. Following the publication of one woman's account of the single life, *Marie-Claire* magazine received a lot of letters (300), and asked me to analyse them in order to provide the basis for a scientific response to them. The raw material was dense, movingly sincere and surprisingly profound. One element was decisive from my point of view. The tightly focused nature of the thematic developed in the letters gave me both the impetus I needed, and a clearer perspective around which I could organize the data. The survey got under way again.

The Letters

Of the 300 letters sent to *Marie-Claire*, 200 were the subject of an initial and rapid analysis; only 91 were archived. Various means (personal contacts, classified advertisements) were then used to organize the collection of a further 63 letters. This gave a total of 154 (125 are cited directly, and their authors are listed below). Some 50 or so letters were removed from the corpus for various reasons. Some were quite beside the point, too short or devoid of content, but most were omitted because their senders requested confidentiality (no letters are quoted when confidentiality was requested, or when the personal content was made clear). They have nonetheless made an anonymous contribution to my general understanding of the question.

The 154 letters that were retained do not constitute a representative sample. In social terms, their distribution is quite good. It is especially noteworthy that having to use the written word did not prevent working-class women from taking part (several letters reveal a poor mastery of the medium, but the desire for self-expression was strong enough to make up for this). It must, however, be pointed out that edu-cated women (teachers and women in managerial and supervisory positions) are clearly over-represented, which comes as no surprise. The criterion of age makes the sample much less representative: the women's ages ranged from 18 to 53. The foregrounding of one theme (the search for a potential conjugal partner) in fact encouraged only one age group to reply; older single women did not feel that the ques-tions were relevant to them. The over-representation of young women also reflected the fact that living alone encourages greater introspec-tion on the part of younger women and women in intermediary cate-gories, and that gives them a special relationship with the written word. The fact that the study focuses on this restricted group does not, however, raise any problems. In fact, the opposite is true to the extent that the subject is not the single life as such, but, more specifically, that moment in its trajectory when the link between the process of reflex-ivity and the conjugal hypotheses is strongest.

Sociological work on letters and other personal documents (includ-ing life histories that have been written up) is not a new practice; indeed, it has a long history (Thomas and Znaniecki 1998). It has given rise to some sharp methodological disagreements, most of them relating to the representative and general nature of the findings (Tripier 1998). This problem can be resolved (as in this study) by cross-checking against other sources of data. Researchers who have handled documents such as these are, however, struck by the high quality of many of them and by their evocative power, the skill with which they can explain details and their ability to provide an insider's description of mental and social mechanisms. William Thomas and Florian Znaniecki have no hesitations about saying that they 'consti-tute perfect sociological raw material' (1998: 46).

We do not, however, find this quality in all cases: the context has to be conducive to contemplation and writing. That is the case here. The letters are not representative of an ordinary postbag. In most cases, the desire to write stemmed from a deeper need to confess, from an attempt to externalize (or even exorcize) certain questions that were tormenting the writers' lives. The letters were simply one further means for expressing their innermost thoughts. They are similar to diaries. That explains their great sincerity, which is never in doubt. Of course they were addressed to someone, but that someone could not be defined. And precisely because that someone could not be defined, the project was taken even more seriously, though that did not detract from its personal nature or its sincerity. 'I had to write this letter to an anonymous reader, even if no one reads it. I had to write it, to make it evaporate, to get it out of my system' (Salomé).

The handwriting is often quite careless (probably because many of the letters were, as some 30 of them state, written in bed). Their content, by contrast, is quite elaborate, and it is obvious that a lot of effort went into writing them. It is unusual to find any chatter, hollow phrases or apologies for what seem, after the event, to be over-long developments (mostly to do with love affairs). It is clear that the writers wanted to say as much as possible in as few words as possible, and to say it well. If there are few words, it is not because the letters are short (on the contrary, some of them are real life histories running to 10–15 pages), but because there was a lot to say. The outcome is that we have some exceptionally dense and concentrated raw material. Unlike taped interviews, they scarcely give the researcher time to breathe. Cutting them down in order to construct the object (Kaufmann 1996) proved to be a delicate task: every one of them, or almost every one, seemed worthy of inclusion.

The style varies. In an earlier study (Kaufmann 1997), in which some of the letters (on the theme of ironing) were used, I noted that the writers used a very poised, academic or even pompous style that was quite different from the more spontaneous oral style of taped interviews. I also underlined the fact that it was a mistake to dwell on the somewhat off-putting nature of that form of expression. It was, after all, no more than another symptom of their propensity for self-analysis and their attempts to provide a systematic explanation: the writers were examining their lives in order to say as much as possible in a well-argued and coherent way. Many of the letters used here also employ the same style, but the tone is less forced than that of the letters about ironing which, because of its practical and technical nature, lends itself more to that style of writing. Less academic but more highly wrought styles tend, rather, to come to resemble literature and poetry, because things that are so difficult to express bluntly are easier to suggest and get across by evoking minor details. Not to mention the other reason: the single life encourages writing and creativity. Writing a beautiful letter is a way of responding to that need.

Many of the letters (and some passages in the same letters) do, however, adopt a very different style that is unusual in written documents. They adopt an oral style similar to that found in taped interviews, and use familiar expressions and turns of phrase typical of spoken language. The reason for this is obvious: these women are quite literally writing down precisely what they are saying to themselves. And we do not use the language of books when we are talking to ourselves (or others).

These turns of phrase have been respected and transcribed, but the spelling has been corrected. A few (rare) details that gave too precise a description of the writers have been replaced by similar elements in order to protect their identity.

In order not to overburden the text, no specific reference is made here to the sources. The data on which I rely to draw this or that conclusion is drawn from a variety of sources (synthetic studies, various statistics, including analyses of household budgets, analyses of letters, and so on). The generalizations are more emphatic when the data is solid, and more cautious when it is not so reliable. It should, however, be pointed out that I did have certain indices, even when my interpretation was very intuitive. One example will illustrate my point. In chapter 2, I said that relations with girlfriends do not mean 'lamentations and tears, which are unusual (they cry in private), but a search for understanding and consolation: warmth, support, a good listener and mutual analysis'. The first part of the sentence is an interpretation based upon fairly reliable indices. No one described it in explicit terms. But countless letters did refer to these conversations without mentioning tears, and that allowed me to deduce that they are, at the very least, uncommon (which is not to say that there never are any). The second part of the sentence is, in contrast, borne out by the raw material: the letters illustrate at considerable length the warmth, support, the importance of having a good listener and the mutual analysis. And that detailed knowledge allowed me to go back to the first half of my sentence and to confirm its high degree of probability.

Constructing Hypotheses

My normal theoretical method is quickly to establish a framework, define a small number of initial hypotheses, and then gradually elaborate a model for a theoretical interpretation that is constructed in the course of a long, slow study of raw materials drawn from interviews (Kaufmann 1996). In this case, however, the first stage (the synthesis) was not just a preliminary part of the survey. It took a long time, and the outcome was a very advanced (albeit fragmentary and disparate) outline of the interpretative model. The letters, which provided both a starting point and a valuable central theme when it came to drafting the book, did not play the same central role when I came to formulate my hypotheses: rather than making a theoretical leap, I was able to reorganize my findings. The letters allowed me to select my hypotheses, to organize them into a hierarchy, and to reduce and condense the initial sketch of the model. They were then used to confirm, refine and illustrate it, to bring it to life and to gain an insider's view. The raw material was, as it happens, well suited to that purpose. Its density and its concise nature, on the other hand, would not have been conducive to the long and problematic familiarity that is established between the researcher and his taped interviews. The model had to be greatly modified. This was mainly because I did not initially foresee that the fairytale prince would play such a major role. The raw material certainly had to be reorganized around and focused on the question of conjugal expectations. But the figure of the Prince encouraged me to go further down that line on investigation, to plunge into the historiography of love and to attempt to describe the complex way in which the imaginary and the concrete interact. Indeed, it led me to organize the book around two possible readings that constantly intersected: an analysis of the lives of single women, and the story of the single woman and the fairytale prince.

The Informants

The letters that were received do not constitute a sample in the academic sense of the term; they were either sent spontaneously or in response to requests that did not ask for any particular information. The data that was gathered and which is presented here is uneven, and that is because each writer felt compelled to identify what she saw as significant points of reference. The way the information was categorized was therefore very telling and must be regarded as data in its own

210

right. The writers often mention their jobs, and even more of them mention their family situation (which is not surprising, given the topic). Age is, however, the detail that is mentioned most often (even though there was no requirement to mention it). Age does indeed play a decisive role in the changes that occur in the lives of single women.

All the names have been changed.

Adeline, 28, senior manager
Adrienne, 42, divorced, retail manager
Agathe, 18, single, high school student
Agnès, 45, divorced, shopkeeper
Albertine, 42, widow
Alexandra, 30, unmarried
Alice, divorced
Alisson, 20, unmarried, student
Amélie, 29, single, care assistant
Angéla, 22, unmarried
Annabelle, 25, unmarried, student
Anne-Laure, 38, unmarried, one child
Aurore, 35, unmarried, nurse
Babette, 35, divorced
Bénédicte, 34, divorced, supervisor
Bérangère, 25, unmarried, supervisor
Betty, 36, unmarried
Brigitte, 39, divorced, worker
Carine, 30
Carmen, divorced
Caroline, 32, divorced
Chantal, married, two children
Charlène, 23, unmarried
Chloé, 20, single, check-out assistant
Claire, 30, unmarried, retail manager
Claudia, 38
Corinne, 25, unmarried, executive secretary
Danièle, 32, divorced, shopkeeper
Delphine, 28, unmarried, student
Diane, 20, unmarried, student
Donatienne, 44
Dorothée, 25, unmarried, unemployed supervisor
Edwige, 33, unmarried, liberal profession
Elisa, 26, single
Elodie, 32, unemployed

Emilienne, 25, unmarried, supervisor
Emma, 31, unmarried, office worker
Ernestine, 52, divorced
Evelyne, 37
Fabienne, 50, widow
Flora, 31, unemployed
Françoise, 38
Gabrielle, divorced, teacher
Gaétane
Geneviève, divorced
Georgina, 39
Geraldine, 29, retail manager
Gisèle, 45, divorced, home help
Gladys, 33, two children
Gwenaëlle
Hélène
Henriette, 44
Hortense, 49, divorced
Hulia, unmarried
Ida, 29, unmarried
Ingrid, 25, unemployed
Isabelle, 37, unemployed
Jacqueline, 47, divorced
Jeanine, divorced
Jeanne, separated, two children
Jenna, unmarried
Joanna, 31, divorced
Joëlle, 41
Judith, 42
Juliette, 31
Justine, 28, unmarried, primary schoolteacher
Karen, 32
Katia, 40
Laura, 40, unmarried, teacher
Laurence, 35
Léa
Leila, 34, divorced, three children
Liliane, divorced, unemployed
Linda, 26, unmarried, youth worker
Lise, 37, unmarried, teacher
Loriane, 24
Lucie, 26, shopworker

Lydia, 27, unmarried
Madeleine, 45, divorced
Maggy, 25, unmarried, secretary
Maïté, 42, married
Malorie
Manon, 37, divorced
Marcelline, 50, divorced
Maria, 52, divorced
Marie-Andrée, divorced
Marie-Christine, 38
Marie-Laure, 33, supervisor
Marie-Line, 29, divorced, two children
Marie-Pierre, 59, council employee
Marina, 23, unmarried
Marjorie, 31, unmarried
Marlène, 36, divorced, two children, supervisor
Martine, married
Mathilde, 20, unmarried
Maud, 24, unmarried, decorator
Michèle, married, two children
Monique, divorced, one child
Nadège, 32, unmarried
Nathalie, 37
Nelly, 32, divorced, one child
Odile, 35, divorced
Olivia, 27, unmarried
Pascale, 48, widow, two children, shopkeeper
Pierrine, 21, unmarried, student
Raphaëlle, 27
Régine, divorced, one child
Roseline, 31, unmarried
Sabine, 34
Salomé, 21, unmarried
Sylvie, 38, unmarried
Tania, 36, office worker
Vanessa, unmarried, worker
Véronique, 42
Violaine, 26
Virginia, 27, unmarried
Viviane, 41, divorced
Yasmine, 32, unmarried
Yvonne, 53, divorced

REFERENCES

Alberoni, F. (1995) 'Enamoration et amour dans le couple', in M. Moulin and A. Eraly (eds), *Sociologie de l'amour. Variations sur le sentiment amoureux.* Brussels: Éditions de l'Université de Bruxelles.

Ariès, P. (1962) *Centuries of Childhood*, tr. Robert Baldrick. London: Cape [original French publication 1960].

Arve-Parès, B. (ed.) (1996) *Reconciling Work and Family Life: A Challenge for Europe.* Stockholm: Swedish Committee on the International Year of the Family.

Bachelard, G. (1969) *The Poetics of Space*, tr. Maria Jolas. Boston: Beacon Press [original French publication 1958].

Bart, J. (1990) 'La famille bourgeoise, héritière de la révolution?', in M.-F. Lévy (ed.), *L'Enfant, la famille. De la fragilité des liens entre des hommes.* Paris: Olivier Orban.

Bauman, Z. (2003) *Liquid Love: On the Frailty of Human Bonds.* Cambridge: Polity.

Beck-Gernsheim, Elizabeth (2002) *Reinventing the Family.* Cambridge: Polity.

Becker, J. (1985) *Outsiders. Etudes de sociologie de la déviance.* Paris: Métailié.

Becker, S., Bentolila, S., Fernandes, A. and Ichino, A. (2005) 'Youth emancipation and perceived job insecurity of parents and children'. www.iue.it/Personal/Ichino/cven0606.pdf.

Belcher, J. (2006) *Online Dating: Whose Space?* New York: E-Marketer.

Berger, P. and Luckmann, T. (1967) *The Social Construction of Reality: A Treatise in the Sociology of Knowledge.* Garden City NY: Anchor Books.

Bidart, C. (1997) *L'Amitié, un lien social.* Paris: La Découverte.

Bihr, A. and Pfefferkorn, P. (1996) *Hommes/femmes, l'introuvable égalité: école, travail, couple, espace publique.* Paris: Éditions de l'Atelier.

Bologne, J.-C. (1998) *Histoire du mariage en Occident.* Paris: Hachette-Pluriel.

Bologne, J.-C. (2004) *Histoire du célibat et des célibataires.* Paris: Fayard.

Bonvalet, C., Gotman, A. and Grafmeyer, Y. (eds, in collaboration with Bertaux-Wiame, I., Maison, D. and Ortalda, L.) (1997) 'Proches et parents: l'aménagement des territoires'. Paris: INED, Dossiers et recherches, no. 64.

Bourdelais, P. (1984) 'Femmes isolées en France. XVIIe–XIXe siècles', in A. Farge and C. Klapisch-Zuber (eds), *Madame ou mademoiselle? Itinéraires de la solitude féminine, XVIIIe–XXe siècles.* Paris: Montalba.

214

REFERENCES

Bourdieu, P. (1984) *Distinction: A Social Critique of the Judgement of Taste*, tr. Richard Nice. London: Routledge & Kegan Paul [original French publication 1979].

Bozon, M. (1990) 'Les femmes et l'art d'âge entre conjoints. Une domination consentie', *Population* 2 and 3.

Bozon, M. (1993) 'L'entrée dans la sexualité adulte: le premier rapport et ses suites', *Population* 5.

Bozon, M. (1998) 'Désenchantement et assagissement: les deux voies de la maturation amoureuse', *Le Journal des Psychologues* 159.

Bozon, M. and Héran, F. (1987) 'La découverte du conjoint', *Population* 6.

Bozon, M. and Héran, F. (2006) *La Formation du couple*. Paris: La Découverte.

Bozon, M. and Léridon, H. (1993) 'Les constructions sociales de la sexualité', *Population* 5.

Bozon, M. and Villeneuve-Gokalp, C. (1994) 'Les enjeux des relations entre générations à la fin de l'adolescence', *Population* 6.

Brown, E., Fougeyrollas-Schwebek, D. and Jaspard, N. (1991) *Le Petit déjeuner: une pratique à la frontière du familier et du travail*. GDR 'Modes de vie' – IRESCO.

Brym, R. and Lenton, R. (2001) *Love Online: A Report on Digital Dating in Canada*. Toronto: MSN.

Burgière, A. (1972) 'De Malthus à Max Weber: le mariage tardif et l'esprit d'entreprise', *Annales: Economies, Sociétés, Civilisations* 4–5.

Burt, R. S. (1992) *Structural Holes: The Social Structure of Competition*. Cambridge, MA: Harvard University Press.

Cacouault, V. (1984) 'Diplôme et célibat: les femmes professeurs de lycée entre les deux guerres', in A. Farge and C. Klapisch-Zuber (eds), *Madame ou mademoiselle? Itinéraires de la solitude féminine, XVIIIe–XXe siècles*. Paris: Montalba.

Caradec, V. (1996) *Le Couple à l'heure de la retraite*. Rennes: Presses Universitaires de Rennes.

Caradec, V. (1997) 'De l'amour à 60 ans', *Mana. Revue de Sociologies et d'Anthropologies* 3.

Cardia-Vonèche, L. and Bastard, B. (1991) *Les Femmes, le divorce et l'argent*. Geneva: Labor et Fides.

Castel, R. (1990) 'Le roman de la désaffiliation. À propos de Tristan et Iseut', *Le Débat* 61.

Castel, R. (1995) *Les Métamorphoses de la question sociale. Une Chronique du salariat*. Paris: Fayard.

Chaland, K. (1994) 'Normalité familiale plurielle. Morcellement des biographies et individualisation', *Revue des Sciences Sociales de la France de l'Est* 21.

Chaland, K. (1996) 'Transformation du lien conjugal. Regard sur le couple contemporain', *Revue des Sciences Sociales de la France de l'Est* 23.

Chaland, K. (1998) 'Les discours familialistes chez les réformateurs et présociologues du XIXe siècle', *Regards sociologiques* 15.

Chalvon-Demersay, S. (1996) 'Une société élective. Scénarios pour un monde de relations choisies', *Terrains* 27.

Chatelain, Y. and Roche, L. (2005) *In Bed with the Web. Internet et le nouvel adultère*. Saint-Quentin-en-Yvelines: Chiron.

Cicchelli-Pugeault, C. and Cicchelli, V. (1998) *Les Théories sociologiques de la famille*. Paris: La Découverte.

Coenen-Huther, J., Kellerhals, J. and Von Allmen, M. (1994) *Les Réseaux de solidarité dans la famille*. Luzern: Réalités sociales.

Coletta, Nancy (1979) 'Support systems after divorce: incidence and impact', *Marriage and the Family* 41.

Commaille, J. (1992) *Les Stratégies des femmes. Travail, famille et politique*. Paris: La Découverte.

Commaille, J. (1996) *Misères de la famille, question d'Etat*. Paris: Presses de la Fondation nationale des sciences politiques.

Commaille, J. and Martin, C. (1998) *Les Enjeux politiques de la famille*. Paris: Bayard.

Constable, N. (2003) *Romance on a Global Stage. Pen Pals, Virtual Ethnography and 'Mail-Order' Marriage*. Berkeley: University of California Press.

Corbin, A. (1990) 'Backstage', in P. Ariès and G. Duby (eds), *A History of Private Life. Vol. IV: From the Fires of Revolution to the Great War*, tr. Arthur Goldhammer. Cambridge, MA: Belknap Press of Harvard University Press [original French publication 1987].

Cordon, Fernandez and Antonio, Juan (1997) 'Youth residential independence and autonomy: a comparative study', *Journal of Family Issues* XVIII (special issue).

Cosson, M.-E. (1990) 'Représentation et évaluation du mariage des enfants par les mères', MA dissertation, Université Rennes 2.

Cott, N. F. (1994) 'La femme moderne. Le style américain des années vingt', in G. Duby and M. Perrot (general eds), *A History of Women in the West. Vol. V: Toward a Cultural Identity in the Twentieth Century*, ed. F. Thébaud, tr. Arthur Goldhammer. Cambridge, MA: Belknap Press of Harvard University Press [original Italian publication 1992].

Daly, M. and Rake, C. (2003) *Gender and the Welfare State. Care, Work and Welfare in Europe and the USA*. Cambridge: Polity Press.

Damasio, A. (1995) *L'Erreur de Descartes. La Raison des émotions*. Paris: Odile Jacob.

Dauphin, C. (1984) 'Un excédent très ordinaire. L'exemple de Châtillon-sur-Seine en 1851', in A. Farge and C. Klapisch-Zuber (eds), *Madame ou mademoiselle? Itinéraires de la solitude féminine, XVIIe–XIXe siècles*. Paris: Montalba.

Déchaux, J.-H. (1997) *Le Souvenir des morts. Essai sur le lien de filiation*. Paris: PUF.

Demar, C. (2001) *Appel d'une femme au peuple sur l'affranchissement de la femme*. Paris: Albin Michel [original French publication 1833].

Di Giorgio, M. (1992) *Le italiane dall'Unità a oggi*. Rome and Bari: Laterza.

Demazière, D. and Dubar, C. (1997) *Analyser les entretiens biographiques. L'Exemple des récits d'insertion*. Paris: Nathan.

Dencik, L. (1995) 'Children in day care and family life', in B. Arve-Parès (ed.), *Building Family Welfare*. Stockholm: The Network of Nordic Focal Points for the International Year of the Family.

Desjeux, D. (1996) 'Tiens bon le concept, j'enlève l'échelle . . . d'observation', *UTINAM* 20.

Desjeux, D., Monjaret, A. and Taponier, S. (1998) *Quand les français déménagent*. Paris: PUF.

Dibie, P. (1987) *Ethnologie de la chambre à coucher*. Paris: Grasset.

Donati, P. (1998) *Manuale di sociologia della famiglia*. Rome and Bari: Laterza.

Draelants, H. and Tatio Sah, O. (2003) 'Femme camerounaise cherche mari blanc: le Net entre eldorado et outil de reproduction', *Esprit Critique* 5(4).

216

Dubar, C. (1991) *La Socialisation. Construction des identités sociales et professionnelles*. Paris: Armand Colin.

Dubar, C. (1998) 'Trajectoires sociales et formes identitaires: clarifications conceptuelles et méthodologiques', *Sociétés contemporaines* 29.

Duby, G. (1983) *The Knight, The Lady and the Priest: The Making of Modern Marriage in Medieval France*, tr. Barbara Bray. New York: Pantheon [original French publication 1981].

Duby, G. and Perrot, M. (general eds) (1992–4) *A History of Women in the West*, 5 vols., tr. Arthur Goldhammer. Cambridge, MA: Belknap Press of Harvard University Press [original Italian publication 1991–2].

Dumont, L. (1986) *Essays on Individualism: Modern Ideology in Anthropological Perspective*. Chicago: University of Chicago Press [original French publication 1986].

Dumont, G.-F. (2005) 'Adaptation des politiques familiales aux évolutions de structures familiales', *Dossiers d'étude* 71, CNAF.

Durand, G. (1969) *Les Structures anthropologiques de l'imaginaire*. Paris: Bordas.

Durkheim, E. (2006) *On Suicide*, tr. Robin Buss. Harmondsworth: Penguin [original publication 1897].

Elias, N. (1991) *The Society of Individuals*, tr. Edmund Jephcott. Oxford: Basil Blackwell [original German publication 1982].

Elias, N. (1993) *Mozart: Portrait of a Genius*, tr. Edmund Jephcott. Cambridge: Polity [original German publication 1991].

Ehrenberg, A. (1995) *L'Individu incertain*. Paris: Calmann-Lévy.

EPHESIA (1995) *La Place des femmes. Les Enjeux de l'identité et de l'égalité au regard des sciences sociales*. Paris: La Découverte.

EUROSTAT (1994) *Statistiques rapides. Populations et conditions sociales*. Luxembourg.

EUROSTAT (2003) 'Évolution des ménages dans l'Union européenne, 1995–2025'. Statistiques en bref.

Fagnani, J. (1998) 'Lacunes, contradictions et incohérences des mesures de "conciliation" travail/famille: bref bilan critique', in I. Théry (ed.), *Couple, filiation et parenté aujourd'hui. Le droit face aux mutations de la famille et de la vie privée*. Paris: Odile Jacob and La Documentation Française.

Farge, A. and Klapisch-Zuber, C. (1984) *Madame ou mademoiselle? Itinéraires de la solitude féminine, XVIIIe–XXe siècles*. Paris: Montalba.

Ferrand, A. and Mounier, L. (1993) 'L'Échange des paroles sur la sexualité: une analyse des relations de confidence', *Population* 5.

Festy, P. (1990) 'Fréquence et durée de la cohabitation. Analyse et collecte des données', in F. Prious (ed.), *La Famille dans les pays développés: permanences et changements*. Paris: INED.

Flahault, E. (1996) 'Femmes seules, trajectoires et quotidiens. Étude sur la monorésidentialité féminine'. PhD dissertation, Université de Nantes.

Flandrin, J.-L. (1981) *Le Sexe et l'Occident. Évolution des attitudes et des comportements*. Paris: Seuil.

Foucault, M. (1979) *The History of Sexuality. Vol. 1: An Introduction*, tr. Robert Hurley. Harmondsworth: Penguin [original French publication 1976].

Foucault, M. (1986) *The History of Sexuality. Vol. 3: The Care of the Self*, tr. Robert Hurley. Harmondsworth: Penguin [original French publication 1984].

Fourier, C. (1967) *Le Nouveau Monde amoureux*. Paris: La Presse du réel.

Fox, R. (1967) *Kinship and Marriage: An Anthropological Perspective*. Harmondsworth: Penguin.

Fraisse, G. (1979) *Femmes toutes mains. Essai sur le service domestique*. Paris: Seuil.

Francescato, D. (1992) *Quando l'amore finisce*. Bologna: Il Mulino.

Galland, O. (1993) ' "Vie solitaire" et "solitude": le cas des jeunes', *L'Année sociologique* 43.

Gauchet, M. (1997) *The Disenchantment of the World: A Political History of Religion*, tr. Oscar Burge, introduction by Charles Taylor. Princeton: Princeton University Press [original French publication 1985].

Geremek, B. (1976) *Les Marginaux parisiens aux XIVe et XVe siècles*. Paris: Flammarion.

Giddens, A. (1991) *Modernity and Self-Identity. Self and Society in the Late Modern Age*. Cambridge: Polity.

Giddens, A. (1992) *The Transformation of Intimacy: Sexuality, Love and Eroticism in Modern Societies*. Cambridge: Polity.

Glodava, M. and Onizuka, R. (1994) *Mail-Order Brides: Women for Sale*. Fort Collins: Alaken Inc.

Goffman, E. (1968) *Asylums. Essays on the Social Situation of Mental Patients and Other Inmates*. Harmondsworth: Penguin [original US publication 1961].

Goffman, E. (1963) *Stigma: Notes on the Management of Spoiled Identity*. Englewood Cliffs, NJ: Prentice-Hall.

Granovetter, M. (1973) 'The Strength of Weak Ties', *American Journal of Sociology* 68(6).

Grimler, G. (1992) 'Les Rythmes quotidiens en France', *INSEE-Résultats* 167–8.

Guibert, C. de, Léridon, H. and Villeneuve-Gokalp, C. (1994) 'La Cohabitation adulte', *Population et sociétés* (September).

Guillais-Maury, J. (1984) 'La Grisette', in A. Farge and C. Klapisch-Zuber (ed.), *Madame ou mademoiselle? Itinéraires de la solitude féminine, XVIIIe–XXe siècles*. Paris: Montalba.

Gullestad, M. (1992) *The Art of Social Relations*. Oslo: Scandinavian University Press.

Hall, R., Ogden, P. and Hill, C. (1997) 'The Pattern and Structure of One-Person Households in England and Wales and France', *International Journal of Population Geography* 3.

Hammadi, Souhila (2004) 'Divorce: la preuve au féminin', *Liberté* (3 November).

Heilborn, M.-L., Aquino, E., Bozon, M. and Knauth, D. (2006) *O prendeizado da sexualidade: un estudo sobre reproduçao e trajectoria de jovens brasileiros*. Rio de Janeiro: Editora Garamond.

Henry, M. (1993) 'Les Nourritures imaginaires de l'amour. Le Roman-photos, une mise en scène de l'amour et de la relation du couple'. Dissertation, Université Rennes 2.

Héran, F. (1988) 'La Sociabilité, une pratique culturelle', *Economie et statistique* 216.

Héran, F. (1990) 'Trouver à qui parler: le sexe et l'âge de nos interlocuteurs', *Données sociales*. Paris: INSEE.

Héritier, F. (1996) *Masculin/féminin. La Pensée de la différence*. Paris: Odile Jacob.

Höpflinger, F. (1991) 'Avenir des ménages et des structures familiales en Europe', *Séminaire sur les tendances démographiques actuelles et modes de vie en Europe*. Strasbourg, Conseil de l'Europe.

Houel, A. (1997) *Le Roman d'amour et sa lectrice. Une si longue passion.* Paris: L'Harmattan.

Hurtubise, R. (1991) 'La Parenté dans les rapports amoureux: analyse d'un siècle des correspondances amoureuses au Québec (1860–1988)', *Relations intergénérationnelles. Parenté. Transmission, Mémoire.* Actes du colloque de Liège, textes réunis par Bernadette Bawin-Legros and J. Kellerhals.

INSEE (1995) *Contours et caractères. Les Femmes.* Paris: INSEE.

Jolivet, M. (2002) *Homo Japonicus.* Paris: Picquier Poche.

Joubert, M., Arene, M., Bruneteaux, P., Lanzarini, C., Perret, A. and Touzé, S. (1997) *Perturbations, Santé mentale et confrontation aux difficultés de la vie quotidienne.* Rapport RESSCOM-MIRE.

Kalesniko, M. (2003) *Mail-Order Bride.* Seattle: Fantagraphics Books.

Kaufmann, J.-C. (1992) *La Trame conjugale. Analyse du couple par son linge.* Paris: Nathan.

Kaufmann, J.-C. (1993) *Célibat, ménages d'une personne, isolement, solitude. Un État des savoirs.* Brussels: Commission des communautés européennes.

Kaufmann, J.-C. (1994a) 'Nuptialité ou conjugalité? Critique d'un indicateur et état des évolutions conjugales en Europe', *Archives européennes de sociologie* XXXV(1).

Kaufmann, J.-C. (1994b) 'Vie hors couple, isolement et lien social. Figures de l'in-scription relationnelle', *Revue française de sociologie* XXXV(4).

Kaufmann, J.-C. (1994c) 'Trois contextes sociaux de l'isolement', *Revue française des affaires sociales* 2.

Kaufmann, J.-C. (1994d) 'Les Ménages d'une personne en Europe', *Population* 4–5.

Kaufmann, J.-C. (1995a) *Corps de femmes, regards d'hommes. Sociologie des seins nus.* Paris: Nathan.

Kaufmann, J.-C. (1995b) 'Les Cadres sociaux du sentiment de solitude', *Sciences sociales et santé* 13(1).

Kaufmann, J.-C. (1995c) 'Isolement choisi, isolement subi', *Dialogue* 12.

Kaufmann, J.-C. (1996) *L'Entretien compréhensif.* Paris: Nathan.

Kaufmann, J.-C. (1997) *Le Coeur à l'ouvrage. Théorie de l'action ménagère.* Paris: Nathan.

Kaufmann, J.-C. (2004) *L'Invention de soi. Une théorie de l'identité.* Paris: Armand Colin.

Kaufmann, J.-C. (2005) *Casseroles, amour et crises. Ce que cuisiner veut dire.* Paris: Armand Colin.

Kellerhals, J., Perrin, J.-F., Steinauer-Cresson, G., Vonèche, L. and Wirth, G. (1982) *Mariages au quotidien. Inégalités sociales, tensions culturelles et organ-isation familiale.* Luzern: Pierre-Marcel Favre.

Knibiehler, Y. (1984) 'Vocation sans voile, les métiers sociaux', in A. Farge and C. Klapisch-Zuber (eds), *Madame ou mademoiselle? Itinéraires de la solitude féminine, XVIIIe–XXe siècles.*

Knibiehler, Y. (1991) 'Le Célibat. Approche historique', in F. de Singly (ed.), *La Famille, l'état des savoirs.* Paris: La Découverte.

Knibiehler, Y. and Fouquet, C. (1977) *Histoire des mères du Moyen Age à nos jours.* Paris: Montalba.

Lagrange, H. (1998) 'Le Sexe apprivoisé ou l'invention du flirt', *Revue française de sociologie* 39(1).

Lagrave, R.-M. (1994) 'A Supervised Emancipation', in G. Duby and M. Perrot (general eds), *A History of Women in the West. Vol. V: Toward A Cultural*

219

Identity in the Twentieth Century, ed. F. Thébaud, tr. Arthur Goldhammer. Cambridge, MA: Belknap Press of Harvard University Press [original Italian publication 1992].

Lahire, B. (1998) *L'Homme pluriel. Les Ressorts de l'action*, Paris: Nathan.

Lardellier, P. (2004) *Le Coeur net. Célibat et amours sur le Web*, Paris: Belin.

Lavertu, J. (1996) 'La Famille dans l'espace française', *Données sociologiques INSEE*.

Lavigne, J.-C. and Arbet, M. T. (1992) *Les Habiter solitaires*. Rapport de recherche pour le plan Construction et Architecture.

Laufer, D. (1987) *Seule ce soir? Le livre des nouvelles célibataires*. Paris: Carrere.

Laurent, A. (1993) *Histoire de l'individualisme*. Paris: PUF.

Le Breton, D. (1991) *Passions du risque*. Paris: Métailié.

Lefaucheur, N. (1994) 'Maternity, Family and the State', tr. Arthur Goldhammer, in G. Duby and M. Perrot (general eds), *A History of Women in the Twentieth Century. Vol. 5: Toward a Cultural Identity in the Twentieth Century*, ed. F. Thébaud, tr. Arthur Goldhammer. Cambridge MA: Belknap Press of Harvard University Press [original Italian publication 1992].

Lefaucheur, N. (1995) 'Qui doit nourrir l'enfant de parents non mariés ou "démariés" ', in N. Lefaucheur and C. Martin (eds) (1995) *Qui doit nourrir l'enfant quand le père est absent?* Rapport pour la CNAF.

Lefaucheur, N. and Schwartz, O. (1995) 'Féminin/masculin, privé/public', in EPHESIA, *La Place des femmes. Les enjeux de l'identité et de l'égalité au regard des sciences sociales*. Paris: La Découverte.

Le Gall, D. (1992) 'Seconds amours: aimer la raison?', *Revue internationale d'action communautaire* 27(67).

Le Gall, D. (1997) 'La Première fois. L'Entrée dans la sexualité adulte d'étudiants en sociologie', *Mana* 3.

Le Goff, J. (1985) 'Jeanne d'Arc', *Encyclopédie Universalis*.

Lombroso, G. (1923) *The Soul of Woman*. London: Cape [original Italian publication 1917–18].

Luhmann, N. (1990) *Amour comme passion. De la Codification de l'intimité*. Paris: Aubier.

Madden, M. and Lenhart, A. (2006) *Online Dating*. Washington, DC: Pew Internet & American Life Project.

Marchand, O. and Thélot, C. (1997) *Le Travail en France (1800–2000)*. Paris: Nathan.

Margueritte, Victor (1923) *The Bachelor Girl*, tr. Hugh Burnaby. London: A. M. Philpot [original French publication 1922].

Markale, J. (1987) *L'Amour courtois, ou le couple infernal*. Paris: Imago.

Marquet, J., Huynen, P. and Ferrand, A. (1997) 'Modèles de sexualité conjugale: de l'influence normative du réseau social', *Population* 6.

Martin, C. (1996) 'Solidarités familiales: débat scientifique, enjeu politique', in J.-C. Kaufmann (ed.), *Faire ou faire faire? Famille et services*. Rennes: Presses Universitaires de Rennes.

Martin, C. (1997) *L'Après-divorce. Lien familial et vulnérabilité*. Rennes: Presses Universitaires de Rennes.

Mauger, G. and Fossé, C. (1977) *La Vie buissonnière. Marginalité, petite-bourgeoisie et marginalité populaire*. Paris: Maspero.

Mead, G. H. (1934) *Mind, Self and Society: From the Standpoint of a Social Behaviourist*. Chicago: University of Chicago Press.

Montreynaud, F. (1992) *Le XXe siècle des femmes*. Paris: Nathan.

Mossuz-Lavau, J. and Kervasdoué, A. (1997) *Les Femmes ne sont pas des hommes comme les autres*. Paris: Odile Jacob.

Mucchielli, L. (1998) 'Clochards et sans-abri: actualité de l'oeuvre d'Alexandre Vexliard', *Revue française de sociologie* 39(1).

Naamane, S. and Gessous, C. (2005) *Grossesses de la honte*. Casablanca: Éditions le Fennec.

Online Publishers Association (2005) *Online Paid Content US Market Spending Report*.

Parent-Lardeur, F. (1984) 'La Vendeuse de grand magasin', in A. Farge and C. Klapisch-Zuber (eds), *Madame ou mademoiselle? Itinéraires de la solitude féminine, XVIIIe–XXe siècles*. Paris: Montalba.

Passeron, J.-C. (1991) *Le Raisonnement sociologique. L'espace non-poppérien du raisonnement naturel*. Paris: Nathan.

Pastrinelli, M. (1998) 'De l'altérité aux familiarités. La vie quotidienne en collocation dans un quartier populaire de Québec'. Communication au Congrès de la Fédération Canadienne des Sciences Humaines et Sociales, Université d'Ottawa, May 1998.

Paugam, S., Zoyem, J.-P. and Charbonnel, J.-M. (1993) 'Précarité et risque d'exclusion en France', *Documents du CERC*, no. 19. Paris: La Documentation française.

Péquignot, B. (1991) *La Relation amoureuse. Analyse sociologique du roman sentimental moderne*. Paris: L'Harmattan.

Perrot, M. (1984) 'Postface', in A. Farge and C. Klapisch-Zuber (eds), *Madame ou mademoiselle? Itinéraires de la solitude féminine, XVIIIe–XXe siècles*. Paris: Montalba.

Perrot, M. (1990a) 'Roles and Characters', in P. Ariès and G. Duby (eds), *A History of Private Life. Vol. 4: From the Fires of Revolution to the Great War*, tr. Arthur Goldhammer. Cambridge, MA: Belknap Press of Harvard University Press [original Italian publication 1987].

Perrot, M. (1990b) 'Introduction to A. Corbin, "Backstage" ', in P. Ariès and G. Duby (eds), *A History of Private Life. Vol. 4: From the Fires of Revolution to the Great War*, tr. Arthur Goldhammer. Cambridge, MA: Belknap Press of Harvard University Press [original Italian publication 1987].

Perrot, M. (1995) 'Identité, égalité, différence. Le regard de l'histoire', in EPHESIA, *La Place des femmes, les enjeux de l'identité et de l'égalité au regard des sciences sociales*. Paris: La Découverte.

Pezerat, P. and Poublon, D. (1984) 'Femmes sans maris, les employées des postes', in A. Farge and C. Klapisch-Zuber (eds), *Madame ou mademoiselle? Itinéraires de la solitude feminine, XVIIIe–XXe siècles*. Paris: Montalba.

Queiroz, J.-M. de (1997) *Individualisme, individus et socialisation*. Mémoire présentée en vue de l'habilitation à diriger des recherches, Université Paris 5-Sorbonne.

Queiroz, J.-M. de and Ziolkovski, M. (1994) *L'Interactionnisme symbolique*. Rennes: Presses Universitaires de Rennes.

Raffin, T. (1987) 'L'Amour Romanesque: mythe et réalité d'un mode féminin d'engagement matrimonial', *Dialogue* 96.

Rheingold, H. (2000) *The Virtual Community: Homesteading on the Electronic Frontier*. Cambridge MA: MIT Press.

Ronsin, F. (1990) 'Le Divorce révolutionnaire', in M.-F. Lévy, *L'Enfant, la famille et la Révolution française*. Paris: Olivier Orban.

Rosenmayr, L. and Kockeis, E. (1965) 'Propositions for a Sociological Theory of Aging and the Family', *International Social Science Journal* 15(3).

Roussel, L. (1983) 'Les Ménages d'une personne: l'évolution récente', *Population* 6.

Roussel, L. (1989) *La Famille incertaine*. Paris: Odile Jacob.

Roussel, L. and Bourguignon, O. (1979) *Générations nouvelles et mariage traditionnel*. Paris: PUF/INED.

Saint-Laurent, L. (1993) 'Le Dynamique de la solitude des néo-célibataires: vers la constitution de nouveaux réseaux de solidarité', *Revue internationale d'action communautaire* 29(69).

Samandi, Z. (2003) 'Pratiques et comportements familiaux. Du système juridique à l'organisation sociale', in G. Botsche, Z. Samandi and C. Villain-Gandossi, *Individu, famille et société en Méditerranée*. Tunis: CERES.

Samandi, Z. (2006) 'L'Interprétation du changement des comportements culturels', *Revue Tunisienne des Sciences Sociales* 130.

Schérer, R. (1996) 'Au Gré des utopies', *Panoramaiques* 25: 'La famille malgré tout', ed. G. Neyrand.

Schultheis, F. de (1991) 'La Famille, le marché et l'état-providence', in F. de Schultheis, *Affaires de famille, affaires d'état*. Jarville-La-Malgrange: Éditions de l'Est.

Scholes, R. (2006) *The 'Mail-Order Bride' Industry and its Impact on US Immigration*. Online report: www.uscis.gov/files/article/MobRept_AppendixA.pdf.

Schurmans, M.-N. and Dominicé, L. (1997) *Le Coup de foudre amoureux. Essai de sociologie compréhensive*. Paris: PUF.

Schwartz, O. (1990) *Le Monde privé des ouvriers. Hommes et femmes du Nord*. Paris: PUF.

Scott, J. W. (1990) ' "L'Ouvrière, mot impie, sordide . . .". Le Discours de l'économie politique française sur les ouvrières (1840–1860)', *Actes de la recherche en sciences sociales* 83.

Segalen, M. (1993) *Sociologie de la famille*. Paris: Armand Colin.

Shorter, E. (1975) *The Making of the Modern Family*. New York: Basic Books.

Shorter, E. (1984) *A History of Women's Bodies*. Harmondsworth: Penguin [original US publication 1982].

Singly, F. de (1987) *Fortune et infortune de la femme mariée*. Paris: PUF.

Singly, F. de (1989) *Lire à 12 ans. Une enquête sur les lectures des adolescents*. Paris: Nathan.

Singly, F. de (1990) 'L'Homme dual. Raison utilitaire, raison humanitaire', *Le Débat* 61.

Singly, F. de (1991) 'Le Célibat contemporain', in T. Hibert and L. Russel (eds), *La Nuptialité: évolution récente en France et dans les pays développés*. Congrès et colloque, no 7, INED-PUF.

Singly, F. de (1996) *Le Soi, le couple et la famille*. Paris: Nathan.

Singly, F. de (1998) 'La Question politique des jeunes adultes', in L. Théry (ed.), *Couple, filiation et parenté aujourd'hui. Le Droit face aux mutations de la famille et de la vie privée*. Paris: La Découverte – La Documentation française.

Singly, F. de (2000) *Libres ensemble. L'individualisme dans la vie commune*. Paris: Nathan.

Sjörgen, A. (1986) 'Les Repas comme architecte de la vie familiale', *Dialogue* 93.

Sohn, A.-M. (1994) 'Between the Wars in France and England', in G. Duby and M. Perrot, (general eds), *A History of Women in the West. Vol. 5. Toward a Cultural Identity in the Twentieth* Century, ed. F. Thébaud, tr. Arthur Goldhammer. Cambridge, MA: Belknap Press of Harvard University Press [original Italian publication 1992].

Storr, A. (1988) *The School of Genius*. London: Deutsch.

Strauss, A. (1992) *La Trame de la négociation. Sociologies qualitatives et interactionnisme*. Paris: L'Harmattan.

Terrail, J.-P. (ed.) (1995) *La Dynamique des générations. Activité individuelle et changement social (1968–1993)*. Paris: L'Harmattan.

Terrail, J.-P. (ed.) (1997) *La scolarisation de la France. Critique de l'état des lieux*. Paris: La Dispute.

Thébaud, F. (1994) 'The Great War and the Triumph of Sexual Division', in G. Duby and M. Perrot (general eds), *A History of Women in the West. Vol. 5. Toward a Cultural Identity in the Twentieth Century*, ed. F. Thébaud, tr. Arthur Goldhammer. Cambridge, MA: Belknap Press of Harvard University Press [original Italian publication 1992].

Théry, J. (1993) *Le Démariage. Justice et vie privée*. Paris: Odile Jacob.

Théry, J. (1996) 'Famille: une crise de l'institution', *Notes de la fondation Saint-Simon* 83.

Théry, J. (1998) *Couple, filiation et parenté aujourd'hui*. Paris: Odile Jacob/La Documentation française.

Thomas, W. I. and Znaniecki, F. (1998) *Le Paysan polonais en Europe et en Amérique. Récit de vie d'un migrant*. Paris: Nathan.

Tisseron, S. (1996) *Le Bonheur dans l'image*. Les Plessis-Robinson: Les Empêcheurs de penser en rond.

Tocqueville, Alexis de (2004) *The Old Regime and the Revolution*, ed. with an introduction by François Furet and Françoise Mélonia, tr. Alan S. Kahan. Chicago: University of Chicago Press [original French publication 1856].

Toulemon, L. (1996) 'La cohabitation hors mariage s'installe dans la durée', *Population* 3.

Tripier, P. (1998) 'Une Sociologie pragmatique: Préface à Thomas W. I. and Znaniecki, I., *Le Paysan polonais en Europe et en Amérique, Récit de vie d'un migrant*. Paris: Nathan.

Ünulan, Turgay (2002) 'Changing Family Structure in Turkey, 1968–1988'. Papers in Demography, No. 6. Institute of Population Studies, Ankara.

Villeneuve-Gokalp, C. (1991) 'Du premier au deuxième couple: les différences de comportement conjugal entre hommes et femmes', in T. Hibert and L. Roussel (eds), *La Nuptialité: évolution récente en France et dans les pays développés*. Congrès et colloques no. 7. Paris: INED-PUF.

Yamada, M. (1999) *Parasito Shinguru no Jidai*. Tokyo: Chikuma Shinsho.

Weinberger-Thomas, C. (1996) *Cendres d'immortalité. La crémation des veuves en Inde*. Paris: Seuil.